W9-BBO-604

TEACHERS AND TEXTS

BY THE SAME AUTHOR

IDEOLOGY AND CURRICULUM

EDUCATION AND POWER

CULTURAL AND ECONOMIC REPRODUCTION IN EDUCATION: ESSAYS ON CLASS, IDEOLOGY AND THE STATE (ED.)

MICHAEL W. APPLE

The University of Wisconsin, Madison

TEACHERS AND TEXTS

A POLITICAL ECONOMY OF CLASS AND GENDER RELATIONS IN EDUCATION

LIBRARY

ROUTLEDGE & KEGAN PAUL

NEW YORK AND LONDON

First published in 1986 by
Routledge & Kegan Paul Inc.
in association with Methuen Inc.
29 West 35th Street, New York, NY 10001

Published in Great Britain by
Routledge & Kegan Paul Ltd
11 New Fetter Lane, London EC4P 4EE

Set in Linotron Bembo 11 on 13 pt
by Input Typesetting Ltd, London
and printed in Great Britain
by T. J. Press (Padstow) Ltd
Padstow, Cornwall

Copyright © Michael W. Apple 1986

No part of this book may be reproduced in
any form without permission from the publisher
except for the quotation of brief passages
in criticism

Library of Congress Cataloging in Publication Data

Apple, Michael W.
Teachers and texts.

Bibliography: p.
Includes index.
1. Education—Social aspects—United States.
2. Discrimination in education—United States.
3. Women teachers—United States—History. 4. Textbooks—Publication and distribution—Social aspects—United States. 5. Computer-assisted instruction—Social aspects—United States. 6. Social structure—United States. I. Title.
LC191.4.A67 1986 370.19'0973 86–13877

British Library CIP Data also available

ISBN 0–7102–0774–3

LC
191.4
.A67
1986

CONTENTS

ACKNOWLEDGMENTS

Teachers and Texts is a book that follows a path I first set out in *Ideology and Curriculum* and *Education and Power*. The aim of this series of volumes has been to inquire into the relationship between the curriculum and teaching that is found in our formal institutions of education, and unequal power in society. These investigations have often been critical of the dominant policies and practices of these institutions; but they have always been guided by a sense that education can be (and in many cases, through a good deal of hard work, is) a liberatory act. There are women and men in schools in the United States and so many other places who constantly try to make and remake the educational institutions in which they work. Yet for this making and remaking to have a lasting effect, these acts need to be linked to a serious analysis of the relations between schooling and the class, race, and gender dynamics that organize our society. Because of this, these books have focused on the always complicated ways schools produce, reproduce, mediate, and transform political, economic, and cultural power. By 'unpacking' these relations and then raising critical questions about them, I have hoped to show not only the limits, but also the possibilities, of politically informed educational action.

Fortunately, there is a relatively large group of other

people in the United States, Canada, England, Australia, New Zealand, Spain, and elsewhere who also take these issues very seriously, with whom I have interacted (and argued) and from whom I have learned no small amount. While any list of people who have offered significant help on a book or who have helped clarify one's ideas is bound to be long, there are individuals who have provided all of the comments anyone would want (and sometimes more). Among these individuals are Sandra Acker, Philip Altbach, Jean Anyon, Harry Apple, Madeleine Arnot, Richard Bates, David Bathrick, Ann Becker, Basil Bernstein, Landon Beyer, Mimi Bloch, Martin Carnoy, John Codd, Bob Connell, Roger Dale, Ian Davey, Miriam David, Gwyn Dow, Liz Ellsworth, Mariano Enguita, Jean Erdman, Rod Fawns, Walter Feinberg, Sara Freedman, Rob Gilbert, Mark Ginsburg, Henry Giroux, Andrew Gitlin, Linda Gordon, Allen Hunter, Lesley Johnson, Carl Kaestle, Gail Kelly, Herbert Kliebard, Richard Lachmann, David Livingstone, Alan Lockwood, Barry MacDonald, Linda McNeil, Barbara Melosh, Alex Molnar, Peter Musgrave, Roy Nash, Fred Newmann, Mary O'Brien, Michael Olneck, Paul Olson, Gary Price, Peter Ramsey, Marcus Raskin, William Reese, Alan Rice, Steven Selden, Douglas Sloan, Robin Small, Richard Smith, Jonas Soltis, Andy Spaull, Ann Stoler, Michael Streibel, Martin Sullivan, Ivan Szelenyi, Joel Taxel, Gary Wehlage, Lois Weis, Philip Wexler, Geoff Whitty, Ann Wilson, Erik Olin Wright, and Kenneth Zeichner.

Many of the arguments in this book were first tried out in public in three arenas. The first was the ongoing Friday Seminar at the University of Wisconsin, Madison. This group continues to provide the political and intellectual climate so necessary for the development of critical work in education. Special thanks go to its former and current participants, including Shigeru Asanuma, Kathleen Casey, Won Choe, Linda Christian-Smith, Esteban de la Torre, Kathleen Densmore, Glenn Hudak, David Hursh, Susan Jungck, Ki Seok Kim, Pat Krueger, Margot Larson, Dan

Liston, Cameron McCarthy, Susan Noffke, Bukwon Park, Yolanda Rojas, Leslie Rothaus, Kenneth Teitelbaum, and Bonnie Trudell.

The second arena was provided by time spent as a visiting professor at Monash University in Melbourne, Australia, and at the Universidad Complutense de Madrid in Spain. The faculty and students (and the leaders of teachers' unions, ministry officials, and members of the State Board of Education) in both Melbourne and Madrid all helped refine my arguments.

Finally, the analysis I shall engage in here also had its genesis in my continual interactions with many progressive teachers, administrators, and curriculum workers in Madison and elsewhere. Their constant struggle to build and defend an education that is both pedagogically and politically worthwhile, sometimes in very difficult circumstances, keeps me optimistic. This is a constant reminder that not only is such an education correct, but it is possible to do. In the present moment, this is no small point.

Other people have also provided important support for this volume. Stratford Caldecott and Robert Paul at Routledge & Kegan Paul continue to demonstrate how editors and publishers should act. Diane Falkner's careful and professional typing of the manuscript is very much appreciated. Joyce Shanks and Peter and Paul Apple worked hard on proofreading and on a multitude of other tasks.

Finally, one of the most important influences on this book was Rima Apple. She continues to be my best and most perceptive critic, not letting me get away with arguments easily and making me realize the implications of what I am saying. A situation in which there are two people living together, each one with firmly held beliefs and each one in the midst of long-term writing commitments, requires love, patience, care, and even sacrifice. Above all, it requires mutual respect. Rima has all of this and I dedicate this book to her.

INTRODUCTION

CHAPTER 1

THE POLITICS OF TEACHERS AND TEXTS

INTRODUCTION

On a trip to Washington, D.C., recently, I visited an elementary school less than a mile from the White House. I arrived at lunch time and witnessed a long line of children, parents, elderly people, and other community members queuing up by a soup kitchen. They were waiting to get food, hoping that there would be enough for everyone on that line that stretched around the block. It looked like 1932, but so much more real. This wasn't in a history book. It was there for all to see. But, of course, the phrase 'to see' is totally inappropriate. For the Black men and women in that community, it wasn't 'seen' at all. It was experienced. It was brutal. And it was (and is) getting worse, exacerbated by economic, political and cultural tendencies that seem to be being self-consciously heightened by national policies in health, education, welfare, defense, the economy, and so on. Thus, this line of women, men, and children in Washington is indicative of something larger than itself. There is a more extensive crisis being built in cities and on farms. It is a crisis that will have a differential impact on the poor, on people of color, and on women. It is covered over a bit too easily by officially optimistic statistics coming out of offices in that same city of Washington, offices so close yet so far away from that long line of people.

Part of the outline of the crisis is visible in the following depiction of the situation by Cohen and Rogers. They analyze the current state of American political and economic life thus:

> The powers of the American state are now deployed in a massive business offensive. Its basic elements are painfully clear. Drastic cutbacks in social spending. Rampant environmental destruction. Regressive revisions of the tax system. Loosened constraints on corporate power. Ubiquitous assaults on organized labor. Sharply increased weapons spending. Escalating threats of intervention abroad.[1]

While these elements may be clear, their ultimate effects are all too often hidden in the political rhetoric of official discourse. Again Cohen and Rogers are helpful in clarifying what these effects may be.

> Together these initiatives promise a profound reduction in the living standards of millions of Americans, and a quantum leap in the militarization and business dominance of national life. Cynically advanced as expressions of the popular will, they constitute a direct attack on the norms of democratic culture. Ceaselessly promoted as a new mandate, they betray a system of conventional politics that thrives on the manipulation of political demand. Advertised as a strategy of general welfare, they seek to detach the exercise of private power from any public constraint, and claim an ever mounting pile-up of victims as their own.[2]

So goes America. But the 'conservative restoration'[3] is not only an American phenomenon. In Britain too there is an ongoing attempt at a thoroughgoing dismantling of the gains for which the majority of people have struggled for decades. This is a story that is being repeated elsewhere as well.

Most educators respond to these conditions in a particular way. They ignore them. The world of capital flight, unemployment, the degradation of labor, disintegrating cities and communities – all of this is not about education, after all. A world in which racism is again on the rise, in which we are attempting to push women both ideologically and economically back into the unpaid labor of the home, in which we warehouse our elderly – these too have little to do with schooling. After all, education is a psychological process, one that is wholly captured by the discourse of learning.

Yet anyone who leaves the lecture halls of the university and works with teachers, parents, and children in, say, local urban communities cannot fail to see how the conditions described by Cohen and Rogers are a large part of a cycle of despair and failure that cannot be separated from the educational experiences of students and teachers. For we do not confront abstract 'learners' in schools in these communities. Instead, we see specific classed, raced, and gendered subjects, people whose biographies are intimately linked to the economic, political, and ideological trajectories of their families and communities, to the political economies of their neighborhoods, and – in an identifiable set of connections – to the exploitative relations of the larger society.

Educators are often protected from recognizing these relations, and their own position in this crisis, by a number of things. By not seeing education relationally, by not seeing it as created out of the economic, political, and cultural conflicts that have historically emerged in the United States and elsewhere, they too often place educational questions in a separate compartment, one that does not easily allow for interaction with the relations of class, gender and racial power that give education its social meaning.[4]

They are also protected in another way, by the research 'tools' they employ. I have set off the word 'tools' in inverted commas for a specific reason. The forms of research many educational scholars employ are not only the logical equivalent of hammers and saws, and, perhaps, microscopes. They are also ways of being with others. They have a politic attached to them.[5] To take people as isolated objects of study is also to risk tearing them out of the fabric of history. The very language employed in a good deal of psychological research – the language of 'subjects', for instance – documents this problem. People can be both the subjects of a ruler (they can be ruled, legislated, and even studied) *and* they can be the subjects of history. That is, they are not simply objects of study but agents of change, of social forces they create beyond themselves. It is the recognition of these social dynamics, the fundamentally socio-political character of educational policy, practice, and outcomes, that seems to be missing in such research.[6]

Do not misconstrue my points. Not all psychological research in education is misguided, and some is truly outstanding. Yet, the capturing of educational discourse by psychology has markedly weakened our ability to respond to the crisis as something that is of crucial importance in an education worthy of its name. Having lost most of its connections with political and ethical debates, education is left nearly powerless in the face of a well-articulated right-wing attack on its very foundations as a public enterprise. Because of this, it is not only the people like those on that line in Washington who will suffer. So too will many of these self-same educators, who will find themselves either out of jobs or working in institutions characterized by worsening economic and intellectual conditions.

Of course, there have been alternative research traditions that have evolved, some of which bring us much closer to the socio-economic and cultural realities of schooling. To take one example, ethnographic work – and in particular such work influenced by a cultural marxist perspective – has provided an important counterbalance to both the unrelational and the more positivist styles that have dominated education. Ethnographies and what has been called 'qualitative research' have their own problems, to be sure, some of which are rather substantial. But it is much harder to ignore the surrounding conditions, the class, gender, and race relations, and the role of the researcher in constructing her or his questions, interpretations, and results here. In fact, these kinds of issues, perhaps especially the latter, seem to evolve naturally in ethnographic and more critically oriented research. The politics of the researcher, how one's 'subjects' are constructed in the act of research, who the research is actually for, the role of the institution one is studying in the larger society, what that larger society looks like – these are often the driving questions that lie behind nearly all critically aware ethnographies. Answers to them are often provisional, but the questions are taken more and more seriously.[7] In a time of social crisis they are especially hard to ignore.

I have my suspicions that some educational researchers turn to ethnography out of a fear of statistics or because they believe it to be simpler. (The former motivation is unfortunate; the latter, as anyone who has done serious ethnographic work undoubtedly knows, is wildly inaccurate.) Yet, both the importance we have given to, say, the work of Paul Willis and R. W. Connell and to the newer investigations of American researchers such as Robert Everhart, Linda Valli, and Lois Weis[8] and the questions they raise show that many educators in a number of countries are more than willing to go beyond the politically blind models that are still too readily available and, as well, are willing to wrestle with the methodological and ideological problems that arise from such ethnographically oriented research and from socially critical research in general. Such questions have been at the heart of my own work and provide the context for this book.

TEACHERS AND TEXTS

In both *Ideology and Curriculum* and *Education and Power*,[9] I set out to illuminate the relationship between the curriculum, pedagogy, and forms of evaluation in schools and the structures of inequality in the larger society. I argued that while we must be very cautious about falling into the trap of economic reductionism, there was a very real set of connections between schooling and economic, cultural, and political power. This could be uncovered best only by getting inside both the school and the workplace to see what actually happens and by examining the relationship between education and 'the state' and between culture and economy in education.

Over the past decade, we have made considerable progress in understanding how our formal institutions of education are situated in the configuration of institutions that surround them. However, while our analytic and political tools have been transformed and made more subtle, we have certainly not eliminated all of our problems of understanding (and misunderstanding) how schools function. One of the problems is that our words have taken on wings, so to speak. The debates over the role of education in the distribution and production of economic, political, and cultural power have all too often remained on a very abstract level, rather than taking the tools and actually applying them to the concrete history and reality of the policies and practices involved in the organization of teaching and curriculum.

Yet the difficult times educators and others are facing today are not abstract. They are very real. In education, we are witnessing a number of tendencies that are gaining considerable momentum. These include attempts (1) to restructure the work of teachers so that it is linked more directly to specific behavioral outcomes and directed by managerial techniques and ideologies, and (2) to more closely specify and monitor curricular goals and materials to bring them into line with the industrial, military, and ideological 'needs' of a relatively small but powerful segment of the American public. When coupled with the conservative restoration, and the continuing financial crisis in education, both of these tendencies are having a profound impact at the level of how teachers have done and are now doing their jobs, on what kinds of knowledge are considered the most important for students to learn, and, finally, on who should make decisions concerning these issues. Like the larger crisis, all of this, of course, is not only happening in the United States.

As one example, throughout the United States, England, Australia, New Zealand, and elsewhere in the last decade there have been strong pressures to gain greater centralized control over curriculum and the teacher. Some countries have been relatively successful in withstanding the restructuring of their educational apparatus; others have not. In the United States, for example, nearly forty states now have some form of state-mandated competency testing. Many national reports have urged even greater centralization of control.

While obviously gaining in sophistication, much of the literature on the relationship between an unequal society and teaching and curriculum has been weakened by other things aside from its tendency toward arid argumentation. It has also tended toward 'class reductionism,' forgetting that class is not the only dynamic in operation here. Race and gender must be taken just as seriously, especially the latter when one is discussing teaching.

Historically, for instance, teaching has been largely women's work. Eighty-seven percent of elementary school teachers and 67 percent of teachers overall are women. The same is true in examining curriculum. Many of the reasons why the texts and other materials made available for school use look the way they do is deeply related not only to class, but to the gender (and race) characteristics of the group of people who actually publish the materials in the first place, as well as to the class and gender characteristics of the teachers for whom curriculum materials and textbooks are produced.

Teachers and Texts will examine this constellation of issues. It will focus on more fruitful ways of thinking about the control of teaching and curriculum and at the same time will apply these ways to what is happening today and how we got there.

The volume is divided into two parts. The first,

'Teachers,' is an analysis of the relationship between class, gender, and teaching. I shall trace out how teaching became 'women's work' in a number of countries and discuss what impact this has had both in the past and today. The argument is that it is nearly impossible to understand why curricula and teaching are controlled the way they are unless we understand *who* is doing the teaching. This will be done in two extensive chapters. The first will provide an examination of how and why we should think of teaching as 'women's work' and its links to other forms of women's labor in which women have been treated markedly unequally. It will also go into some empirical detail about how many teachers are responding to current attempts to rationalize and control their jobs. The second will move backwards in time and document how teaching (especially elementary school teaching) became women's work in the first place. It will demonstrate the long history of the attempts to place managerial constraints on women's labor in general and teaching in particular both through the external control of the curriculum and through the creation of administrative techniques to guarantee standardized outcomes and behaviors. Particular attention will be paid to the resulting deskilling, reskilling, intensification, and resistance that evolve. This analysis continues but goes considerably beyond the arguments developed in *Education and Power*, where I related the deskilling and transformation of teaching and curriculum to changes in the labor process and class location of teachers. I now believe that this is only half the story.

Much of this section of the volume will be historical for a particular set of reasons. By focusing only on the current situation, on the current attempts to restructure curriculum and teaching, we lose a sense of what these attempts grow out of. Very importantly, we can also miss some of the major political dynamics that are embodied within such attempts. In so doing, the efficacy of real groups of people who successfully acted against such earlier periods of rationalization is lost.

Gerald Grace makes these points well in his discussion

of the importance of grounding current problems in their history:

> Our critical understanding of . . . contemporary developments will be enhanced if we locate our analysis . . . historically. One of the most promising developments in contemporary sociology of education has been the re-discovery of the heuristic power of historically located inquiry. Such inquiry, the virtues of which were well known to the founding fathers of sociology and which were proclaimed in a later period by writers such as C. Wright Mills, has many advantages. It guards against . . . an unfortunate tendency towards a disembodied structuralism on the one hand or an unrelated world of consciousness on the other. More positively it has the advantage of sensitizing us to the principles and procedures which have been dominant in the past so that we are alert to the mode of their reproduction, reconstitution or change. It has the advantage also of concretely exemplifying and making visible the relations between educational structures and processes and wider structures of power, economy and control in particular periods of social change. Such exemplification and such making visible can provide us with suggestive hypotheses and useful models in our attempts to clarify the present form of those relations.[10]

Since a good deal of the argument I make in the second section of the book depends on an understanding of the past linkages between class, gender, and teaching, it is important that we do situate 'the present form of these relations' within that history.

While the first part of the book examines the history and current status of the control of teaching, by linking it to changes in the sexual division of labor over time and to economic and gender dynamics, the second part of the book, 'Texts,' examines the other side, the process by which the curriculum gets to those teachers. It looks at the concrete process by which certain knowledge, usually the knowledge of dominant groups, gets to be legitimate for use by teachers in their classrooms. It examines, as well, the politics and economics of the national proposals that reinforce this process.

The notion of 'texts' is construed broadly to include two elements. First is the actual textbook itself. Whether we like it or not, in the United States and an increasing range of other countries, the curriculum in most schools is defined by the standardized, grade-level-specific textbook in reading, mathematics, social studies, science, and so forth. Yet we know almost nothing of its forms of production, distribution, and consumption. A significant portion of this section of the volume, then, will focus on the economics and politics of the process by which textbooks are produced and sold. How does text publishing operate? Who decides? What are the ideological and economic reasons behind decisions about textbooks? How, *specifically*, are culture, economy, and the state interrelated in the production of official knowledge? This is the task of Chapter 4.

Second, the idea of texts not only includes what students are to read in our classrooms or what teachers confront in making (or not making) choices. It also includes books and proposals made available to educators and the general public by specific groups to influence our decisions about what should be taught in schools and what teachers' jobs should look like. Two sets of documents are gaining the most attention: (1) *The Paideia Proposal*,[11] which argues that we must in essence return to the 'great books' and the 'life of the mind,' excluding all electives and focusing only on academic knowledge that has met the test of time, and (2) government and national commissions' reports, such as *A Nation at Risk*,[12] which propose that curricula be more closely linked to the needs of national security, reindustrialization, new technology and 'hi-tech' jobs, and international competition. The first involves returning our schools to a vision of the academy. The second involves turning the educational system into an overt arm of conservative elements in government and industry. Both need serious critical discussion. A chapter is devoted to each.

These official and semi-official reports are occurring at a particular time – a time when both the school and the larger society are feeling the impact of major technological shifts. The 'texts' students are often being asked to work with now come with a keyboard attached to them as computers enter many classrooms. The texts that teachers, administrators, parents, and others read call for a major shift not only to a technologized classroom, but to a technologized workplace. These tendencies too need serious, and critical, scrutiny, since they are so closely tied to transformations in teachers' working conditions and to the current efforts to link the school more closely to the technological 'requirements' of the economy. Chapter 7 is devoted to exactly that scrutiny. I shall claim that given the changes now occurring in teachers' work and the economy, the technologization of the classroom may, in fact, actually increase inequalities, not lessen them.

Each of the chapters in this section, then, aims at clarifying what the pressures are that educators are being placed under. Each examines what the implications of these pressures will be in class, gender, and race terms.

There are countervailing, and more democratic, proposals and movements that are in fundamental disagreement both with the ways texts are produced and used and with the policies advocated by such things as *The Paideia Proposal* and *A Nation at Risk.* The concluding chapter will assess these and will propose ways of more adequately dealing with the more control-oriented tendencies surrounding teaching and curriculum so that democratic policies and practices will not be lost.

While I shall deepen this discussion in the next section of this chapter, the analysis of teachers and texts presented in the following chapters needs to be seen as having its roots in particular analytic and political traditions. Analytically, it has been influenced by positions in cultural studies that examine cultural products not as isolated entities but as 'things' that have a circuit of production, circulation, and consumption.[13] These 'things,' though, are not physical objects, but are actually made up of relations among specific groups of people with different power. In essence, the examination of the political economy of textbook publishing, of the ideological and economic roots of the current pressures to transform teaching and curricula into appendages of national economic policy, of technology, and of the historical and current responses of school personnel and, especially, teachers to these pressures, corresponds to particular moments in the circuit of cultural products and relations. These moments occur at a specific conjuncture, in which the always complicated relations among culture, economy, and the state in education (and among the class, gender, and race dynamics within each of these) are being rearticulated. Thus, part of what needs to be told is the story of these changing relations and dynamics in education.

As I just noted, though, the volume stands upon more than an analytic tradition. In general, behind a good deal of the analysis in this book is a distinct sense of how power operates in our society. Because of this, a number of political/economic questions will come to the fore. Who benefits? In what ways? How are relations of domination and subordination reproduced and challenged in existing cultural, political, and economic forms of interaction? These two traditions are not new to this book, of course. They have guided my work for the better part of two decades and have influenced many other educators as well. They will have a slightly different emphasis here, though – one that is somewhat more 'empirical' than my previous investigations.

In each chapter, not only shall I make conceptual and political arguments, but I also want to synthesize varying historical, economic, political, and ethnographic data to show these patterns of differential benefits in the control of teaching and curriculum, the political economics of publishing, in terms of class, gender, and race dynamics in the economy, and in relation to the technological restructuring that is occurring in the labor process both inside and outside the school. I shall use these data for two reasons. First, all too many of us simply do not have a sufficiently accurate picture of what is actually happening, to identifiable groups of people, in the current conservative restoration. Because of this, we are too easily swayed by official statements that are often politically self-serving and less than accurate.

Second, because of the many cogent criticisms of scientism and positivism in education and social research in general, some of which I mentioned earlier – the tendency to measure anything that moves, the neglect of the latent political commitments in research questions and designs, the inclination to simply provide technical expertise for hire[14] – we have overstated our case with a vengeance at times. The Habermasian criticism that science is a form of domination, while partly justifiable, has led to an unfortunate circumstance. It has caused many people to neglect the empirical economic, political, cultural, and educational data that are available and that could provide important support for our arguments about the growing inequalities in the larger society and in schools themselves.

I am, of course, using the concept of 'empirical' in its broadest sense, to include historical and ethnographic, and qualitative as well as quantitative, knowledge. I am also employing it in a way that denies the idea of 'raw empiricism,' of theory-less seeing. The evidence I shall bring to bear was not gathered randomly, nor is it unguided by particular theories and sensibilities. While rooted in a search for a more adequate picture of the way education functions in our social formation, it is organized around a set of questions that speak to an understanding of the dynamics of unequal power that lie at the heart of this society. And it is nurtured in the soil of many very real memories of things like that line outside the school in Washington, D.C.

Now, it is important that we recognize that empirical data, even broadly conceived, cannot provide the final justification for ideological or political criticisms or claims about justice in education or anywhere else. After all, leftist arguments can be just as subject to the logical problems associated with the naturalistic fallacy as other positions. It is a logical leap of considerable proportions from a specification of what current conditions are, no matter how lamentable, to what should replace them. Justifying particular positions requires fairly detailed and concise ethical and political arguments.[15] However, even given this, to ignore empirical detail as *part* of a larger process of justification and criticism is to weaken one's case considerably.

A good deal of the data I shall draw upon will be of a specific kind. For the purposes of my arguments in this book, I shall privilege two particular kinds of knowledge: about economic and class tendencies, and about gender relations. Those readers who are familiar with my previous work know that in a number of my volumes I have argued against seeing schools in an overly economistic fashion. Not everything is explained by economic power. Capitalism is not only an economic system, but a form of life, 'a structured totality.' It is not reducible to the bare bones of economic relations. Indeed, it is hard to locate any relations that are only economic. Instead, I argued that we need to see our kind of social formation as built up out of a constantly changing and contradictory set of interconnections among the economic, political, and cultural 'spheres.' These spheres are themselves arenas for the working out of three kinds of dynamics – class, gender, and race.[16] In fact, most of the recent work in education over the past decade on the state, on critical culturalist theories, in critical ethnographies, and so on, by many individuals, has been about exactly these kinds of positions. Current arguments have nearly all been involved in or have evolved from, in a word, an *anti-reductionist* program.[17] This is a program I have not only been influenced by and have contributed to, but continue to support unequivocally.

Once again, however, in making arguments against economic reductionism, we want to be careful not to overstate our case. We *do* live in a particular kind of economy. Relations of economic and political inequality *are* being widened.[18] Schools and their curricular and teaching policies and practices *are* increasingly being pressured to conform to economic needs as defined by the powerful. Because of these conditions, economic relations and the increasingly close connections between official and dominant culture and economic power *will* play a large part in the story I wish to tell, especially in the second half of the book when I examine many of the current pressures on schools. My aim is not to contradict my earlier work, but to have us focus more directly on a major constitutive element that is very powerful at this time. Cultural form and content and the state may be 'relatively autonomous' from economic relations. But in times of real crisis, the stress may need to be more on the first half of that phrase – *relatively* – than on the second.

For example, as I showed in *Education and Power*, one of the tendencies of corporate economies when they are in crisis is to *export* the blame from the economy to the state.[19] Instead of examining the role of our dominant mode of economic organization in producing unemployment, instead of looking at how our economic arrangements 'naturally' generate such inequalities, our attention is diverted from the economy to government. The economy isn't the problem. Government interference is. At the same time, however, it is 'government interference' that will help us solve the problem, or so say many corporate leaders. If legislation can be passed, for instance, that gives the corporate sector considerably more power politically, culturally, and economically, that sector will solve all of our problems. This tendency is clearly seen in the current ways our educational system is being restructured. Thus, when millions of people are jobless or can only find part-time low-paying work, we blame the school. Standards have fallen. Our teachers are poorly trained. Our students haven't enough work discipline. They too are technically unprepared. These are the reasons why there is unemployment, or so the explanation goes. The answer? Don't alter the economy; 'simply' change the schools so that the ultimate arbiter of the content of the curriculum and the teaching practices within them is a set of needs defined more and more by capital.

Recognizing how such a crisis is exported is helpful, yet this particular kind of reading of the relationship between our educational system and the larger society can itself have the latent effect of privileging class and economic relations to the exclusion of other major components. Because of this, I shall want to pay special attention in the chapters that follow to data on gender relations as well, for the crisis has also been exported onto *women* to a considerable degree. 'They are taking men's jobs.' 'They are destroying the family by not staying at home.' Their long and continuing struggle for both economic and person rights 'has gone too far.' Gender, then, will play a large part in my analysis at both an economic and a cultural level.[20]

I do not wish to argue that these are the only dynamics at work; but they provide significant entry points into uncovering what is happening inside and outside our institutions of formal education. By privileging both economic power and class and gender relations, I want to open doors to our understanding that would be closed were these elements not stressed. Thus, the dual relations in education between economy and culture and between class and gender, and the tensions and contradictions embodied in these relations, are very much a part of what I shall focus upon. As I shall argue, it is very hard to appreciate the conditions surrounding either teachers or texts without such a dual focus.

STRUCTURES AND AGENTS

In order to set the stage for the chapters that follow, it may be helpful at this point to go into the political and theoretical background of this book in somewhat more depth. As I noted, the analysis does come out of a particular history of critical scholarship in education – one that has been strongly influenced by questions about class inequalities and now more strongly by feminist positions. It also stems from a debate about the relationship among culture, politics, and economy.

Though brief, this section of my introductory chapter will be somewhat technical, dealing as it does with some of the theoretical disputes on which I shall take a stand. While any author thinks that everything she or he writes is eminently worthy of close study, it is possible that some readers may wish to come back to this discussion after reading the chapters in the next sections. Most of the following chapters will be understandable without this theoretical gloss, I believe. But a grounding in the historical debates will be helpful to many readers who want to understand how and why particular claims are being made.

A significant portion of the program of analysis that stands behind this work has been influenced (not determined) by a *culturalist* marxism – one that is self-critical and that has been considerably tempered and made much more flexible. This influence is usually based on three main premises.

> The first is that cultural processes are intimately connected with social relations, especially with class and class formations, with sexual divisions, with the racial structuring of social relations and with age oppressions as a form of dependency. The second is that culture involves power and helps to produce asymmetries in the abilities of individuals and social groups to define and realize their needs. And the third, which follows the other two, is that culture is neither an autonomous nor

> an externally determined field, but a site of social differences and struggles.[21]

Certain important elements should be noticed here: the anti-determinist position of the last sentence in the quotation; and the emphasis not only on struggles over economy but culture, not only class but sex and race. These premises bear in important ways on how we think about education, since, as a primary agency in the production and reproduction of 'legitimate' culture, education has not only been one of the things that is struggled over, but is a major institutional site in which these struggles take place.

Usually, however, the way we have talked about these things historically has not been particularly 'culturalist.' Culture has taken a back seat and most of the examinations have stressed the connections between our institutions of education and the 'occupational ladder' in the economy. Formal schooling, it has been argued, corresponds to and helps reproduce the social division of labor in the economy.

Even though, as a number of people have demonstrated, this research has been conceptually and empirically problematic and rather too deterministic,[22] this has been a progressive step. For instance, so much has been written about the connections between the school and the labor market that it is hard not to think about schooling in class terms. From the early functionalist work of Bowles and Gintis to the later analyses of Bernstein, Willis, Giroux, and myself, there has been a clearer recognition that our educational system can only be understood 'relationally.'[23] Its meaning, what it does culturally, politically, and economically, is missed if our analysis does not situate the school back into the nexus of dominant class relations that help shape our society. (I shall not go into detail on the historical growth of relational analyses of class in education, since this has been done elsewhere.)[24]

The recognition that schools need to be understood in this way has had its benefits, to be sure. But it has also led to a number of problems as well. Less attention has been paid to the other constitutive dynamics around which our society has been organized. Here I am talking about gender and race. It would be impossible, for example, to understand the history of the United States labor market, its urban economies and governmental policies, its popular cultural forms, and so much more, without integrating an analysis of racial formation into one's assessment. As Michael Omi and Howard Winant put it, racial formation is a complex process that is at once political, cultural, and economic.[25] Economic and class analysis, while indeed providing important elements of understanding, cannot do justice to the realities of racial oppression. Furthermore, by directing our attention to the primacy of class relations, it undervalues political processes and actions that have their roots in racial identity and the cultural forms of people of color, thereby repelling 'many politically active persons whose awareness of racism it cannot address, but only distort and deny.'[26]

These same points about class need to be made about gender relations as well, and will be of considerable import to my discussion of teaching later on. We do gain insights into women's realities by talking in class terms. For instance, in our kind of society, women have a double relation to wage labor. They are both paid and unpaid workers. Unpaid domestic labor, relations of consumption, and their connections to paid work are all critically important in illuminating both how our economy functions and the 'shaping of women's consciousness.'[27] This consciousness and these relations have a long history, of course, for women's ties to wage labor and the unpaid labor in the home or on the farm have changed markedly over time. We need to remember, for example, that at the end of the eighteenth and the beginning of the nineteenth century, the lack of an 'adequate supply of workers' and the continuing need for cheap labor in the early mills in New England created conditions that made *women* the first industrial proletariat in the United States.[28]

It is essential that we know this, but stopping there would cause us to underemphasize the role that cultural forms played in the formation of a specifically women's response to certain of these economically and class-based conditions. Thus, for instance, for many working-class and middle-class women in later periods of American history, the definition of themselves as, say, the primary purchasers of commodities for the home was used by these women to expand their sphere of control outside as well as inside the home. Consumption practices, the 'labor of purchasing' (and it *is* a labor process), were not only a way in which the economy locked them into their class location. These practices were employed by women to increase their social space and freedom, and to remove themselves from patriarchal relations in the home.[29] A specifically women's cultural politics evolved – one that is missed in discussions of class and economy.

Two things are worthy of note from this discussion. First, cultural forms and practices often have their own politics. They may be related to and limited by class relations and the economy, but they are also 'relatively autonomous.' They have something of a life of their own and provide important grounding for action that may not simply reproduce existing relations of domination and exploitation. Second, there are at least *two* elements operating in this situation: class *and* gender. Thus, an analysis of dominant power relations in our society needs not only a theory of class but just as much of a sensitivity to patriarchy and race as well. For my purposes here I shall focus primarily on class and gender, but in no way do I want to minimize the significance of racial domination.

Patriarchal structures and class structures are both subtle, complex, and wide-ranging. As I shall show in Chapters 2 and 3, they have their own dynamics and are not reducible to each other, though unfortunately those scholars on the left who stress class as the fundamental category of analysis tend to merge feminist issues back into the 'real' problems of class relations. As Heidi Hartmann has put it in arguing against such reductive tendencies, 'The marriage of marxism and feminism has been like the marriage of husband and wife depicted in English common law: Marxism and feminism are one, and that one is marxism.'[30] Such a position has, of course, been challenged conceptually and politically. These criticisms have caused a particular set of questions to come to the forefront of our investigations in a number of fields. What is the relationship between gender and class? How are these relationships produced and reproduced in particular sites such as the home, the paid workplace, and the school? Are these dominant relationships contested by real women and men as they go about their daily lives or are they largely accepted as the way the world really is?[31] One cannot study teaching or texts without taking these issues very seriously. They provide the evident undergirding for my analysis of 'teachers' in the next section, but will be clearly present in the discussions of 'texts' in the later part of the book as well.

These are complicated issues, as you would imagine. But the attempt to deal with class and gender together, without slighting either, is one of the most serious agendas we face. However, these attempts face other difficulties if they are to do justice to the actual people who are in these sets of relations. This bears on the point I made a few pages ago about cultural forms and practices.

For example, the problem is not only how we might fruitfully examine both class and gender together, but also how we combine structuralist insights about the relationship between the school and the social and sexual division of labor with a culturalist perspective that places human agency and the concrete experiences of people at the center. How do we show the role of the educational system in the production of these divisions without at the same time falling into the many traps that bedevilled earlier attempts at doing this – attempts that often turned people into the puppets of structural forces?[32] Can we get inside institutions and illuminate what actually happens, how people act (often in contradictory ways) within the conditions set by the institution and the larger society, and point out possibilities that exist for altering dominant relations?

In the past, only a handful of books have been able to successfully combine a structuralist focus on the objective conditions within a social formation and the culturalist insistence on seeing these conditions as ongoingly built, and contested, in our daily lives. All too often, authors either see culture as a mere reflex of economic relations or else tend to fall into a naive romanticism about the power of 'resistance' by women or men on the shop floor, the home, the office, or the school. Unfortunately (or, perhaps, fortunately) reality is much more dense and contradictory than that, as I shall show in my analysis of both teachers and textbook publishing later on.

Oddly, progress in discerning the relationship between class and gender and between, say, culture and economy has been stimulated by advances in and debates about the class analytic program itself in education. While the literature in class analysis in education has progressed rapidly over the past decade, it is in two areas that the most headway seems to have been made. The first is the growth of understanding of the labor process. Originally stimulated in large part by Harry Braverman's work and the debates this engendered,[33] the actual work settings of educators have been explored more and more rigorously. Forms of control of the curriculum, of the teaching act itself, and specific administrative strategies have been situated within the larger dynamics of the transformation of labor over time and the contradictory needs of the state to support capital accumulation and to legitimate both itself and the accumulation process.[34] Discussions of how teachers are being deskilled as more and more of the curriculum, pedagogy, and evaluation is standardized or prepackaged, of the 'proletarianization' of teaching as teachers' working conditions, control, and autonomy worsen, and of the accompanying ideological tensions that result from these processes have all become increasingly visible.[35]

I believe that these were significant gains in our understanding, and a number of the chapters in this volume, especially Chapters 2, 3, and 7, rest directly on the recent work on the deskilling and proletarianization of teaching and other workers that has been produced. Paradoxically, however, though focusing largely on teachers as classed actors, these gains have led to some very important challenges to the limitations of class analysis *per se*, since it has become increasingly clear that the labor that is being 'degraded' and controlled in schools is largely women's labor in a whole array of cases. Thus, once again, the need to integrate class and gender together has been seen as a very real issue.

The second area in which considerable progress has been made concerns a rejection of imposition theory. In early formulations of the problem in education, it was often assumed that dominant classes had self-identified and coherent interests. These powerful groups identified institutions that were not meeting these interests and then imposed equally coherent strategies on those institutions to guarantee that dominant interests were in fact met. Now, of course, some of this strategizing does go on. Witness the growing influence of capital on the bulk of the national reports on education and in many of the state legislatures throughout the United States and elsewhere that I shall discuss later on.

Yet, this kind of theory also assumes too easily that institutions like the school or in the larger state are populated by mere homunculi, puppets whose strings are pulled by classes in dominance. What it forgets is that most institutions not only came about because of conflict, but are continually riven by conflicts today. Furthermore, people employed in these institutions at all levels often have their own interests that they try to pursue based on their own material circumstances and histories. Many times, these interests will cohere with those of dominant groups, perhaps especially now when capital and the right are resurgent. At times, though, these same people will mediate, transform, and attempt to generally set limits on what is being imposed from the outside. They will also try to employ such 'impositions' for their own ends – ends that will have a good deal to do with their own class and gender location. This will be a key point in my argument in the next two chapters, for instance. I shall show how the class and gender positions of women teachers work together in exactly these ways.

The same must be said not only about the position of teachers, but about other groups' position as well. Right now definitions of 'legitimate' culture are being fought over in education. The school and the state in general are part of a 'contested terrain.' Many groups within that terrain are struggling to maintain their positions or increase their power. These points will provide an important building block in my analysis of textbook publishing, documents such as *The Paideia Proposal* and *A Nation at Risk*, and the attempt to computerize classrooms. Not only capital, but the new middle class and the 'old humanist' fraction of the middle class that resides largely in the universities, right-wing populist groups (who are normally made up of individuals from the working class or lower-middle class whose moral and economic world seems threatened as capitalism transforms their public and private lives), as well as teachers and other groups of women, people of color, workers, and so on – all are contesting the balance of power and culture in education. Capital and the right may be in the ascendant, but that doesn't mean that their ability to pressure textbook publishers, educational policy-makers, the government, and teachers will be unmediated by groups with their own ideological and economic interests.

Thus, while impositions may be tried, they do not occur without a struggle. The key to winning, to establishing hegemony, is usually that group which can establish the parameters of the terms of the debate, that group which can incorporate the competing claims of other groups under its own discourse about education and social goals. As we shall see, this discourse is increasingly framed in economic terms – in the language of production, rationalization, and standardization. The voice of democracy, participation, and equality is being muted. This more democratic voice is still alive, to be sure, but it is harder to hear above the machinery of the mechanization of education.

The dominant discourse is not only increasingly economic. It is also framed in gender terms. For the conservative restoration rests not only on an ethic of the accountant's profit and loss sheet and on 'productivity' and accumulation. It rests on a return to past moments of gender and race relations, a return to a romanticized past when people 'knew their place.'

The reconstruction of gender relations that accompanies the current conservative restoration is nowhere more evident than in the changes in the literature publishers are producing for, say, adolescents. There has been a rapid growth of such things as adolescent romance novels – novels that are pushing other kinds of books out of the market. Thus, as one example, school book clubs that market paperback books directly to the classroom are becoming more likely to have a significant portion of their list taken up by teenage romance novels in series titled 'Sweet Dreams,' 'First Love,' and the like. In essence, these are simply junior Harlequin books, written in such a way as to construct a model of femininity that is overtly 'classless' and 'raceless' and that harks back to definitions of women or girls as only finding fulfillment in the world of romance and commodities.[36]

Women are visible here, but only in roles that are more than a little bounded by a reemerging and partly transformed conservative partriarchal and economic discourse. The feminization of poverty, the history of struggles to gain political and economic (and bodily) rights, the current changes in women's paid and unpaid labor – these are noted only by their invisibility. This is heightened considerably by the invisibility of race as well. In transfigured form, this may be exactly what is happening in the educational reports, in the production of texts and technology, and the reconstruction of the context in which teaching takes place. The ways class, race, and gender are made visible *and* invisible in teaching and in texts may tell us a great deal about who is really profiting and who is really losing during the conservative restoration. The hungry people such as those on that line in America's capital are not the only ones who are finding themselves on the losing side of that social ledger. The next two chapters' examination of class and gender in teaching may make that clear.

TEACHERS

CHAPTER 2

CONTROLLING THE WORK OF TEACHERS

PROLETARIANIZATION: CLASS AND GENDER

An examination of changes in class composition over the past two decades points out something quite dramatically. The process of proletarianization has had a large and consistent effect. There has been a systematic tendency for those positions with relatively little control over their labor process to expand during this time period. At the same time, there was a decline in positions with high levels of autonomy.[1]

This should not surprise us. In fact, it would be unusual if this did not occur, especially now. In a time of general stagnation and of crises in accumulation and legitimation, we should expect that there will also be attempts to further rationalize managerial structures and increase the pressure to proletarianize the labor process. This pressure is not inconsequential to educators, both in regard to the kinds of positions students will find available (or not available) after completing (or not completing) schooling, and also in regard to the very conditions of working within education itself. The labor of what might be called 'semi-autonomous employees' will certainly feel the impact of this. Given the fiscal crisis of the state, this impact will be felt more directly among state employees such as teachers as well. One should expect to see a rapid growth of plans and pressures for the rationalization of administration and labor within the state itself.[2] This is one of the times when one's expectations will not be disappointed.

In earlier work, I argued that teachers have been involved in a long but now steadily increasing restructuring of their jobs. I claimed that they were more and more faced with the prospect of being deskilled because of the encroachment of technical control procedures into the curriculum in schools. The integration together of management systems, reductive behaviorally based curricula, pre-specified teaching 'competencies' and procedures and student responses, and pre and post testing, was leading to a loss of control and a separation of conception from execution. In sum, the labor process of teaching was becoming susceptible to processes similar to those that led to the proletarianization of many other blue-, pink-, and white-collar jobs. I suggested that this restructuring of teaching had important implications given the contradictory class location of teachers.[3]

When I say that teachers have a contradictory class location, I am *not* implying that they are by definition within the middle classes, or that they are in an ambiguous position somehow 'between' classes. Instead, along with Wright, I am saying that it is wise to think of them as located simultaneously in two classes. They thus share the interests of both the petty bourgeoisie and the working class.[4] Hence, when there is a fiscal crisis in which many teachers are faced with worsening working conditions, layoffs, and even months without being paid – as has been the case in a number of urban areas in the United States – and when their labor is restructured so that they lose control, it is possible that these contradictory interests will move closer to those of other workers and people of color who have historically been faced with the use of similar procedures by capital and the state.[5]

Yet, teachers are not only classed actors. They are gendered actors as well – something that is too often neglected by investigators. This is a significant omission. A striking conclusion is evident from the analyses of proletarianization. In every occupational category, *women* are more apt to be proletarianized than men. This could be because of sexist practices of recruitment and promotion, the general tendency to care less about the conditions under which women labor, the way capital has historically colonized patriarchal relations, the historical relation between teaching and domesticity, and so on. Whatever the reason, it is clear that a given position may be more or less proletarianized depending on its relationship to the sexual division of labor.[6]

In the United States, it is estimated that over 90 percent of women's (paid) work falls into four basic categories: (1) employment in 'peripheral' manufacturing industries and retail trades, and considerably now in the expanding but low-paid service sector of the economy; (2) clerical work; (3) health and education; and (4) domestic service. Most women in, say, the United States and the United Kingdom are concentrated in either the lowest-paid positions in these areas or at the bottom of the middle-pay grades when there has been some mobility.[7] One commentator puts it both bluntly and honestly: 'The evidence of discrimination against women in the labour market is considerable and reading it is a wearing experience.'[8]

This pattern is, of course, largely reproduced within education. Even given the years of struggle by progressive women and men, the figures – most of which will be quite familiar to many of you – are depressing. While the overwhelming majority of school teachers are women (a figure that becomes even higher in the primary and elementary schools), many more men are heads or principals of primary and elementary schools, despite the proportion of women teachers.[9] As the vertical segregation of the workforce increased, this proportion actually increased in inequality. In the United States in 1928, women accounted for 55 percent of the elementary school principalships. Today, with nearly 90 percent of the teaching force in elementary schools being women, they account for only 20 percent of principals.[10] This pattern has strong historical roots – roots that cannot be separated from the larger structures of class and patriarchy outside the school.

In this chapter, I shall want to claim that unless we see the connections between these two dynamics – class and gender – we cannot understand the history of and current attempts at rationalizing education or the roots and effects of proletarianization on teaching itself. Not all teaching can be unpacked by examining it as a labor process or as a class phenomenon, though as I have tried to demonstrate in some of my previous work much of it is made clearer when we integrate it into theories of and changes in class position and the labor process. Neither can all of teaching be understood as totally related to patriarchy, though why it is structured the way it is is due in very large part to the history of male dominance and gender struggles,[11] a history I shall discuss in considerably more detail in the next chapter. The two dynamics of class and gender (with race, of course) are not reducible to each other, but intertwine, work off, and co-determine the terrain on which each operates. It is at the intersection of these two dynamics that one can begin to unravel some of the reasons why procedures for rationalizing the work of teachers have evolved. As we shall see, the ultimate effects of these procedures, with the loss of control that accompanies them, can bear in important ways on how we think about the 'reform' of teaching and curriculum and the state's role in it.

ACADEMIC KNOWLEDGE AND CURRICULAR CONTROL

So far I have made a number of general claims about the relationship between proletarianization and patriarchy in the constitution of teaching. I want to go on to suggest ways we can begin to see this relationship in operation. Some sense of the state's role in sponsoring changes in curricular and teaching practice in the recent past is essential here.

The fact that schools have tended to be largely organized around male leadership and female teachers is simply that – a social fact – unless one realizes that this means that educational authority relations have been formally patriarchal. As in the home and the office, male dominance is there; but teachers – like wives, mothers, clerical workers, and other women engaged in paid and unpaid labor – have carved out spheres of power and control in their long struggle to gain some autonomy. This autonomy only becomes a problem for capital and the state when what education is for needs revision.

To take one example outside of education: in offices clerical work is in the process of being radically transformed with the introduction of word-processing technologies, video display terminals, and so on. Traditional forms of control – ones usually based on the dominance of the male boss – are being altered. Technical control, where one's work is deskilled and intensified by the 'impersonal' machinery in the office, has made significant inroads. While certainly not eliminating patriarchal domination, it has in fact provided a major shift in the terrain on which it operates. Capital has found more efficient modes of control than overt patriarchal authority.[12]

Similar changes have occurred in schools. In a time when the needs of industry for technical knowledge and technically trained personnel intersect with the growth in power of the new petty bourgeoisie (those people in technical and middle management positions) and the reassertion of academic dominance in the curriculum, pressures for curricular reform can become quite intense. Patience over traditional forms of control will lessen.

Patriarchal relations of power, therefore, organized around the male principal's relations to a largely female teaching staff, will not necessarily be progressive for capital or the state. While they once served certain educational and ideological ends, they are less efficient than what has been required recently. Gender relations must be partly subverted to create a more efficient institution. Techniques of control drawn from industry will tend to replace older styles which depended more on a sexual division of power and labor within the school itself.

Perhaps an example will document the long and continuing history of these altered relationships. In the United States, for instance, during the late 1950s and the 1960s, there was rather strong pressure from academics, capital, and the state to reinstitute academic disciplinary knowledge as the most 'legitimate' content for schools. In the areas of mathematics and science especially, it was feared that 'real' knowledge was not being taught. A good deal of effort was given to producing curricular programs that were systematic, based on rigorous academic foundations, and, in the elementary school material in particular, were teacher-proof. Everything a teacher was to deal with was provided and prespecified. The cost of the development of such programs was socialized by the state (i.e., subsidized by tax dollars). The chance of their being adopted by local school districts was heightened by the National Defense Education Act, which reimbursed school districts for a large portion of the purchase cost. That is, if a school system purchased new material of this type and the technology which supported it, the relative cost was minimal. The bulk of the expense was repaid by the state. Hence, it would have seemed irrational not to buy the material – irrational in two ways: (1) the chance of getting new curricula at low cost is clearly a rational management decision within industrial logic, and (2) given its imprimatur of science and efficiency, the material itself seemed rational.

All of this is no doubt familiar to anyone who lived through the early years of this movement, and who sees the later, somewhat less powerful, effects it had in, say, England and elsewhere. Yet this is not only the history of increasing state sponsorship of and state intervention in teaching and curriculum development and adoption. *It is the history of the state, in concert with capital and a largely male academic body of consultants and developers, intervening at the level of practice into the work of a largely female workforce.* That is, ideologies of gender, of sex-appropriate knowledge, need to be seen as having possibly played a significant part here. The loss of control and rationalization of one's work forms part of a state/class/gender 'couplet' that works its way out in the following ways. Mathematics and science teaching are seen as abysmal. 'We' need rapid change in our economic responsiveness and in 'our' emerging ideological and economic struggle with the Soviet Union.[13] Teachers (who just happen to be almost all women at the elementary level) aren't sophisticated enough. Former ways of curricular and teaching control are neither powerful nor efficient enough for this situation. Provide both teacher-proof materials and financial incentives to make certain that these sets of curricula actually reach the classroom.

One must integrate an analysis of the state, changes in the labor process of state employees, and the politics of patriarchy to comprehend the dynamics of this history of curriculum. It is not a random fact that one of the most massive attempts at rationalizing curricula and teaching had as its target a group of teachers who were largely women. I believe that one cannot separate out the fact of a sexual division of labor and the vision of who has what kinds of competence from the state's attempts to revamp and make more 'productive' its educational apparatus. In so doing, by seeing these structurally generated relationships, we can begin to open up a door to understanding part of the reasons behind what happened to these curriculum materials when they were in fact introduced.

As numerous studies have shown, when the material was introduced into many schools, it was not unusual for the 'new' math and 'new' science to be taught in much the same manner as the old math and old science. It was altered so that it fitted into both the existing regularities of the institution and the prior practices that had proven successful in teaching.[14] It is probably wise to see this as not only the result of a slow-to-change bureaucracy or a group of consistently conservative administrators and teachers. Rather, I think it may be just as helpful to think of this more structurally in labor process and gender terms. The supposed immobility of the institution, its lack of significant change in the face of the initial onslaught of such material, is at least partly tied to the resistances of a female workforce against external incursions into the practices they had evolved over years of labor. It is in fact more than a little similar to the history of ways in which other women employees in the state and industry have reacted to past attempts at altering traditional modes of control of their own labor.[15]

A NOTE ON THE STATE

The points I have just made about the resistances of the people who actually work in the institutions, about women teachers confronted by external control, may seem straightforward. However, these basic arguments have very important implications not only about how we think about the history of curriculum reform and control, but more importantly about how many educators and political theorists have pictured the larger issue of the state's role in supporting capital. In the historical example I gave, state intervention on the side of capital and for 'defense' is in opposition to other positions within the state itself. The day-to-day interests of one occupational position (teachers) contradict the larger interests of the state in efficient production.[16] Because of instances such as this, it is probably inappropriate to see the state as a homogeneous entity, standing above day-to-day conflicts.

Since schools *are* state apparatuses, we should expect them to be under intense pressure to act in certain ways, especially in times of both fiscal and ideological crises. Even so, this does not mean that people employed in them are passive followers of policies laid down from above. As Roger Dale has noted:

> Teachers are not merely 'state functionaries' but do have some degree of autonomy, and [this] autonomy will not necessarily be used to further the proclaimed ends of the state apparatus. Rather than those who work there fitting themselves to the requirements of the institutions, there are a number of very important ways in which the institution has to take account of the interests of the employees and fit itself to them. It is here, for instance, that we may begin to look for the sources of the alleged inertia of educational systems and schools, that is to say what appears as inertia is not some immutable characteristic of bureaucracies but is due to various groups within them having more immediate interests than the pursuit of the organization's goals.[17]

Thus, the 'mere' fact that the state wishes to find 'more efficient' ways to organize teaching does not guarantee that this will be acted upon by teachers who have a long history of work practices and self-organization once the doors to their rooms are closed. As we shall see in a moment, however, the fact that it is primarily women employees who have faced these forms of rationalization has meant that the actual outcomes of these attempts to retain control of one's pedagogic work can lead to rather contradictory ideological results.

LEGITIMATING INTERVENTION

While these initial attempts at rationalizing teaching and curricula did not always produce the results that were anticipated by their academic, industrial, and governmental proponents, they did other things that were, and are, of considerable import. The situation is actually quite similar to the effects of the use of Tayloristic management strategies in industry. As a management technology for deskilling workers and separating conception from execution, Taylorism was less than fully successful. It often generated slowdowns and strikes, exacerbated tensions, and created new forms of overt and covert resistance. Yet, its ultimate effect was to legitimate a particular ideology of management and control both to the public and to employers and workers.[18] Even though it did not succeed as a set of techniques, it ushered in and finally brought acceptance of a larger body of ideological practices to deskill pink-, white-, and blue-collar workers and to rationalize and intensify their labor.

This too was one of the lasting consequences of these earlier curriculum 'reform' movements. While they also did not completely transform the practice of teaching, while patriarchal relations of authority which paradoxically 'gave' teachers some measure of freedom were not totally replaced by more efficient forms of organizing and controlling their day-to-day activity, they legitimated both new forms of control and greater state intervention using industrial and technical models and brought about a new generation of more sophisticated attempts at overcoming teacher 'resistance.' Thus, this new generation of techniques that are being instituted in so many states in the United States and elsewhere currently – from systematic integration of testing, behavioral goals and curriculum, competency-based instruction and prepackaged curricula, to management by objectives, and so forth – has not sprung out of nowhere, but, like the history of Taylorism, has grown out of the failures, partial successes, and resistances that accompanied the earlier approaches to control. As I have claimed, this is not only the history of the control of state employees to bring about efficient teaching, but a rearticulation of the dynamics of patriarchy and class in one site, the school.

INTENSIFICATION AND TEACHING

In the first half of this chapter, we paid particular attention to the historical dynamics operating in the schools. I would like now to focus on more current outgrowths of this earlier history of rationalization and control.

The earlier attempts by state bureaucrats, industry, and others to gain greater control of day-to-day classroom operation and its 'output' did not die. They have had more than a decade to grow, experiment, and become more sophisticated. While gender will be less visible in the current strategies (in much the same way that the growth of management strategies in industry slowly covered the real basis of power in factories and offices), as we shall see it will be present in important ways once we go beneath the surface to look at changes in the labor process of teaching, how some teachers respond to current strategies, and how they interpret their own work.

Since in previous work I have focused on a number of elements through which curricula and teaching are controlled – on the aspects of deskilling and reskilling of labor, and on the separation of conception from execution in teachers' work – here I shall want to concentrate more on something which accompanies these historically evolving processes: what I shall call *intensification*. First, let me discuss this process rather generally.

Intensification 'represents one of the most tangible ways in which the work privileges of educational workers are eroded.' It has many symptoms, from the trivial to the more complex – ranging from being allowed no time at all even to go to the bathroom, have a cup of coffee or relax, to having a total absence of time to keep up with one's field. We can see intensification most visibly in mental labor in the chronic sense of work overload that has escalated over time.[19]

This has had a number of notable effects outside of education. In the newspaper industry, for example, because of financial pressures and the increased need for efficiency in operation, reporters have had their story quotas raised substantially. The possibility of doing non-routine investigative reporting, hence, is lessened considerably. This has had the effects of increasing their dependence 'on prescheduled, preformulated events' in which they rely more and more on bureaucratic rules and surface accounts of news provided by official spokespersons.[20]

Intensification also acts to destroy the sociability of non-manual workers. Leisure and self-direction tend to be lost. Community tends to be redefined around the needs of the labor process. And, since both time and interaction are at a premium, the risk of isolation grows.[21]

Intensification by itself 'does not necessarily reduce the range of skills applied or possessed by educated workers.' It may, in fact, cause them to 'cut corners' by eliminating what seems to be inconsequential to the task at hand. This has occurred with doctors, for instance; many examinations now concentrate only on what seems critical. The chronic work overload has also caused some non-manual workers to learn or relearn skills. The financial crisis has led to shortages of personnel in a number of areas. Thus, a more diverse array of jobs must be done that used to be covered by other people – people who simply do not exist within the institution any more.[22]

While this leads to a broader range of skills having to be learned or relearned, it can lead to something mentioned earlier – the loss of time to keep up with one's field. That is, what might be called 'skill diversification' has a contradiction built into it. It is also part of a dynamic of intellectual deskilling[23] in which mental workers are cut off from their own fields and again must rely even more heavily on ideas and processes provided by 'experts.'

While these effects are important, one of the most significant impacts of intensification may be in reducing the *quality*, not the quantity, of service provided to people. While, traditionally, 'human service professionals' have equated doing good work with the interests of their clients or students, intensification tends to contradict the traditional interest in work well done, in both a quality product and process.[24]

As I shall document, a number of these aspects of intensification are increasingly found in teaching, especially in those schools which are dominated by behaviorally prespecified curricula, repeated testing, and strict and reductive accountability systems. (The fact that these kinds of curricula, tests, and systems are now more and more being mandated should make us even more cautious.) To make this clear, I want to draw on some data from recent research on the effects of these procedures on the structure of teachers' work.

I have argued here and elsewhere that there has been a rapid growth in curricular 'systems' in the United States – one that is now spreading to other countries.[25] These curricula have goals, strategies, tests, textbooks, worksheets, appropriate student response, etc., integrated together. In schools where this is taken seriously,[26] what impact has this been having? We have evidence from a number of ethnographic studies of the labor process of teaching to be able to begin to point to what is going on. For example, in one school where the curriculum was heavily based on a sequential list of behaviorally defined competencies and objectives, multiple worksheets on skills which the students were to complete, with pre-tests to measure 'readiness' and 'skill level' and post-tests to measure 'achievement' that were given often and regularly, the intensification of teacher work is quite visible.

In this school, such curricular practice required that teachers spend a large portion of their time evaluating student 'mastery' of each of the various objectives and recording the results of these multiple evaluations for later discussions with parents or decisions on whether or not the student could 'go on' to another set of skill-based worksheets. The recording and evaluation made it imperative that a significant amount of time be spent on administrative arrangements for giving tests, and then grading them, organizing lessons (which were quite often standardized or pre-packaged), and so on. One also found teachers busy with these tasks before and after school and, very often, during their lunch hour. Teachers began to come in at 7:15 in the morning and leave at 4:30 in the afternoon. Two hours' more work at home each night was not unusual, as well.[27]

Just as I noted in my general discussion of the effects of intensification, here too getting done became the norm. There is so much to do that simply accomplishing what is specified requires nearly all of one's efforts. 'The challenge of the work day (or week) was to accomplish the required number of objectives.' As one teacher put it, 'I just want to get this done. I don't have time to be creative or imaginative.'[28] We should not blame the teacher here. In mathematics, for example, teachers typically had to spend nearly half of the allotted time correcting and recording the worksheets the students completed each day.[29] The situation seemed to continually push the workload of these teachers up. Thus, even though they tended to complain at times about the long hours, the intensification, the time spent on technical tasks such as grading and record-keeping, the amount of time spent doing these things grew inexorably.[30]

Few of the teachers were passive in the face of this, and I shall return to this point shortly. Even though the elements of curricular control were effective in structuring major aspects of their practice, teachers often responded in a variety of ways. They subtly changed the pre-specified objectives because they couldn't see their relevance. They tried to resist the intensification as well: first by trying to find some space during the day for doing slower-paced activities; and second by actually calling a halt temporarily to the frequent pre- and post-tests, worksheets and the like and merely having 'relaxed discussions with students on topics of their own choosing.'[31]

This, of course, is quite contradictory. While these examples document the active role of teachers in attempting to win back some time, to resist the loss of control of their own work, and to slow down the pace at which students and they were to proceed, the way this is done is not necessarily very powerful. In these instances, time was fought for simply to relax, if only for a few minutes. The process of control, the increasing technicization and intensification of the teaching act, the proletarianization of their work – all of this was an absent presence. It was misrecognized as a symbol of their increased *professionalism*.

PROFESSION AND GENDER

We cannot understand why teachers interpreted what was happening to them as the professionalization of their jobs unless we see how the ideology of professionalism works as part of both a class and gender dynamic in education. For example, while reliance on 'experts' to create curricular and teaching goals and procedures grew in this kind of situation, a wider range of technical skills had to be mastered by these teachers. Becoming adept at grading all those tests and worksheets quickly, deciding on which specific skill group to put a student in, learning how to 'efficiently manage' the many different groups based on the tests, and more, all became important skills. As responsibility for designing one's own curricula and one's own teaching decreased, responsibility over technical and management concerns came to the fore.

Professionalism and increased responsibility tend to go hand in hand here. The situation is more than a little paradoxical. There is so much responsibility placed on teachers for technical decisions that they actually work harder. They feel that since they constantly make decisions based on the outcomes of these multiple pre- and post-tests, the longer hours are evidence of their enlarged professional status. Perhaps a quote will be helpful here.

One reason the work is harder is we have a lot of

> responsibility in decision-making. There's no reason not to work hard, because you want to be darn sure that those decisions you made are something that might be helpful . . . So you work hard to be successful at these decisions so you look like a good decision maker.[32]

It is here that the concept of professionalism seemed to have one of its major impacts. Since the teachers thought of themselves as being more professional to the extent that they employed technical criteria and tests, they also basically accepted the longer hours and the intensification of their work that accompanied the program. To do a 'good job,' you needed to be as 'rational' as possible.[33]

We should not scoff at these perceptions on the part of the teachers. First, the very notion of professionalization has been important not only to teachers in general but to women in particular. It has provided a contradictory yet powerful barrier against interference by the state; and just as critically, in the struggle over male dominance, it has been part of a complex attempt to win equal treatment, pay, and control over the day-to-day work of a largely female labor force.[34]

Second, while we need to remember that professionalism as a social goal grew at the same time and was justified by the 'project and practice of the market professions during the liberal phase of capitalism,'[35] the strategy of professionalism has historically been used to set up 'effective defenses against proletarianization.'[36] Given what I said earlier about the strong relationship between the sexual division of labor and proletarianization, it would be not only ahistorical but perhaps even a bit sexist as well wholly to blame teachers for employing a professional strategy.

Hence, the emphasis on increasing professionalism by learning new management skills and so on today and its partial acceptance by elementary school teachers can best be understood not only as an attempt by state bureaucrats to deskill and reskill teachers, but as part of a much larger historical dynamic in which gender politics have played a significant role.

Yet the acceptance of certain aspects of intensification is not only due to the history of how professionalism has worked in class and gender struggles. It is heightened by a number of internal factors as well. For example, in the school to which I referred earlier, while a number of teachers believed that the rigorous specification of objectives and teaching procedures actually helped free them to become more creative, it was clear that subtle pressures existed to meet the priorities established by the specified objectives. Even though in some subject areas they had a choice of how they were to meet the objectives, the objectives themselves usually remained unchallenged. The perceived interests of parents and their establishment of routines helped assure this. Here is one teacher's assessment of how this occurs.

> Occasionally you're looking at the end of the book at what the unit is going to be, these are the goals that you have to obtain, that the children are going to be tested on. That may affect your teaching in some way in that you may by-pass other learning experiences simply to obtain the goal. These goals are going home to parents. It's a terrible thing to do but parents like to see 90's and 100's rather than 60's on skills.[37]

In discussing the use of the skills program, another teacher points out the other element besides parents that was mentioned: 'It's got a manual and you follow the manual and the kids know the directions and it gets to be routine.'[38]

Coupled with perceived parental pressure and the sheer power of routine is something else: the employment practices surrounding teaching. In many schools, one of the main criteria for the hiring of teachers is their agreement with the overall curricular, pedagogic, and evaluative framework which organizes the day-to-day practice. Such was the case in this study. Beyond this, however, even though some investigators have found that people who tend to react negatively to these pre-packaged, standardized, and systematized curricular forms often leave teaching,[39] given the depressed market for new teachers in many areas that have severe fiscal problems and the conscious decision by some school districts to hire fewer teachers and increase class size, fewer jobs are available right now. The option of leaving or even protesting seems romantic, though current teacher shortages may change this.

GENDERED RESISTANCE

At this point in my argument it would be wise to return to a claim I made earlier. Teachers have not stood by and accepted all this. In fact, our perception that they have been and are passive in the face of these pressures may reflect our own tacit beliefs in the relative passivity of women workers. This would be an unfortunate characterization. Historically, for example, as I shall demonstrate in the following chapter, in England and the United States the picture of women teachers as non-militant and middle-class in orientation is not wholly accurate. There have been periods of exceptional militancy and clear political commitment.[40] However, militancy and political commitment are but one set of ways in which control is contested. It is also fought for on the job itself in subtle and even 'unconscious' (one might say 'cultural') ways – ways which will be contradictory, as we shall now see. Once again, gender will become of prime importance.

In my own interviews with teachers it has become clear that many of them feel rather uncomfortable with their role as 'managers.' Many others are less than happy with the emphasis on programs which they often feel 'lock us into a rigid system.' Here the resistance to rationalization and the loss of historically important forms of self-control of one's labor has very contradictory outcomes, partly as a result of sexual divisions in society. Thus, a teacher using a curricular program in reading and language arts that is very highly structured and test-based states:

> While it's really important for the children to learn these skills, right now it's more important for them to learn to feel good about themselves. That's my role, getting them to feel good. That's more important than tests right now.

Another primary grade teacher, confronted by a rationalized curriculum program where students move from classroom to classroom for 'skill groups,' put it this way:

> Kids are too young to travel between classrooms all the time. They need someone there that they can always go to, who's close to them. Anyway, subjects are less important than their feelings.

In these quotes, discomfort with the administrative design is certainly evident. There is a clear sense that something is being lost. Yet the discomfort with the process is coded around the traditional distinctions that organize the sexual division of labor both within the family and in the larger society. The *woman's* sphere is that of providing emotional security, caring for feelings, and so on.

Do not misconstrue my points here. Teachers should care for the feelings and emotional security of their students. However, while these teachers rightly fight on a cultural level against what they perceive to be the ill-effects of their loss of control and both the division and the intensification of their labor, they do so at the expense of reinstituting categories that partly reproduce other divisions that have historically grown out of patriarchal relations.[41]

This raises a significant point: much of the recent literature on the role of the school in the reproduction of class, sex, and race domination has directed our attention to the existence of resistances. This realization was not inconsequential and was certainly needed to enable us to go further than the overly deterministic models of explanation that had been employed to unpack what schools do. However, at the same time, this literature has run the risk of romanticizing such resistances. The fact that they exist does not guarantee that they will necessarily be progressive at each and every moment. Only by uncovering the contradictions within and between the dynamics of the labor process *and* gender can we begin to see what effects such resistances may actually have.[42]

LABOR, GENDER, AND TEACHING

I have paid particular attention here to the effects of the restructuring of teachers' work in the school. I have claimed that we simply cannot understand what is happening to teaching and curriculum without placing it in a framework which integrates class (and its accompanying process of proletarianization) and gender together. The impact of deskilling and intensification occurs on a terrain and in an institution that is populated primarily by women teachers and male administrators – a fact that needs to be recognized as being historically articulated with both the social and sexual divisions of labor, knowledge, and power in our society.

Yet, since elementary school teachers are primarily women, we must also look beyond the school to get a fuller comprehension of the impact of these changes and the responses of teachers to them. We need to remember something in this regard: women teachers often work in *two* sites – the school and then the home. Given the modification of patriarchal relations and the intensification of labor in teaching, what impact might this have outside the school? If so much time is spent on technical tasks at school and at home, is it possible that less time may be available for domestic labor in the home? Other people in the family may have to take up the slack, thereby partly challenging the sexual division of household labor. On the other hand, the intensification of teachers' work, and the work overload that may result from it, may have exactly the opposite effect. It may increase the exploitation of unpaid work in the home by merely adding more to do without initially altering conditions in the family. In either case, such conditions will lead to changes, tensions, and conflicts outside of the sphere where women engage in paid work.[43] It is worth thinking very carefully about the effects that working in one site will have on the other. The fact that this dual exploitation exists is quite consequential in another way. It opens up possible new avenues for political intervention by socialist feminists, I believe. By showing the relationship between the home and the job and the intensification growing in both, this may provide for a way of demonstrating the ties between both of these spheres and between class and gender.

Thinking about such issues has actually provided the organizing framework for my analysis. The key to my investigation in this chapter has been reflecting about changes in *how* work is organized over time and, just as significantly, *who* is doing the work. A clearer sense of both of these – how and who – can enable us to see similarities and differences between the world of work in our factories and offices and that of semi-autonomous state employees such as teachers.

What does this mean? Historically the major struggles labor engaged in at the beginning of the use of systematic management concerned resistance to speed-ups.[44] That is, the intensification of production, the pressure to produce more work in a given period, led to all kinds of interesting responses. Craft workers, for example, often simply refused to do more. Pressure was put on co-workers who went too fast (or too slow). Breaks were extended. Tools and machines suddenly developed 'problems.'

Teachers – given their contradictory class location, their relationship to the history of patriarchal control and the sexual division of labor, and the actual conditions of their work – will find it difficult to respond in the same way. They are usually isolated during their work, and perhaps more so now given the intensification of their labor. Further, machinery and tools in the usual sense of these terms are not visible.[45] And just as importantly, the perception of oneself as professional means that the pressures of intensification and the loss of control will be coded and dealt with in ways that are specific to that workplace and its own history. The ultimate effects will be very contradictory.

In essence, therefore, I am arguing that – while similar labor processes may be working through institutions within industry and the state which have a major impact on women's paid work – these processes will be responded to differently by different classes and class segments. The ideology of professional discretion will lead to a partial acceptance of, say, intensification by teachers on one level, and will generate a different kind of resistance – one specific to the actual work circumstances in which they have historically found themselves. The fact that these changes in the labor process of teaching occur on a terrain that has been a site of patriarchal relations plays a major part here.

My arguments here are not to be construed as some form of 'deficit theory.' Women have won and will continue to win important victories, as I will demonstrate in the following chapter. Their action on a cultural level, though not overtly politicized, will not always lead to the results I have shown here. Rather, my points concern the inherently *contradictory* nature of teachers' responses. These responses are victories and losses at one and the same time. The important question is how the elements of good sense embodied in these teachers' lived culture can be reorganized in specifically feminist ways – ways that maintain the utter importance of caring and human relationships without at the same time reproducing other elements on that patriarchal terrain.

I do not want to suggest that once you have realized the place of teaching in the sexual division of labor, you have thoroughly understood deskilling and reskilling, intensification and loss of control, or the countervailing pressures of professionalism and proletarianization in teachers' work. Obviously, this is a very complex issue in which the internal histories of bureaucracies, the larger role of the state in a time of economic and ideological crisis,[46] and the local political economy and power relations of each school play a part. What I do want to argue quite strongly, however, is the utter import of gendered labor as a constitutive aspect of the way management and the state have approached teaching and curricular control. Gendered labor is the absent presence behind all of our work. How it became such an absent presence is the topic of the next chapter.

CHAPTER 3

TEACHING AND 'WOMEN'S WORK'

The arguments I made in the previous chapter need to be seen in a much wider historical context. As I claimed, women's work is very often the target of both rationalization and attempts to gain control over it. Such attempts and the resistances to them become quite significant economically and politically, to say nothing of educationally, in schools. In this chapter, I would like to inquire into how it came about that women were in the position to be so targeted. Not only here in the United States, but in other countries as well, the control of teaching and curricula had a strong relationship to sexual and class divisions. I shall focus historically here on the United States and England, though the arguments I shall present are not necessarily limited to these countries.

THE STRUCTURE OF WOMEN'S WORK

As one of the very best historians of women's labor has recently argued, most historical analyses of the rationalization and control of labor have been 'preoccupied with artisans or skilled workers' such as weavers, shoemakers, or machinists, or with those people who worked in heavy industry such as miners and steelworkers. Almost by definition, this is the history of men's work. Only a relatively few individuals – though luckily this number is growing rapidly – 'have considered the implications of rationalization for women workers, despite the steadily growing number of women in the workforce.'[1]

Let me begin by going into even more detail about what the shape of women's paid work currently looks like. Such work is constructed around not one but two kinds of divisions. First, women's work is related to a *vertical* division of labor in which women as a group are disadvantaged relative to men in pay and in the conditions under which they labor. Second, such work is involved in the *horizontal* division of labor where women are concentrated in particular kinds of work.[2] Thus, 78 percent of all clerical workers, 67 percent of service workers, 67 percent of teachers (but a much higher proportion in the elementary school), and so on are women in the United States. Less than 20 percent of all administrative, executive, or managerial workers in the United States, and up to a decade ago less than 10 percent in England, are women.[3]

The connections between these two divisions, however, are quite striking. Low-wage, competitive sector employment contains a large share of women in both countries. In England, 41 percent of jobs women hold are part-time, thereby guaranteeing lower wages and benefits and less control, and also documenting the linkages between patriarchal relations in the home (it is the woman's place to only work part-time and take care of children) and the kinds of work made available in the wage labor market.[4]

We can get an even better idea of the concentration of women in certain occupations in the following data. As of 1979, in England, two-thirds of all women engaged in paid work were found in three occupational groups. Over 31 percent were working in clerical and related jobs; 22 percent worked in personal service occupations; and approximately 12 percent were employed in 'professional' and related occupations in health and welfare. Within nearly all occupations, however, 'women were over-represented in the less-skilled, lower status or lower-paid jobs, while men were over-represented in the highly-skilled and managerial jobs.'[5]

Though showing some differences, the figures are similar in the United States. Clerical work constitutes 35 percent of women's paid labor, followed by service work at 21 percent, educators, librarians, and social workers at 8 percent, retail sales at 6 percent, nurses and health technicians at 5 percent, and clothing and textile work at 4 percent.[6] Michele Barrett and others have pointed to the close correspondence between the kinds of paid work women tend to do and the division of labor in the family. Service work, the 'caring professions,' domestic service, clothing, human needs, and so forth, all remain part of this relationship between work inside and outside the home.[7] As I shall document in the next section, this relationship has a long history in education.

While these statistics are important in and of themselves, what they do not reveal is the working conditions and class dynamics themselves. Historically, as I noted in Chapter 2, women's jobs have been much more apt to be 'proletarianized' than men's. There have been constant pressures to rationalize them. With the growth of positions with little autonomy and control, one of the most interesting findings has been that these proletarianized positions are largely filled by women.[8] Evidence of this is given by the fact that the majority of working-class positions (54 percent) in the United States are held by women, and the figure is increasing.[9] These figures are actually evidence of a complicated and dialectical process. As the labor market changes over time, the decrease in jobs with autonomy is closely related to changes in the sexual division of labor. Women will tend to fill these jobs. Just as importantly, as jobs – either autonomous or not – are filled by women, there are greater attempts to control both the content of that job and how it is done from the outside. Thus, the separation of conception from execution and what has been called the deskilling and depowering of jobs have been a particularly powerful set of forces on women's labor. (The current transformation of clerical work by word processing technologies, with its attendant loss of office jobs and mechanization of those jobs that remain, offers a good example here.)[10]

These points have important implications for the analysis I am presenting. The sex-typing of a job is not likely to change unless the job itself undergoes substantial alteration in some respects. Either the surrounding labor market needs to change and/or the tasks of the job itself are restructured.[11] But sex-typing when it has occurred has had a distinct impact on conflicts in the workplace and on negotiations over such things as the definition of jobs and pay level, and determining whether or not a job is considered skilled.[12]

In general, there seems to be a relatively strong relationship between the entry of large numbers of women into an occupation and the slow transformation of the job. Pay is often lowered and the job is regarded as low-skilled so that control is 'needed' from the outside. Added to this is the fact that 'those occupations which became defined as female were expanded at a time when the skills needed to do them were [seen as being] commonly held or easily learned and when there was a particularly high demand for labour, or an especially large pool of women seeking work.'[13]

Of course, sometimes the very tasks associated with a job reinforce such sex-typing. Since teaching, for instance, does have a service and nurturing component to it – as evidenced by the experience of the teachers I described in the previous chapter – this reconstitutes in action the definition of it as women's work. And given 'our' association of service and nurturing activity as less skilled and less valued than other labor, we thereby revivify patriarchal hierarchies and the horizontal and vertical divisions of labor in the process.[14] In many ways, the very perception of an activity is often saturated with sexual bias. Women's work is considered somehow inferior or of less status simply because it is women who do it.[15] Because of these conditions, it has been exceptionally difficult for women to establish recognition of the skills required in their paid and unpaid work.[16] They must fight not only against the ideological construction of women's work, but against the tendencies for the job to become something different and for its patterns of autonomy and control to change as well.

In my presentation of data to show the progression of teaching from being largely men's work to women's work, in many ways we shall want to pay close attention to how teaching may have changed and to the economic and gender conditions surrounding this. In essence, we may not be describing quite the same occupation after elementary school teaching became women's work. For jobs *are* transformed, often in significant ways, over time. A good example here is again clerical work. Like teaching, this changed from being a masculine occupation in the nineteenth century to being a largely female one in the twentieth. And the labor process of clerical work was radically altered during this period. It was deskilled, came under tighter conditions of control, lost many of its paths of upward mobility to managerial positions, and lost wages at the end of the nineteenth century in the United States and England as it became 'feminized.'[17] Given this, it is imperative that we ask whether what has been unfortunately called the feminization of teaching actually concerns the same job. I will claim, in fact, that in some rather substantive economic and ideological aspects it is not the same job. This transformation is linked in complex ways to alterations in patriarchal and economic relations that were restructuring the larger society.

GENDER AND TEACHING OVER TIME

Where does teaching fit in here? Some facts may be helpful. What has been called the 'feminization' of teaching is clearly seen in data from England. Before the rapid growth of mass elementary education, in 1870, men actually outnumbered women slightly in the teaching profession. For every 100 men there were only 99 women employed as teachers. This, however, is the last time men have a numerical superiority. Just ten years later, in 1880, for every 100 males there are now 156 women. This ratio rose to 207 to 100 in 1890 and to 287 in 1900. By 1910, women outnumbered men by over three to one. By 1930, the figure had grown to closer to four to one.[18]

Yet these figures would be deceptive if they were not linked to changes in the actual numbers of teachers being employed. Teaching became a symbol of upward mobility for many women, and as elementary schooling increased so did the numbers of women employed in it – points I shall go into in more detail later on. Thus, in 1870, there were only 14,000 teachers in England, of which more were men than women. By the year 1930, 157,061 teachers worked in state-supported schools in England and Wales, and close to 120,000 of these were women.[19] The definition of teaching as a female enclave is given further substantiation by the fact that these numbers signify something quite graphic. While the 40,000 men employed as teachers around 1930 constitute

TABLE 1
TEACHERS IN PUBLIC ELEMENTARY SCHOOLS IN ENGLAND AND WALES, 1870–1930

Year	Total number	Number of women teachers per 100 men teachers
1870	13,729	99
1880	41,428	156
1890	73,533	207
1900	113,986	287
1910	161,804	306
1920	151,879	315
1930	157,061	366

Source: Reconstructed from Barry Bergen, 'Only a Schoolmaster: Gender, Class, and the Effort to Professionalize Elementary Teaching in England, 1870–1910,' *History of Education Quarterly* 22 (Spring 1982), p. 4.

less than 3 percent of the occupied male workers, the 120,000 women teachers account for nearly 20 percent of all women working for pay outside the home.[20]

If we compare percentages of male to female teachers in the United States with those of England for approximately the same time period, similar patterns emerge. While there was clear regional variation, in typical areas in, say, 1840, only 39 percent of teachers were women. By 1850, the figure had risen to 46 percent.[21] The increase later on is somewhat more rapid than the English experience. The year 1870 finds women holding approximately 60 percent of the public elementary school teaching positions. This figure moves up to 71 percent by 1900. It reaches a peak of fully 89 percent in 1920 and then stabilizes within a few percentage points over the following years.

TABLE 2
TEACHERS IN PUBLIC ELEMENTARY SCHOOLS IN THE UNITED STATES, 1870–1930

Year	Number of men	Number of women	Total number of teachers	Percentage of women
1870	–	–	–	59 (estimate)
1880	–	–	–	60 (estimate)
1890	121,877	232,925	354,802	65.6
1900	116,416	286,274	402,690	71.1
1910	91,591	389,952	481,543	81.0
1920	63,024	513,222	576,246	89.1
1930	67,239	573,718	640,957	89.5

Source: Adapted from Willard S. Elsbree, *The American Teacher*, (New York: American Book Co., 1939), p. 554, and Emery M. Foster, 'Statistical Summary of Education, 1929–30,' *Biennial Survey of Education 1928–1930, Vol. 2* (Washington: US Government Printing Office, 1932), p. 8.

Given the historical connection between elementary school teaching and the ideologies surrounding domesticity and the definition of 'women's proper place,' in which teaching was defined as an extension of the productive and reproductive labor women engaged in at home,[22] we should not be surprised by the fact that such changes occurred in the gendered composition of the teaching force. While there are clear connections between patriarchal ideologies and the shift of teaching into being seen as 'women's work,' the issue is not totally explained in this way, however. Local political economies played a large part here. The shift to non-agricultural employment in male patterns of work is part of the story as well. Just as important was the relationship between the growth of compulsory schooling and women's labor. As we shall see, the costs associated with compulsory schooling to local school districts were often quite high. One way to control such rising costs was in changing accepted hiring practices.[23] One simply hired cheaper teachers – women. Let us examine both of these dynamics in somewhat more detail. In the process, we shall see how class and gender interacted within the limits set by the economic needs of our social formation.

Some simple and well-known economic facts need to be called to mind at the outset. In the U.K., although women teachers outnumbered their male colleagues, the salaries they were paid were significantly lower. In fact, from 1855 to 1935, there was a remarkably consistent pattern. Women were paid approximately two-thirds of what their male counterparts received.[24] Indeed, Bergen claims that one of the major contributing factors behind the schools' increased hiring of women was that they would be paid less.[25]

In the United States, the salary differential was often even more striking. With the rapid growth of schooling stimulated by large rates of immigration as well as by struggles by a number of groups to win free compulsory education, school committees increased their rate of hiring women, but at salaries that were originally half to a third as much as those given to men.[26] But how did it come about that there were positions to be filled in the first place? What happened to the people who had been there?

Elementary school teaching became a women's occupation

in part because men *left* it. For many men, the 'opportunity cost' was too great to stay in teaching. Many male teachers taught part-time (e.g., between harvests) or as a stepping stone to more lucrative or prestigious jobs. Yet with the growth of the middle class in the United States, with the formalization of schools and curricula in the latter half of the nineteenth century, and with the enlarged credentialling and certification requirements for teaching that emerged at this time, men began to, and were often able to, look elsewhere.

Strober summarizes these points nicely:

> All of these changes tended to make teaching less attractive to men. When teaching was a relatively casual occupation that could be engaged in for fairly short periods of time, it was attractive to men in a variety of circumstances. A farmer could easily combine teaching in the winter with caring for his farm during the rest of the year. A potential minister, politician, shopkeeper or lawyer could teach for a short period of time in order to gain visibility within a community. However, once standards rose for teacher certification and school terms were lengthened and combined into a continuous year, men began to drop out of teaching. In urban areas, where teaching was first formalized, and then, later, in rural areas, most men found the opportunity cost of teaching was simply too great, especially since although annual salaries were higher once standards were raised and the school term lengthened, the average teaching salary remained inadequate to support a family. Men also disliked losing their former classroom autonomy. And at the same time attractive job opportunities were developing for men in business and in other professions.[27]

Thus, patriarchal familial forms in concert with changes in the social division of labor of capitalism combine here to create some of the conditions out of which a market for a particular kind of teacher emerges. (In England, we should add, a considerable number of men sought employment both there and abroad in the civil service. Many of the men who attended 'training colleges,' in fact, did so as a point of entry into the civil service, not into teaching.[28] The 'Empire,' then, had a rather interesting effect on the political economy of gendered labor.)

Faced with these 'market conditions,' school boards turned increasingly to women. Partly this was a result of women's successful struggle. More and more women were winning the battles over access to both education and employment outside the home. Yet partly it is the result of capitalism as well. Women were continuing to be recruited to the factories and mills (often, by the way, originally because they would sometimes be accompanied by children who could also work for incredibly low wages in the mills).[29] Given the exploitation that existed in the factories and given the drudgery of paid and unpaid domestic labor, teaching must have seemed a considerably more pleasant occupation to many single women. Finally, contradictory tendencies occurred at an ideological level. While women struggled to open up the labor market and alter patriarchal relations in the home and the paid workplace, some of the arguments used for opening up teaching to women were at the expense of reproducing ideological elements that had been part of the root causes of patriarchal control in the first place. The relationship between teaching and domesticity was highlighted. 'Advocates of women as teachers, such as Catherine Beecher, Mary Lyon, Zilpah Grant, Horace Mann and Henry Barnard, argued that not only were women the ideal teachers of young children (because of their patience and nurturant qualities) but that teaching was ideal preparation for motherhood.'[30] These same people were not loath to argue something else. Women were 'willing to' teach at lower wages than those needed by men.[31] When this is coupled with the existing social interests, economic structures, and patriarchal relations that supported the dominance of an ideology of domesticity in the larger society, we can begin to get a glimpse at the conditions that led to such a situation.

Many men did stay in education, however. But as Tyack, Strober, and others have demonstrated, those men who stayed tended to be found in higher-status and higher-paying jobs. In fact, as school systems became more highly bureaucratized, and with the expansion of management positions that accompanied this in the United States, many more men were found in positions of authority than before. Some men stayed in education; but they left the classroom. This lends support to Lanford's claim that from 1870 to 1970, the greater the formalization of the educational system, the greater the proportion of women teachers.[32] It also tends to support my earlier argument that once a set of positions becomes 'women's work,' it is subject to greater pressure for rationalization. Administrative control of teaching, curricula, and so on increases. The job *itself* becomes different.

Thus, it is not that women had not been found in the teaching ranks before; of course they had. What is more significant is the increasing numbers of women at particular levels 'in unified, bureaucratic, and public schools' with their graded curricula, larger and more formally organized districts, growing administrative hierarchies,[33] and, just as crucially, restructuring of the tasks of teachers themselves.

Such sex segregation was not an unusual occurrence in the urban graded school, for instance. At its very outset, proponents of these school plans had a specific labor force and labor process in mind. 'Hiring, promotion and salary schedules were routinized.' Rather than leaving it up to teachers, the curriculum was quite standardized along grade level lines, with both teachers and students divided into these grades. New managerial positions were created – the superintendent and non-teaching principal, for instance – thereby moving responsibility for managerial concerns out of the classroom. Again, women's supposed nurturing capabilities and 'natural' empathic qualities and their relatively low salaries made them ideally suited for teaching in such schools. Even where there were concerns about women teachers' ability to discipline older students, this too could be solved. It was the principal and/or superintendent who handled such issues.[34]

This sexual division of labor within the school had other impacts. It enhanced the ability of urban school boards to maintain bureaucratic control of their employees and over curriculum and teaching practices. The authors of a recent historical analysis of the relationship between gender division and control demonstrate this rather well. As they argue:

> By structuring jobs to take advantage of sex role stereotypes about women's responsiveness to rules and male authority, and men's presumed ability to manage women, urban school boards were able to enhance their ability to control curricula, students and personnel. Male managers in nineteenth-century urban schools regulated the core activities of instruction through standardized promotional examinations on the content of the prescribed curriculum and strict supervision to ensure that teachers were following mandated techniques. Rules were highly prescriptive. Normal classes in the high schools of the cities prepared young women to teach in a specified manner; pictures of the normal students in Washington, D.C., for example, show women students performing precisely the same activities prescribed for their future pupils, even to the mid-morning 'yawning and stretching' session. Given this purpose of tight control, women were ideal employees. With few alternative occupations and accustomed to patriarchal authority they mostly did what their male superiors ordered. [This by the way is partly questionable.] Difference of gender provided an important form of social control.[35]

Given these ideological conditions and these unequal relations of control, why would women ever enter such labor? Was it the stereotypical response that teaching was a temporary way-station on the road to marriage for women who loved children? While this may have been partly accurate, it is certainly overstated since in many instances this was not even remotely the case.

In her collection of teachers' writings from the nineteenth and twentieth centuries, Nancy Hoffman makes the point that most women did not enter teaching with a love of children or with marital plans as the main things in mind. Rather, uppermost in their minds was one major concern. They entered teaching in large part because they needed work. The teachers' comments often document the following facts:

> Women had only a few choices of occupation; and compared with most – laundering, sewing, cleaning, or working in a factory – teaching offered numerous attractions. It was genteel, paid reasonably well, and required little special skill or equipment. In the second half of the century and beyond, it also allowed a woman to travel, to live independently or in the company of other women, and to attain economic security and a modest social status. The issue of marriage, so charged with significance among male educators, emerges in stories of schoolmarms pressured reluctantly into marriage by a family fearful of having an 'old maid' on their hands, rather than in teachers' accounts of their own eagerness or anxiety over marriage. There are also explicit statements, in these accounts, of teachers *choosing* work and independence over a married life that appeared, to them, to signify domestic servitude or social uselessness. Finally, the accounts of some women tell us that they chose teaching not because they wanted to teach children conventional right from wrong, but in order to foster social, political, or spiritual change: they wanted to persuade the young, move them to collective action for temperance, for racial equality, for conversion to Christianity. What these writings tell us, then, is that from the woman teacher's perspective, the continuity between mothering and teaching was far less significant

> than a paycheck and the challenge and satisfaction of work.[36]

We should be careful about overstating this case, however. Not a few women could and did train to be teachers and then worked for a relatively short period. As Angela John puts it, 'Because the dominant ideology argued that woman's place was in the home, it conveniently enabled elementary teaching to be viewed in theory (if not in practice) as a profession for which women could train and work for a limited time.'[37] Obviously, constructing the image of teaching as a transient occupation 'permitted the perpetuation of low wages,' since such waged labor was merely a way of 'tiding women over until they were married.'[38] Many women teachers in England, the United States, and elsewhere, however, never married and, hence, the situation is considerably more complicated than conventional stereotypes would have it.[39]

Yet while many teachers in the United States and undoubtedly in the U.K. approached their jobs with a sense that did not necessarily mirror the stereotypes of nurturance and preparation for marriage, this did not stop such stereotypes from creating problems. The increase in women teachers did not occur without challenge. Conservative critics expressed concern over the negative effects women teachers might have on their male pupils. Such concerns increased as the proportion of students going on to secondary schools rose. 'While recognizing the beneficial effects on primary-level pupils, the continuation of the female teacher–male student relation into higher grades was viewed as potentially harmful.'[40] (The longer tradition of single-sex schools in England partially mediated these pressures.) That this is not simply a historical dynamic is evident by the fact that even today the proportion of male teachers in high school is considerably higher than in the elementary school.

CLASS DYNAMICS AND TEACHING

The general picture I have painted so far has treated the constitution of teaching as primarily a part of the sexual division of labor over time. While this is crucially important, we need to remember that gender was not the only dynamic at work here. Class played a major part, especially in England, but most certainly in the United States as well.[41] Class dynamics operated at the level of who became teachers and what their experiences were.

It was not until the end of the nineteenth century and the outset of the twentieth that middle-class girls began to be recruited into teaching in England. In fact, only after 1914 do we see any large influx of middle-class girls entering state-supported elementary school teaching.[42]

Class distinctions were very visible. While the concept of femininity *idealized* for middle-class women centered around an image of the 'perfect wife and mother,' the middle-class view of working-class women often entailed a different sense of femininity. The waged labor of working-class women 'tarnished' them (though there is evidence of between-class feminist solidarity).[43] Such waged labor was a departure from bourgeois ideals of domesticity and economic dependence. With the emergence of changes in such bourgeois ideals toward the end of the nineteenth century, middle-class women themselves began to 'widen their sphere of action and participate in some of the various economic and social changes that accompanied industrialization' and both the restructuring of capitalism and the division of labor. Struggles over legal and political rights, over employment and education, came to be of considerable import. Yet because of a tension between the ideals of domesticity and femininity on the one hand and the struggle to enlarge the middle-class woman's economic sphere on the other, particular jobs were seen as appropriate for women. Teaching (and often particular kinds of stenographic and secretarial work) was one of the predominant ones.[44] In fact, of the white women who worked outside the home in the United States in the mid- to late nineteenth century, fully 20 percent were employed at one time or another as teachers.[45]

This entrance of women, and especially of middle-class women, into paid teaching created important pressures for improvements in the education of women in both the United States and England.[46] Equalization of curricular offerings, the right to enter into traditional male enclaves within universities, and so on, were in no small part related to this phenomenon. Yet we need to remember an important social fact here. Even though women were making gains in education and employment, most, say, middle-class women still found themselves *excluded* from the professions and other areas of employment.[47] Thus, a dynamic operated that cut both ways. In being limited to and carving out this area of employment, women 'held on to it as one of the few arenas in which they could exert any power, even at the expense of further reinforcing stereotypes about women's sphere.'[48]

Having said this, we again should not assume that teachers were recruited primarily from middle-class homes in the United States or England. Often quite the opposite was the case. A number of studies demonstrate that working-class backgrounds were not unusual. In fact, one American study completed in 1911 presents data on the average woman teacher's economic background. She came from a family in which the father's income was approximately $800 a year, a figure that places the family among skilled workers or farmers rather than the middle class.[49]

These class differences had an impact not only on an ideological level, but in terms of education and employment within education as well. Girls of different class backgrounds often attended different schools, even when they might both wish to be teachers.[50] Furthermore, by the end of the nineteenth century in England, class differences created clear distinctions in patterns of where one might teach. While middle-class women teachers were largely found working in private secondary and single-sex schools 'which catered especially to middle class girls' or as governesses, women teachers from working-class backgrounds were found elsewhere. They dominated positions within state-supported elementary schools – schools that were largely working-class and mixed-sex.[51] In many ways these were simply different jobs.

These class distinctions can hide something of considerable significance, however. Both groups still had low status.[52] To be a woman was still to be involved in a social formation that was defined in large part by the structure of patriarchal relations. But again patriarchal forms were often colonized and mediated by class relations.

For example, *what* was taught to these aspiring teachers had interesting relationships to the social and sexual divisions of labor. Many aspiring working-class 'pupil teachers' in England were recruited to teach in working-class schools. Much of what they were expected to teach centered around domestic skills such as sewing and needlework in addition to reading, spelling, and arithmetic. For those working-class pupil teachers who might ultimately sit for an examination to enter one of the teacher training colleges, gender divisions were most pronounced. In Purvis's comparison of these entrance tests, the different expectations of what men and women were to know and, hence, teach are more than a little visible. Both men and women were examined in dictation, penmanship, grammar, composition, school management, history, geography, French, German, Latin, and Welsh. Yet only men were tested in algebra, geometry, Euclid, and Greek. Only women took domestic economy and needlework.

The focus on needlework is a key here in another way, for not only does it signify clear gender dynamics at work but it also points again to class barriers. Unlike the 'ornamental sewing' that was more common in middle-class households, these working-class girls were examined on 'useful sewing.' Questions included how to make the knee part of 'knickerbocker drawers' and the sewing together of women's petticoats of a gored variety. (This was one of the most efficient uses of material, since less material is needed if the fabric is cut and sewn correctly.)[53] The dominance of utility, efficiency, and cost saving is once more part of the vision of what working-class girls would need.[54] As Purvis notes, 'it would appear then that female elementary teachers were expected to teach those skills which were linked to that form of feminity deemed appropriate for the working classes.'[55]

But teaching, especially elementary school teaching, was not all that well paid, to say the least, earning somewhat more than a factory operative but still only the equivalent of a stenographer's wages in the United States or England.[56] What would its appeal have been for a working-class girl? In England, with its very visible set of class relations and articulate class culture, we find answers similar to but – given these more visible class relations – still different from the United States. First, the very *method* by which girls were first trained in the 1870s to become teachers was a system of apprenticeship – a system that was 'indigenous to working class culture.' This was especially important since it was evident at the time that female pupil teachers were usually the daughters of laborers, artisans, or small tradesmen. Second, and here very much like the American experience, compared to occupations such as domestic service, working in factories, dressmaking, and so on – among the only jobs realistically open to working-class women – teaching had a number of benefits. It did increase status, especially among working-class girls who showed a degree of academic ability. Working conditions, though still nothing to write home about, were clearly better in many ways. They were relatively clean and, though often extremely difficult given the overcrowded conditions in schools, had that same potential for job satisfaction that was evident in my earlier quotation from Hoffman and that was frequently missing in other employment. And, just as significantly, since teaching was considered to be on the mental side of the mental/manual division of labor, it gave an opportunity – though granted a limited one – for a certain amount of social mobility.[57] (This question of social mobility and 'respectability' may have been particularly important to those women and families newly within a 'lower-middle-class' location, as well, given the increasing proportion of such people in teaching in England by the beginning of the second decade of this century.)

There was a price to pay for this 'mobility' and the promise of improved working conditions that accompanied it. Women elementary school teachers became less connected to their class origins, and at the same time class differences in ideals of femininity still kept them from being totally acceptable to these classes above them. This contradictory situation is not an abstraction. The fact that it was lived out is made clear in these teachers' frequent references to their social isolation.[58] Such isolation was of course heightened considerably by other lived conditions of teachers. The formal and contractual conditions under which teachers were hired were not the most attractive. As many of you already know, women teachers in the United States, for example, could be fired for getting married, or if married, getting pregnant. There were prohibitions about being seen with men, about clothes, about makeup, about politics, about money, about nearly all of one's public (and private) life.

It would be wrong to trace all of this back to economic motives and class dynamics. For decades married women were prohibited from teaching on both sides of the Atlantic. While single women were often young, and hence were paid less, the notion of morality and purity as powerful symbols of a womanly teaching act undoubtedly played a large part. The above-mentioned array of controls of women's physicality, dress, living arrangements, and morals shows the importance of these concerns. Ideologies of patriarchy, with the teacher being shrouded in a domestic and maternal cloak – possibly combined with a more deep-seated male suspicion of female sexuality – are reproduced here.[59] It is the very combination of patriarchal relations and economic pressures that continue to work their way through teaching to this day.

These controls are strikingly evident in a relatively standard teacher's contract from the United States for the year 1923. I reproduce it in its entirety since it condenses within itself so many of the ideological conditions under which women teachers worked:

TEACHERS CONTRACT 1923

This is an agreement between Miss __________, teacher, and the Board of Education of the __________ School, whereby Miss __________ agrees to teach for a period of eight months, beginning Sept. 1, 1923. The Board of Education agrees to pay Miss __________ the sum of ($75) per month.
Miss __________ agrees:

1. Not to get married. This contract becomes null and void immediately if the teacher marries.
2. Not to keep company with men.
3. To be home between the hours of 8:00 p.m. and 6:00 a.m. unless in attendance at a school function.
4. Not to loiter downtown in ice cream stores.
5. Not to leave town at any time without the permission of the chairman of the Board of Trustees.
6. Not to smoke cigarettes. This contract becomes null and void immediately if the teacher is found smoking.
7. Not to drink beer, wine, or whiskey. This contract becomes null and void immediately if the teacher is found drinking beer, wine, or whiskey.
8. Not to ride in a carriage or automobile with any man except her brother or father.
9. Not to dress in bright colors.
10. Not to dye her hair.
11. To wear at least two petticoats.
12. Not to wear dresses more than two inches above the ankles.
13. To keep the schoolroom clean
    a. to sweep the classroom floor at least once daily.

b. to scrub the classroom floor at least once weekly with hot water and soap.
c. to clean the blackboard at least once daily.
d. to start the fire at 7:00 so the room will be warm at 8:00 a.m. when the children arrive.

14. Not to use face powder, mascara, or paint the lips.

In many ways, the contract speaks for itself. It is important to note, though, that this sort of thing did not end in 1923. Many of these conditions continued for decades, to be ultimately transformed into the more technical and bureaucratic forms of control I analyzed in Chapter 2.

Let me give one further concrete example. The larger political economy, in combination with patriarchal ideological forms, shows its power once again whenever the question of married women who engage in waged work appears historically. By the turn of the century hundreds of thousands of married women had begun to work outside the home. Yet during the Depression, it was very common for married women to be fired or to be denied jobs if they had working husbands. The state played a large role here. In England, governmental policies and reports gave considerable attention to women's domestic role.[60] In the United States, in 1930–31 the National Association of Education reported that of the 1,500 school systems in the country 77 percent refused to hire married women teachers. Another 63 percent dismissed any woman teacher who got married during the time of her employment. This did not only occur at the elementary and secondary levels. Some universities asked their married women faculty to resign. Lest we see this as something that only affected women teachers, the Federal government itself required in 1932 that if a married couple worked for the government, one must be let go. This law was applied almost invariably to women only.[61]

The very fact that these figures seem so shocking to us now is eloquent testimony of the sacrifices made and the struggles that women engaged in for decades to alter these oppressive relations. These struggles have been over one's control of one's labor and over the control of one's very life. Given the past conditions I have just pointed to, these historically significant struggles have actually brought no small measure of success. It is to these activities that I shall briefly turn in the concluding section of my analysis.

BEYOND THE MYTH OF THE PASSIVE TEACHER

Women teachers were not passive in the face of the class and gender conditions I described in the previous sections of this chapter. In fact, one of the major but lesser-known stories is the relationship between socialist and feminist activity and the growth of local teachers' organizations and unions in England and the United States.

Even while they worked internally to alter the frequently awful conditions they faced in urban schools on both sides of the Atlantic – such as crowded, unsanitary buildings, a teacher/student ratio that was often incredibly high, and an impersonal bureaucracy that, especially in the United States, was daily attempting to transform, rationalize, and control their work – a good deal of the unified action teachers took was concerned with their economic well-being. For example, grade school teachers in Chicago worked long and hard for adequate pensions. Out of this experience, the Chicago Teachers Federation headed by Catherine Goggin and Margaret Haley was born in 1897. It soon led a successful fight for salary increases and succeeded in organizing more than half the city's teachers in less than three years. Still an organization made up primarily of elementary school teachers, it was quite militant on economic matters. And while the women leaders and rank-and-file teachers were not necessarily as radical as some other leftist unions in cities such as Chicago, they still actively supported women's issues, municipal ownership of all utilities, popular elections and recalls, and labor solidarity. They did this in the face of middle- and upper-class resentment of unions. There was a constant struggle between the school board and the CTF, with the school board voting in 1905 to condemn the teachers for affiliating with the Chicago Federation of Labor. Such an affiliation was, according to the board, 'absolutely unjustifiable and intolerable in a school system of a democracy.'[62]

While these teachers were never totally successful either in their economic demands or in organizing plans,[63] they did succeed in forcing school boards to take elementary teachers – women – seriously as a force to be reckoned with. In the process, too, they partially challenged the economic and ideological relations surrounding women's work.

For many others in England and the United States, the conditions under which they labored had a radicalizing effect. Thus, many of the leaders of feminist groups were originally teachers who traced their growing awareness of the importance of the conflict over patriarchal domination to their experience as teachers. Their resentment over salary differentials, over interference in their decisions, over the very ways they were so tightly controlled, often led in large part to their growing interest in feminist ideas.[64]

These examples offer us a glimpse of politicized activities. But a large portion of the teachers in London or New York, Birmingham or Chicago, Liverpool or Boston, struggled in 'cultural' ways. They developed practices that gave them greater control of the curriculum; they fought to have a much greater say in *what* they taught, *how* they were to teach it, and how and by *whom* their work was to be evaluated. These everyday efforts still go on as teachers continue to defend themselves against external encroachments from the state or from capital.

The history of elementary school teaching (and curriculum in part, as well) *is* the history of these political/economic and cultural struggles. It is the history of a gendered workforce who, in the face of attempts to restructure their jobs, fought back consciously and unconsciously. Sometimes these very battles reinforced the existing definitions of women's work. Sometimes, perhaps more so in England, they led to a cutting of ties to one's class background. And sometimes, in ways similar to the teachers in Chapter 2, they supported class-specific ideals of work and professionalism. Just as often, however, these efforts empowered women by radicalizing some of them, or by giving them much more say in the actual control of what they taught and how they taught it, or by demonstrating that patriarchal forms could be partially fractured in equalizing both salaries and hiring and firing conditions.

What ultimately shapes how curricula and teaching are controlled at the level of classroom practice is, hence, an *ongoing* process. It involves a complex interplay among the ideological and material structures of control of gendered labor that arise from bureaucratic management, the forms of resistance and self-organization of teachers, and then employer counter-pressures,[65] which once again produce a response by teachers themselves. I have shown one moment in this process. As teaching changes from a predominantly male to a predominantly female occupation, the constitution of the job itself changes as well. It entails significantly greater controls over teaching and curriculum at the level of teacher education and in the classroom. It is structured around a different set of class and gender dynamics. Finally, women are active, not passive, figures in attempting to create positions for women as teachers based on their own positions in the social and sexual divisions of labor. These efforts may have had contradictory results, but they were part of a much larger movement – and one that is still so necessary today – to challenge aspects of patriarchal relations within both the home and the workplace.

Yet, as I have also argued, the transformation of teaching also led to the job itself becoming a breeding ground for further struggles. Many women were politicized. Some created unions. And others fought 'silently' every day on their jobs to expand or retain control of their own teaching and curriculum. In a time when the state and capital, as we shall see, are once more searching for ways to rationalize and control the day-to-day work of teachers, these overt and covert efforts from the past are of more than historical interest. For elementary school teaching *is* still gendered labor.[66] It is not too odd to end this section of the volume by saying that the past is still ahead of us.

TEXTS

CHAPTER 4

THE CULTURE AND COMMERCE OF THE TEXTBOOK

INTRODUCTION

The previous chapters examined how current and past policies and practices for the control of teaching grew out of the intersection of class and gender dynamics and out of the political/economic conditions of which schools were a part. They stressed the interplay between structure and agency, showing the contradictory causes and results of the ways teaching was constituted over time as well as pointing to the continuing effects of the constitution of elementary school teaching as 'women's work.' While the focus there was on teachers, our attention in this next section of the book will be on texts. The issue will be not only on the control of who should do the teaching and under what conditions, but on *what should be taught* in the first place.

How do the pressures on teachers I analyzed get built through the curricula and textbooks themselves, through policies articulated by national reports that have had such a major effect on state and local educational authorities, and by economic and technological structures in the larger society? Who stands to benefit from these curricular pressures and policies? Since it is the textbook which establishes so much of the material conditions for teaching and learning in classrooms in many countries throughout the world, and since it is the textbook that often defines what is elite and legitimate culture to pass on, that is where we shall start.

The textbook in the United States is now increasingly 'systems managed.' It is more and more rationalized and geared to testing programs and competency measures, especially at the elementary level; but with the growth of statewide high school competency tests, this rationalization and standardization is growing rapidly there as well. The economic and ideological pressures on texts are very intense. Though the textbook can be partly liberatory since it can provide needed knowledge where that information is missing, the text often becomes one aspect of the systems of control I discussed earlier. Little is left to the teacher's discretion as the state becomes even more intrusive into the kinds of knowledge that must be taught, the end products and goals of that teaching, and the ways it must be carried on. Even with these intrusions, however, here too we shall see that culture, state, and economy have complicated interrelationships – ones that have been and are mediated by class and gender dynamics.

CULTURE AND COMMERCE

We can talk about culture in two ways: as a lived process, as what Raymond Williams has called a whole way of life, or as a commodity.[1] In the first, we focus on culture as a constitutive social process through which we live our daily lives. In the second, we emphasize the products of culture, the very thingness of the commodities we produce and consume. This distinction can of course be maintained only on an analytic level, since most of what seem to us to be things – like lightbulbs, cars, records, and, in the case of this chapter, books – are really part of a larger social process. As Marx, for example, spent years trying to demonstrate, every product is an expression of embodied human labor. Goods and services are relations among people – relations of exploitation often, but human relations nevertheless. Turning on a light when you walk into a room is not only using an object, it is also to be involved in an anonymous social relationship with the miner who worked to dig the coal burned to produce the electricity.

This dual nature of culture poses a dilemma for those individuals who are interested in understanding the dynamics of popular and elite culture in our society. It makes studying the dominant cultural products – from films, to books, to television, to music – decidedly slippery, for there are sets of relations behind each of these 'things.' And these in turn are situated within the larger web of the social and market relations of capitalism.

While there is a danger of falling into economic reductionism, it is essential that we look more closely at this political economy of culture. How do the dynamics of class, gender, and race 'determine' cultural production? How is the organization and distribution of culture 'mediated' by economic and social structures?[2] What is the relationship between a cultural product – say a film or a book – and the social relations of its production, accessibility, and consumption? These are not easy questions to deal with. They are not easy in at least two ways. First, the very terms of the language and concepts we use to ask them are notoriously difficult to unpack. That is, words such as 'determine', 'mediate', 'social relations of production', and so on – and the conceptual apparatus that lies behind them – are not at all settled. There is as much contention over their use currently as there has ever been.[3] Thus, it is hard to grapple with the issue of the determination of culture without at the same time being very self-conscious about the tools one is employing to do it.

Second, and closely related to the first, perhaps because of the theoretical controversies surrounding the topic and the anti-positivist positions I mentioned in Chapter 1, there have been fewer detailed and large-scale empirical investigations of these relations recently than is necessary. While we may have interesting ideological or economic analyses of a television show, film, or book,[4] there are really only a few well-designed empirical studies that examine the economics and social relations involved in films and books in general. It is hard to get a global picture because of this.

This lack is a problem in sociological analysis in general; yet it is even more problematic in the field of education. Even though the overt aim of our institutions of schooling has more than a little to do with cultural products and processes, with cultural transmission, it has only been in the last decade or so that the politics and economics of the culture that actually *is* transmitted in schools has been taken up as a serious research problem. It was almost as if Durkheim and Weber, to say nothing of Marx, had never existed. In the area that has come to be called the sociology of the curriculum, however, steps have been taken to deal with this issue in some very interesting ways. A good deal of progress has in fact been made in understanding whose knowledge is taught and produced in our schools.[5]

While not the only questions with which we should be concerned, it is clear that major curriculum issues are those of content and organization. What should be taught? In what way? Answering these questions is difficult. For not only does the first, for example, involve some very knotty epistemological issues – what should be granted the status of knowledge? – but it is a politically loaded problem as well. To borrow the language of Pierre Bourdieu and Basil Bernstein, the 'cultural capital' of dominant classes and class segments has been considered the most legitimate knowledge.[6] This knowledge, and one's 'ability' to deal with it, has served as one mechanism in a complex process in which the economic and cultural reproduction of class, gender, and race relations is accomplished. Therefore, the choice of particular content and ways of approaching it in schools is related both to existing relations of domination and to struggles to alter these relations. Not to recognize this is to ignore a wealth of evidence in the United States, England, Australia, France, Sweden, Germany, and elsewhere that links school knowledge – both commodified and lived – to class, gender, and race dynamics outside as well as inside our institutions of education.[7]

Even where there is recognition of the political nature of the curriculum, this does not solve all of our problems. The statement that school knowledge has some (admittedly complex) connections to the larger political economy merely restates the issue. It does not in itself explain how these connections operate. Though the ties that link curricula to the inequalities and social struggles of our social formation are very complicated, occasionally research is available that helps illuminate this nexus, even when it may not be overtly aimed at an educational audience. I want to draw on this research to help us begin to uncover some of the connections between curriculum and the larger political economy. The most interesting of this research is about the culture and commerce of publishing. It wants to examine the relationship between how publishing operates internally – its social relations and composition – and the cultural and economic market within which it is situated. What do the social and economic relations within the publishing industry have to do with schools, with the politics of knowledge distribution in education? Perhaps this can be made clearer if we stop and think about another question.

How is this 'legitimate' knowledge made available in schools? By and large it is made available through something to which we have paid far too little attention – the textbook. Whether we like it or not, the curriculum in most American schools is not defined by courses of study or suggested programs, but by one particular artifact, the standardized, grade-level-specific text in mathematics, reading, social studies, science (when it is even taught), and so on. The impact of this on the social relations of the classroom is also immense. It is estimated, for example, that 75 percent of the time elementary and secondary students are in classrooms and 90 percent of their time on homework is spent with text materials.[8] Yet, even given the ubiquitous character of textbooks, they are one of the things we know least about.

While the text dominates curricula at the elementary, secondary, and even college levels, very little critical attention has been paid to the ideological, political, and economic sources of its production, distribution, and reception.[9]

In order to make sense out of this, we need to place the production of curricular materials such as texts back in the larger process of the production of cultural commodities, such as books, in general. There are approximately 40,000 books published each year in the United States.[10] Obviously, these are quite varied, with only a small portion of them being textbooks. Yet, even with this variation, there are certain constants that act on publishers.

We can identify four 'major structural conditions' that by and large determine the shape of publishing currently in the United States.

> (1) The industry sells its products – like any commodity – in a market, but a market that, in contrast to that for many other products, is fickle and often uncertain. (2) The industry is decentralized among a number of sectors whose operations bear little resemblance to each other. (3) These operations are characterized by a mixture of modern mass-production methods and craft-like procedures. (4) The industry remains perilously poised between the requirements and restraints of commerce and the responsibilities and obligations that it must bear as a prime guardian of the symbolic culture of the nation. Although the tensions between the claims of commerce and culture seem to us always to have been with book publishing, they have become more acute and salient in the last twenty years.[11]

These conditions are not new phenomena, by any means. From the time printing began as an industry, books were pieces of merchandise. They were, of course, often produced for scholarly or humanistic purposes, but before anything else their prime function was to earn their producers a living. Book production, hence, has historically rested on a foundation where from the outset it was necessary to 'find enough capital to start work and then to print only those titles which would satisfy a clientele, and that at a price which would withstand competition.' Similarly to the marketing of other products, then, finance and costing took an immensely important place in the decisions of publishers and booksellers.[12] Febvre and Martin, in their analysis of the history of book printing in Europe, argue this point exceptionally clearly:

> One fact must not be lost sight of: the printer and the bookseller worked above all and from the beginning for profit. The story of the first joint enterprise, Fust and Schoeffer, proves that. Like their modern counterparts, 15th-century publishers only financed the kind of book they felt would sell enough copies to show a profit in a reasonable time. We should not therefore be surprised to find that the immediate effect of printing was merely to further increase the circulation of those works which had already enjoyed success in manuscript, and often to consign other less popular texts to oblivion. By multiplying books by the hundred and then thousand [compared to, say, the laborious copying of manuscripts], the press achieved both increased volume and at the same time more rigorous selection.[13]

Drawing upon Pierre Bourdieu's work, we can make a distinction between two types of 'capital': *symbolic* and *financial*. This enables us to distinguish among the many kinds of publishers one might find. In essence, these two kinds of capital are found in different kinds of markets. Those firms that are more commercial, that are oriented to rapid turnover, quick obsolescence, and to the minimization of risks, are following a strategy for the accumulation of financial capital. Such a strategy has a strikingly different perspective on time, as well. It has a short time perspective – one that focuses on a particular group of readers' current interests. In contradistinction to those publishers whose market embodies the interests of finance capital, those firms whose goal is to maximize the accumulation of symbolic capital operate in such a way that their time perspective is longer. Immediate profit is less important. Higher risks may be taken and experimental content and form will find greater acceptance. These publishers are not uninterested in the 'logic of profitability,' but long-term accumulation is more important. One example is provided by Beckett's *Waiting for Godot*, which only sold 10,000 copies in the first five years after its publication in 1952, yet then went on to sell 60,000 copies as its rate of sales increased yearly by 20 percent.[14]

This conceptual distinction based on varying kinds of capital does not totally cover the differences among publishers regarding the kinds of books they publish, however. Coser, Kadushin, and Powell, for example, further classify publishers according to the ways in which editors themselves carry out their work. In so doing, they distinguish among trade, or text, or finally the various scholarly monograph or university presses. Each of these various labels refers not only to editorial policy. It speaks to a whole array of differences concerning the kind of technology that is employed by the press, the bureaucratic and organizational structures that coordinate and control the day-to-day work of the company, and the different risks and monetary and marketing policies involved. Each label also refers to important differences in relations with authors, in time scheduling, and ultimately in what counts as 'success.'[15] Behind the commodity, the book, there stands, indeed, a whole set of human relations.

These structural differences in organization, technology, and economic and social relations structure the practices of the people involved in producing books. This includes editors, authors, agents, and to a lesser extent sales and marketing personnel. Digging deeper into these relations also enables us to better understand the political economy of culture. By integrating analyses of internal decision-making processes and external market relations within publishing we can gain a good deal of insight into how particular aspects of popular and elite culture are presented in published form and become the 'what' that is taught in schools.

Let us set the stage for our further discussion historically. From the period just after the Civil War to the first decade of the twentieth century, fictional books led in the sheer quantity of titles that were published. We can see this if we take one year as an example. In 1886, *Publishers Weekly* took the nearly 5,000 books published and broke them down into various categories. The ten categories with the most volumes were: fiction (1,080), law (469), juvenile (458), literary history and miscellaneous (388), theology (377), education and language (275), poetry and drama (220), history (182), medical science (177), and social and political science (174).[16] These data do not account for the many informal political booklets and pamphlets that were published. But who the readership actually was, what the rates of literacy were between particular classes and genders, what the economic conditions of publishing and purchasing were – all of this had an impact on what was published.

These figures are interesting since they have tended to change markedly over the years. Yet it is not just the type of book that is published that is of import either historically or currently. Form and content have been subject to the influences of the larger society as well. To take one example, market constraints have often had a profound impact on what gets published and even on what authors will write. Again, certain aspects of fiction writing and publishing offer an interesting case in point. Wendy Griswold's analysis of the manner in which different market positions occupied by various authors and publishers had an impact documents this nicely.

In the nineteenth century, the topics that European writers were dealing with had a distinct market advantage in the United States due to the oddities of our copyright laws. As Griswold put it:

> During most of the 19th century, American copyright laws protected citizens or permanent residents of the United States but not foreign authors. The result was that British and other foreign works could be reprinted and sold in the United States without royalties being paid to their authors, while Americans did receive royalty payments. Many interests in the United States benefited from this literary piracy and lobbied to maintain the status quo. (Actually piracy is something of a misnomer, for the practice was perfectly legal.) The nascent printing industry was kept busy. Publishers made huge profits from reprinting foreign books. Readers had available the best foreign literature at low prices; for example, in 1843 *A Christmas Carol* sold for 6c in the United States and the equivalent of $2.50 in England.[17]

Clearly, such a situation could lead to some rather difficult circumstances for authors. American publishers had little inducement to publish 'original native works,' since a copyright had to be paid to their authors. American authors were largely left, then, unable to earn their living as fiction writers because they were excluded from the fiction market. This had an impact on the content of their writing as well. Since they were discouraged from dealing with subjects already treated in the cheaper editions of European works, American authors often had to stake out a different terrain, areas that were unusual but would still have enough market appeal to convince publishers to publish them.[18]

These influences did not constitute a new phenomenon. In fact, the growth of particular genres and styles of books themselves has been linked closely to similar social forces operating earlier. As Ian Watt and Raymond Williams have argued, the rise of something as common today as the novel is related to changes in political economies and class structures and to the growth of ideologies of individualism, among other things.[19] In the eighteenth century, for instance, 'the rapid expansion of a new audience for literature, the literate middle class, especially the leisured middle class women,' also led to novels focusing on 'love and marriage, economic individualism, the complexities of modern life, and the possibility of personal morality in a corrupting world.' The economic conditions of publishing also changed a good deal. There was a decline in patronage and the growth of the bookseller who combined publishing, printing, and selling together. Authors were often paid by the page. Speed and the number of pages became of no small value, as you would imagine.[20]

These small examples can give a sense of the historical complexity of the influences on publishing and on its content, readership, and economic realities. Book publishing today lives in the shadow of this past and the social, ideological, and economic conditions that continued their development out of it. This must be particularly borne in mind in endeavoring to understand the commercial and cultural structures involved in the publication of textbooks for schools. An excellent case in point is the production of texts for tertiary-level courses. As we shall see, the 'culture and commerce' of college and other text production can provide some important insights into how the cultural commodification process works.

THE POLITICAL ECONOMY OF THE TEXTBOOK

While we may think of book publishing as a relatively large industry, by current standards it is actually rather small compared to other industries. A comparison may be helpful here. The *entire* book publishing industry with its 65,000 or so employees would rank nearly forty to fifty positions below a single one of the highest grossing and largest employing American companies. While its total sales in 1980 were approximately $6 billion, and this does in fact sound impressive, in many ways its market is much less certain and is subject to greater economic, political, and ideological contingencies than is the case for these large companies.

Six billion dollars, though, is still definitely not a pittance. Book publishing *is* an industry, and one that is divided up into a variety of markets. Of the total, $1.2 billion was accounted for by reference books, encyclopedias, and professional books; $1.5 billion came from the elementary, secondary, and college text market; $1 billion was taken in from book clubs and direct mail sales; nearly $660 million was accounted for by mass market paperbacks; and finally books intended for the general public – what are called trade books – had a sales level of $1 billion. With its $1.5 billion sales, it is obvious that the textbook market is no small segment of the industry as a whole.[21]

The growing concentration of power in text publishing has been marked. There has been increased competition recently; but this has been among a small number of the larger firms. The competition has also reduced the propensity to take risks. Instead, many publishers now prefer to expend most of their efforts on a smaller selection of 'carefully chosen "products".'[22]

Perhaps the simplest way to illuminate part of this dynamic is to quote from a major figure in publishing who, after thirty-five years' involvement in the industry, reflected on the question 'How competitive is book publishing?' His answer, succinct and speaking paragraphs that remained implicit, was only one word – 'Very.'[23]

A picture of the nature of the concentration within text publishing can be gained from a few facts. Seventy-five percent of the total sales of college textbooks was controlled by the ten largest text publishers, with 90 percent accounted for by the top twenty. Prentice-Hall, McGraw-Hill, the CBS Publishing Group, and Scott, Foresman – the top four – accounted for 40 percent of the market.[24] In what is called the 'elhi' (elementary and high school) market, the figures are also very revealing. It is estimated that the four largest textbook publishers of these materials account for 32 percent of the market. The eight largest firms control 53 percent. And the twenty largest control over 75 percent of sales.[25] This is no small amount, to be sure. Yet concentration does not tell the entire story. Internal qualities concerning who works in these firms, what their backgrounds and characteristics are, and what their working conditions happen to be, also play a significant part.

What kind of people make the decisions about college and other texts? Even though many people find their way into publishing in general by accident, as it were, this is even more the case for editors who work in firms that deal with, say, college texts. 'Most of them entered publishing simply because they were looking for some sort of a job, and publishing presented itself.'[26] But these people are not all equal. Important divisions exist within the houses themselves.

In fact, one thing that recent research makes strikingly clear is the strength of sex-typing in the division of labor in publishing. Women are often found in subsidiary rights and publicity departments. They are often copy editors. While they outnumber men in employment within publishing as a whole, this does not mean that they are usually a powerful overt force. Rather, they tend largely to be hired as 'secretaries, assistants, publicists, advertising managers, and occupants of other low- and mid-level positions.' Even though there have been a number of women who have moved into important editorial positions in the past few years, by and large women are still not as evident in positions that actually 'exercise control over the goals and policy of publishing.' In essence, there is something of a dual labor market in publishing. The lower-paying, replaceable jobs, with less possibility for advancement, are the characteristics of the 'female enclaves.'[27]

What does this mean for this particular discussion? Nearly 75 percent of the editors in college text publishing either began their careers as sales personnel or held sales or marketing positions before being promoted to editor.[28] Since there are many fewer women than men who travel around selling college or other level texts or holding positions of authority within sales departments that could lead to upward mobility, this will have an interesting effect both on the people who become editors and on the content of editorial decisions as well.

These facts have important implications. Most editorial decisions concerning which texts are to be published – that is, concerning what is to count as legitimate content within particular disciplines that students are to receive as 'official knowledge' – are made by individuals who have specific characteristics. These editors will be predominantly male, thereby reproducing patriarchal relations within the firm itself. Second, their general background will complement the existing market structure that dominates text production. Financial capital, short-term perspectives, and high profit margins will be seen as major goals.[29] A substantial cultural or educational vision or the concerns associated with strategies based on symbolic capital will necessarily take a back seat, where they exist at all.

The influence of profit, of the power of what they call commerce, in text production, is recognized by Coser, Kadushin, and Powell. As they note about college text publishing, the major emphasis is on the production of books for introductory level courses that have high student enrollments. A good deal of attention is paid to the design of the book itself and to marketing strategies that will cause it to be used in these courses.[30] Yet unlike most other kinds of publishing, text publishers define their markets not as the actual reader of the book but as the teacher or professor.[31] The purchaser, the student, has little power in this equation, except where it may influence a professor's decision.

Based on the sense of sales potential and on their 'regular polling of their markets,' a large percentage of college text editors actively search for books. Contacts are made, suggestions given. In essence, it would not be wrong to say that text editors create their own books.[32] This is probably cheaper in the long run.

In the United States it is estimated that the production costs of an introductory text for a college-level course is usually between $100,000 and $250,000. Given the fact that text publishers produce relatively few titles compared to large publishers of, say, fiction, there is considerable pressure on the editorial staff and others to guarantee that such books sell.[33] For the 'elhi' market the sheer amount of money and the risks involved are made visible by the fact that, nearly a decade ago, for every $500,000 invested by a publisher in a text 100,000 copies needed to be sold merely to break even.[34]

These conditions will have ramifications in the social relations within the firm besides the patriarchal structure I noted earlier. Staff meetings, meetings with other editors, meetings with marketing and production staff to coordinate the production of a text, and so on – those kinds of activities tend to dominate the life of the text editor. As Coser and his co-authors so nicely phrase it, 'text editors practically live in meetings.'[35] Hence, text publishing will be much more bureaucratic and will have more formalized decision-making structures. This is partly due to the fact that textbook production is largely a routine process. Formats do not markedly differ from discipline to discipline. And as I mentioned, the focus is primarily on producing a limited number of large sellers at a comparatively high price compared to fiction. Lastly, the emphasis is often on marketing a text with a standard content, which, with revisions and a little bit of luck, will be used for years to come.[36]

All of these elements are heightened even more in one other aspect of text publishing that contributes to bureaucratization and standardization: the orchestrated production of 'managed' texts. These are volumes that are usually written by professional writers, with some 'guidance' from graduate students and academics, though such volumes often bear the name of a well-known professor. Written text and graphics are closely coordinated, as are language and reading levels and an instructor's manual. In many ways, these are books without formal authors. Ghost-written under conditions of stringent cost controls, geared to what will sell, not necessarily what is most important to know, managed texts have been taking their place in many college classrooms. While the dreams of some publishers that such texts will solve their financial problems have not been totally realized, the managed text is a significant phenomenon and deserves a good deal of critical attention not only at the college level but in elementary and secondary schools as well, since the managed text is by no means absent in these areas.[37] Its introduction in many ways complements the styles and techniques of managing teachers' work I analyzed earlier and needs to be linked in important ways to the restructuring of women's labor that has been such a prime component in the constitution of the role of teaching.

Despite the difficulty some managed texts have had in making the anticipated high profits, there will probably be more centralized control over writing and over the entire process of publishing material for classroom use. The effect, according to Coser, Kadushin, and Powell, will be 'an even greater homogenization of texts at a college level'[38] – something we can expect at the elementary and high school level as well,[39] especially given the growing pressures to standardize both curricula and teaching.

These points demonstrate some of the important aspects of day-to-day life within publishing. One would expect that all of the meetings, the planning, the growing sampling of markets, the competition, and so forth, would have a profound impact on the content of volumes. This is indeed the case, but perhaps not quite in the way one might think. We need to be very careful here about assuming that there is simple and overt censorship of material. The process is much more complicated than that. Even though existing research does not go into detail about such things within the college text industry specifically, one can infer what happens from its discussion of censorship in the larger industry.

In the increasingly conglomerate-owned publishing field as a whole, censorship and ideological control as we commonly think of them are less of a problem than might be anticipated. It is not ideological uniformity or some political agenda that accounts for many of the ideas that are ultimately made or not made available to the larger public. Rather, it is the infamous 'bottom line' that counts. 'Ultimately . . . if there is any censorship, it concerns profitability. Books that are not profitable, no matter what their subject, are not viewed favorably.'[40]

This is not an inconsequential concern. In the publishing industry as a whole only three out of every ten books are marginally profitable; only 30 percent manage to break even. The remainder lose money.[41] Further, it has become clear that sales of texts in particular have actually been decreasing. If we take as a baseline the years 1968 to, say, 1976, costs rose considerably, but sales at a college level fell by 10 percent. The same is true for the 'elhi' text market; coupled with rising costs was a drop in sales of 11.2 percent[42] (though this may have changed for the better given recent sales figures). Thus, issues of profit are in fact part of a rational set of choices within corporate logic.

If this is the case for publishing in general and probably in large part for college text production, is it generalizable to those standardized secondary and, especially, elementary textbooks I pointed to earlier? Are market, profit, and internal relations more important than ideological concerns? Here we must answer that this is so only in part.

The economics and politics of text production are somewhat more complicated when one examines what is produced for sale in our elementary and secondary schools. While there is no official federal government sponsorship of specific curriculum content in the United States in quite the same way as there is in those countries where ministries of education mandate a standard course of study, the structures of a national curriculum are produced by the market place and by state intervention in other ways. Perhaps the most important aspect of this is the various models of state adoption now extant.

As many of you know from personal experience, in many states – most often in the Southern tier around to the Western sun belt – textbooks for use in the major subject areas must be approved by state agencies or committees. Or, they are reviewed and a limited number are selected as recommended for use in schools. If local school districts select material from such an approved list, they are often reimbursed for a significant portion of the purchase cost. Because of this, even where texts are not mandated, there is a good deal to be gained by local schools in a time of economic crisis if they do in fact ultimately choose an approved volume. The cost savings here are obviously not inconsequential.

Yet, it is not only here that the economics of cultural distribution operate. Publishers themselves, simply because of good business practice, must by necessity aim their text publishing practices towards those states with such state adoption policies. The simple fact of getting one's volume on such a list can make all the difference for a text's profitability. Thus, for instance, sales to California and Texas can account for over 20 percent of the total sales of any particular book – a considerable percentage in the highly competitive world of elementary and secondary school book publishing and selling. Because of this, the writing, editing, promotion, and general orientation and strategy of such production is quite often aimed toward guaranteeing a place on the list of state-approved material. Since this is the case, the political and ideological climate of these primarily Southern states often determines the content and form of the purchased curriculum throughout the rest of the nation. And since a textbook series often takes years to write and produce and, as I noted earlier, can be very costly when production costs are totalled up, 'publishers want assurance of knowing that their school book series will sell before they commit large budgets to these undertakings.'[43]

Yet even here the situation is complicated considerably, especially by the fact that agencies of the state apparatus are important sites of ideological struggle. These very conflicts may make it very difficult for publishers to determine a simple reading of the needs of 'financial capital.' Often, for instance, given the uncertainty of a market, publishers may be loath to make decisions based on the political controversies or 'needs' of any one state, especially in highly charged curriculum areas. A good example is provided by the California creationism vs. evolutionism controversy, where a group of 'scientific creationists,' supported by the political and ideological Right, sought to make all social studies and science texts give equal weight to creationist and evolutionary theories.

Even when California's Board of Education, after much agonizing and debate, recommend 'editorial qualifications' that were supposed to meet the objections of creationist critics of the textbooks, the framework for text adoption was still very unclear and subject to many different interpretations. Did it require or merely allow discussion of the theory of creation? Was a series of editorial changes that qualified the discussions of evolution in the existing texts all that was required? Given this ambiguity, and the volatility of the issue, in which the 'winning position' was unclear, publishers 'resisted undertaking the more substantial effort of incorporating new information into their materials.'[44] In the words of one observer of the process, 'Faced with an unclear directive, and one that might be reversed at any moment, publishers were reluctant to invest in change. They eventually yielded to the minor editorial adjustments adopted by the board, but staunchly resisted the requirement that they discuss creation in their social science texts.'[45] Both economic and ideological forces come into play here in important ways, both between the firms and their markets and undoubtedly within the firms themselves.

Notice what this means if we are to fully understand how specific cultural goods are produced and distributed for our public schools. We would need to unpack the logic of a fairly complicated set of interrelationships. How does the political economy of publishing itself generate particular economic and ideological needs? How and why do publishers respond to the needs of the 'public'? Who determines what this 'public' is?[46] How do the internal politics of state adoption policies work? What are the processes used in selecting the people and interests that make up the state textbook committees? How are texts sold at a local level? What is the actual process of text production, from the commissioning of a project to revisions and editing to promotion and sales? How and for what reasons are decisions on this made? Only by going into considerable detail on each of these questions can we begin to see how particular groups' cultural capital is commodified and made available (or not made available) in schools throughout the country.[47]

My discussion of the issues of state adoption policies and my raising of the above questions are not meant to imply that all of the material found in our public schools will be simply a reflection of existing cultural and economic inequalities. After all, if texts were totally reliable defenders of the existing ideological, political, and economic order, they would not be such a contentious area as they are currently. Industry and conservative groups have made an issue of what knowledge is now taught in schools precisely because there *are* progressive elements within curricula and texts.[48] This is partly due to the fact that the authors of such material often belong to a particular segment of the new petty bourgeoisie with its own largely liberal ideological interests, its own contradictory consciousness, its own elements of what Gramsci might call good and bad sense, which will not be identical with those embodied in profit maximization or ideological uniformity. To speak theoretically, there will be relatively autonomous interests in specific cultural values within the groups of authors and editors who work for publishers. These values may be a bit more progressive than one might anticipate from the market structure of text production. This will surely militate against total standardization and censorship.[49]

These kinds of issues concerning who writes and edits texts, whether they are totally controlled by the complicated market relations and state policies surrounding text publishing, and what are the contradictory forces at work all clearly need further elaboration. My basic aim has been to demonstrate how recent research on the ways in which culture is commodified can serve as a platform for thinking about some of our own dilemmas as teachers and researchers in education concerned with the dynamics of cultural capital and the ways texts see the light of day.

THE RELATIVE AUTONOMY OF THE TEXT

So far, I have employed some of the research on book publishing to help clarify an issue that is of great import to educators – how and by whom the texts which dominate the curriculum come to be the way they are. As I mentioned at the very outset of this chapter, however, we need to see such analyses as constituting a serious contribution to a larger theoretical debate about cultural processes and products as well. In this concluding section, let me try to make clear this part of my argument about the political economy of culture.

External economic and political pressures are not somewhere 'out there' in some vague abstraction called the economy. As recent commentators have persuasively argued, in our society hegemonic forms are not often imposed from outside by a small group of corporate owners who sit around each day plotting how to do in workers, women, and people of color. Some of this plotting may go on, of course. But just as significant are the routine grounds of our daily decisions, in our homes, stores, offices, and factories. To speak somewhat technically, dominant relations are ongoingly reconstituted by the actions we take and the decisions we make in our own small local areas of life. Rather than an economy being out there, it is right here. We rebuild it routinely in our social interaction. Rather than ideological domination and the relations of cultural capital being something we have imposed on us from above, we reintegrate them within our everyday discourse merely by following our commonsense needs and desires as we go about making a living, finding entertainment and sustenance, and so on.[50]

These arguments are abstract but they are important for the points I want to make. For while a serious theoretical structure is either absent or is often hidden within the data presented by the research I have drawn upon, a good deal of this research does document some of the claims I made in the above paragraph. As the authors of *Books* put it in their discussion of why particular decisions are made:

> For the most part, what directly affects an editor's daily routine is not corporate ownership or being one division of a large multi-divisional publishing house. Instead, on a day-to-day basis, editorial behavior is most strongly influenced by the editorial policies of the house and the relationship among departments and personnel *within* the publishing house or division.[51]

This position may not seem overly consequential, yet its theoretic import is great. Encapsulated within a changing set of market relations which set limits on what is considered rational behavior on the part of its participants, editors and other employees have 'relative autonomy.' They are partly free to pursue the internal needs of their craft and to follow the logic of the internal demands within the publishing house itself. The past histories of gender, class, and race relations and the actual 'local' political economy of publishing set the boundaries within which these decisions are made and in large part determine who will make the decisions. To return to my earlier point about text editors usually having their prior roots in sales, we can see that the internal labor market in text publishing, the ladder upon which career mobility depends, means that sales will be in the forefront ideologically and economically in these firms. 'Finance capital' dominates, not only because the economy out there mandates it, but because of the historical connections among mobility patterns within firms, rational decision-making based on external competition, political dynamics (of which more will be said later), and internal information, and, because of these things, the kinds of discourse which tend to dominate the meetings and conversations among all the people involved within the organizational structure of the text publisher.[52] This kind of analysis makes it more complicated, of course. But surely it is more elegant and more grounded in reality than some of the more mechanistic theories about the economic control of culture that have been a bit too readily accepted. It manages to preserve the efficacy of the economy while granting some autonomy to the internal bureaucratic and biographical structure of individual publishers, while at the same time recognizing the political economy of gendered labor that exists as well.

Many areas remain that I have not focused upon here, of course. Among the most important of these is the alteration in the very technology of publishing. Just as the development and use of print 'made possible the growth of literary learning and journals' and thereby helped create the conditions for individual writers and artists to emerge out of the more collective conditions of production that dominated guilds and workshops,[53] so too one would expect that the changes in the technology of text production and the altered social and authorial relations that are evolving from them will also have a serious impact on books. At the very least, given the sexual division of labor in publishing, new technologies can have a large bearing on the deskilling and reskilling of those 'female enclaves' I mentioned earlier.[54]

Further, even though I have directed my attention primarily to the 'culture and commerce' surrounding the production of one particular cultural commodity – the standardized text used for tertiary and elhi level courses – it still remains an open question how exactly the economic and ideological elements I have outlined actually work through some of the largest of all text markets – those found in the elementary and secondary schools. However, in order to go significantly further we clearly need a more adequate theory of the relationship between the political and economic (to say nothing of the cultural) spheres in education. Thus, the state's position as a site for class, race, and gender conflicts, how these struggles are 'resolved' within the state apparatus, how publishers respond to these conflicts and resolutions, and ultimately what impact these resolutions or accords have on the questions surrounding officially sponsored texts and knowledge – all of these need considerably more deliberation.[55] Carnoy's and Dale's recent work on the interrelations between education and the state and Offe's analyses of the state's role in negative selection may provide important avenues here.[56]

This points to a significant empirical agenda as well. What is required now is a long-term *and* theoretically and politically grounded ethnographic investigation that follows a curriculum artifact such as a textbook from its writing to its selling (and then to its use). Only then will we have a more accurate portrayal of the complete circuit of cultural production, circulation, and consumption. Not only would this be a major contribution to our understanding of the relationship among culture, politics and economy, it is also absolutely essential if we are to act in ways that alter the kinds of knowledge considered legitimate for transmission in our schools.[57] As long as the text dominates curricula, to ignore it as being simply not worthy of serious attention and serious struggle is to live in a world divorced from reality.

The textbook does not stand alone, however. There are pressures from a variety of groups – mostly conservative – to redefine both the ways teachers teach and the knowledge considered legitimate for the curriculum. These groups have themselves authored a number of 'texts,' not for children but for adults, in an effort to convince the public that both teaching and curriculum need to be reoriented in significant ways. The first of these ways is largely based on a restoration of academic knowledge, on the text as a set of 'classics.' The second is a transformation of teachers and texts into more economically efficient aspects of the movement to reindustrialize America. The next two chapters will focus directly on these movements. As we shall see, both these positions and their outcomes are rather contradictory.

CHAPTER 5

OLD HUMANISTS AND NEW CURRICULA

COMMON CURRICULUM AND THE EDUCATIONAL CRISIS

During the past few years, we in the United States have witnessed a shift of major proportions in the attention being given to one set of institutions. From being seen as something of marginal interest in public discussions and in the media, schools are now directly in the spotlight of public scrutiny. At the time of writing, in fact, it is hard to find newspapers or magazines that do *not* devote considerable space to detailing 'problems' with the American school system. A sense of the depth of these problems that many rather powerful groups find in our schools can be seen in the final report of the National Commission on Excellence in Education, *A Nation at Risk*. In language that leaves no room for the false hope that things are all right educationally, the report's authors state:

> Our nation is at risk. Our once unchallenged preeminence in commerce, industry, science, and technological innovation is being taken over by competitors throughout the world . . . We report to the American people that while we can take justifiable pride in what our schools and colleges have historically accomplished and contributed to the United States and the well-being of its people, the educational foundations of our society are presently being eroded by a rising tide of mediocrity

> that threatens our very future as a nation and a people. What was unimaginable a generation ago has begun to occur – others are matching and surpassing our educational attainments.[1]

The report goes on, making its conclusions even more graphic:

> If an unfriendly foreign power had attempted to impose on America the mediocre educational performance that exists today, we might well have viewed it as an act of war. As it stands, we have allowed this to happen to ourselves. We have even squandered the gains in student achievement made in the wake of the Sputnik challenge . . . We have, in effect, been committing an act of unthinking, unilateral educational disarmament.[2]

What has been the root cause of this disarmament? The report concludes that the educational system and the society as a whole have 'lost sight of the basic purpose of schooling, and of the high expectations and disciplined effort needed to attain them.'[3]

Though published before *A Nation at Risk*, *The Paideia Proposal*[4] is part of this larger movement to define again the 'basic purpose of schooling' and to recommit our classrooms to 'excellence' and 'discipline.' Like the report of the National Commission, it too is addressed to 'the public.' The problems it wants to speak to are wide and varied. Many of them are real issues, as we shall see. Yet its construction of what some of these problems are, and their root causes, may lead us to misrecognize effects for causes and may divert our attention to actions that may not be as effective as its proponents might wish.

Who is this public that *The Paideia Proposal* addresses? It is everyone who is 'most concerned with the future of our public schools.' 'Who,' though, is coupled with 'why.' Adler, speaking for the members of the Paideia Group, offers a list of such 'whos' and 'whys.' There are ten constituencies.[5]

1 Parents – 'who believe that the decline in the quality of public schooling is damaging the future of their children.'
2 Teachers – who are 'troubled that the increasing time spent in keeping basic order in the classroom undermines the real business of schooling: to teach and to learn.'
3 School boards – who are 'frightened by the flight of middle-class children and youth to private and parochial schools.'
4 College educators – who are 'burdened by the increasing need to provide remedial education which detracts from their ability to offer a meaningful higher education.'
5 Elected public officials – who are 'searching for ways to improve the quality of education without increasing the cost to taxpayers.'
6 Employers – whose concerns include 'the effects on productivity in a work force lacking skills in reading, writing, speaking, listening, observing, measuring, and computing.'
7 Minority groups – who are 'angered by widening gulfs between the better educated and the poorly educated, and between the employed and the unemployed.'
8 Labor leaders – who must attempt 'to deal with workers who lack skills to find jobs in the new high-technology industries.'
9 Military leaders – who need 'brainpower among the troops capable of coping with sophisticated weaponry.'
10 American citizens in general – who are 'alarmed by the prospects of democracy in which a declining

proportion of the people vote or endeavor to understand the great issues of our time.'

Thus, all of these groups have a major interest in radically altering the way our schools are functioning today. Without such alterations, we shall be condemned to low productivity, middle-class flight, high unemployment, horrible discipline problems, racial animosities, stupid warriors, higher costs, and a shriveling of democracy.

This of course leads Adler to the question of what we must do to avoid these problems. What would this altered educational process look like? First, our school system must eliminate tracking. There should be a one-track system in which the education of all children must have the same objectives, with no exception, for the twelve or so years of elementary and secondary schooling.[6] These objectives center around three broad and basic goals. First, their schooling should prepare all students to 'take advantage of every opportunity for personal development that our society offers.'[7] It should prepare all of our children for the continuation of learning not only now but throughout their adult lives. Second, our schools must prepare enfranchized citizens. They must provide 'an adequate preparation for discharging the duties and responsibilities of citizenship.'[8] Third, rather than training students for specific jobs, schools must give students the 'basic skills that are common to all work in a society such as ours.'[9] Thus, the positive goals of formal education require it to be both general and liberal. Speaking negatively, education should be *non-specialized* and *non-vocational*. This is a vision that is very similar to that held by such figures as Charles Eliot in earlier periods of curricular debate.[10]

These three objectives are to be met by instituting a common course of study based largely on academic knowledge that eliminates nearly all electives. The common curriculum is divided into three interconnected areas, thus continuing *The Paideia Proposal*'s seemingly magical faith in the number three. Each of these areas is associated with different modes of teaching and learning that are seen as constitutive of the ways in which 'the mind can be improved.' These include the acquisition of organized knowledge, the development of intellectual skills, and the enlargement of understanding, insight, and aesthetic appreciation.[11] This division roughly corresponds to the traditional analytic distinctions between knowledge 'that,' 'how,' and 'to' through which a number of philosophers have urged us to think about the knowledge we should teach in schools.[12] It also again speaks directly to the roots *The Paideia Proposal* has in mental disciplinary forms of curriculum,[13] to what Kliebard and Williams have called the educational position of the old humanists.[14]

Minds cannot be improved if 'thats,' 'hows,' and 'tos' are approached through the same pedagogical arrangements, according to Adler. Therefore, the style of teaching corresponding to each will be decidedly distinct. For organized knowledge in language, literature, and the fine arts, in mathematics and natural sciences, and in history, geography, and social studies – these three groupings are considered the indispensable areas of organized knowledge – the dominant method of instruction is 'teaching by telling.' 'It employs textbooks and other instructional materials and is accompanied by laboratory demonstrations.'[15] The linguistic, mathematical, and scientific skills of reading, writing, speaking, listening, observing, measuring, estimating, and calculating, however, require another style of teaching. This is not didactic teaching but coaching. It is the 'backbone of basic schooling' and requires a significantly smaller teacher–pupil ratio. Finally, only a discussion method, a Socratic mode of teaching based on rigorous questioning, enables understanding, appreciation, and insight to evolve. 'Great' music and art and 'great' books of poetry, fiction, history, science, philosophy, and so on are to be examined carefully and discussed. Participation in learning is the key here.[16]

While these are the basics, there are 'auxiliary studies' as well. These include such things as health, physical education and sports, manual activities for both girls and boys in typing, cooking, sewing, and automobile driving and repair, and an introduction to 'the wide range of human work.'[17] Anything else is extracurricular and should be done after the school day is over, though one can see here in these auxiliary studies an attempt by the Paideia Group not to alienate anyone. They obviously include a good deal of content that is less 'mindful' than the theory behind *The Paideia Proposal* might logically allow.

The above then are the common elements for all students. For those students who cannot keep up or are deficient in any of the three areas of improving one's mind, a rigorous program of remediation is to be established. They will be given more time and help; but they will still be expected to complete the common course of study, not only because it is expected but also because nearly all students are seen optimistically. All are viewed as being basically capable of dealing with even relatively sophisticated cultural resources in an adequate way. This optimistic position, its belief in the potential of all children and rejection of the stereotypical labels that are so prevalent and damaging in education today, is actually quite powerful and remains as one of the strongest points in the Paideia Group's outlook.

INSIDE THE CLASSROOM

As I noted in my introductory remarks to this chapter, *The Paideia Proposal* is responding to some very real issues about education. Perhaps a number of the most important of these concern the dynamics of classroom life, for if one enters many classrooms one is not always immediately struck by the power of the existing curriculum content and teaching, the former often being driven by publishers' concerns over financial capital.

What is the empirical status of curricular and teaching practice in classrooms? While perhaps not totally generalizable, the findings from the study conducted by John Goodlad and his associates do enable us to gain a much better picture. The 'modal classroom' exhibits the following characteristics: 'a lot of teacher talk and a lot of student listening, unless students are responding to teachers' questions or working on written assignments; almost invariably closed and factual questions; little corrective feedback and no guidance; and predominantly total class instructional configurations around traditional activities – all in a virtually affectless environment.'[18]

But it is not only the standardized teaching practice that should concern us. *What* is taught is surely just as important as the manner in which the pedagogy proceeds. Here it is clear that certain subject areas are often nearly ignored or are given much less time than others.

This differential curricular emphasis is quite visible in the elementary school, for example. Overwhelming emphasis is found in the teaching of English, reading, and language arts. Next in importance, though still with less stress placed upon it, is mathematics. Finally, science, social studies, and the arts account for a relatively small portion of classroom time. At the lower elementary grade levels, these differences are even greater.[19]

My own research, and that of Gitlin and others, documents how a good deal of the newer curriculum models and materials now in use also tend to reduce the actual content down to atomistic units. Their effects on teaching as a labor process and on curricular quality are profound, often resulting in the deskilling of teaching and a neglect of all but the most surface and reductive knowledge to be studied.[20]

At the high school level, McNeil's interesting ethnographic work has revealed similar patterns. In history classes, for instance, nearly all topics to be studied 'were reduced to simplistic teacher-controlled information.' Aside from a relatively small amount of text material, little or no reading or writing was required on the part of students. Serious class discussions on the material were few and far between. And even in those schools with extensive resources that could have been used to enhance the study of these topics, little use was made of them.[21]

This gives one side of the coin, the structures of both time and curriculum in classrooms. Yet what of the experiences of teachers? Since all too much educational research tends to ignore what teachers themselves think, it is not surprising that in most documents the real lives of teachers – their hopes, fears, frustrations, and sense of success – are absent. Interviews done by the Boston Women's Teachers' Group, however, partially overcome this lack. They point to a number of the reasons, though not all, why classrooms may look the way they do. For many committed teachers, existing structures within the educational system – including its characteristic overadministration, its differential power in decision-making, the lack of interpersonal contact among teachers, and so on – seem to inexorably produce what has been called 'teacher burn-out,' especially in our more urban school systems.[22] As they put it:

> The conditions elementary school teachers encounter in their day-to-day school lives – conditions such as the overwhelming emphasis on quantification (both in scoring children and in keeping records), the growing lack of control over curriculum (separating conception from execution) and over other aspects of their work, the isolation from their peers, the condescending treatment by administrators, and the massive lay-offs of veteran teachers – underlie teachers' frustration and anger, as well as their feelings that there are no realistic alternatives to the current institutional structure.[23]

Based on these interviews and their own experiences, the question is put quite bluntly by the Boston Women's Teachers' Group: 'Can we expect schools to educate, encourage, and expand the horizons of our children if these same institutions serve to restrict and retard the growth of teachers?'[24] As Chapters 2 and 3 demonstrated, the fact that at the elementary school level it is primarily *women* teachers who make up this labor force – 'given' the sexual division of labor – and who are experiencing this loss of control and overadministration points to a real issue that should be of concern to us. It documents once again the close relationship over time between the control of curriculum and teaching and patriarchal relations both inside and outside the school. The gendered constitution of the teaching force is totally ignored by *The Paideia Proposal*, thereby both effectively adding an elitist element to it and losing a possible base of support for its recommendations.

Now many schools will differ from the characterizations given above. There will be classrooms, and entire buildings, in which both the subject matter and the pedagogy are of the highest quality, where the environment is such that serious discussion, probing, and debate that test the limits of existing curricula go on. If, however, the data collected by Goodlad and others and the personal experiences documented by the Boston Women's Teachers' Group are even partly representative, then it should be clear that the Paideia Group are not totally off the mark in their recognition that a good deal of the current conditions of teaching, learning, and curriculum leave something to be desired. This is true even though they have ignored the issue of gender and teaching. Whether their prescriptions or the assumptions that lay behind them are fully adequate to change these conditions is open to question, though. And it is to this that we shall now turn.

CURRICULUM AS A SLOGAN SYSTEM

It is important to ask *why* this proposal – the affirmation of the old humanists' view of culture – is so widely discussed, and sponsored, today. What are the social conditions of its writing, dissemination, and reception? Only when we know that can we understand its social as well as its educational functions. Some of this can be illuminated by focusing directly on the kind of document it is and on its arrival on the scene where the issue of 'the basics' has already been established as a political and educational issue by the political right in the United States, Canada, Australia, and elsewhere.

The Paideia Proposal is a classic example of a particular kind of curriculum document, a *slogan system.*[25] By calling it by this name, I do not mean to denigrate it; after all, some of the most powerful literature in curriculum, from Ralph Tyler's classic little text, *Basic Principles of Curriculum and Instruction,*[26] to Jerome Bruner's almost poetic arguments for discipline-centered education, *The Process of Education,*[27] have been of the same genre. Rather, what I want to do is have us focus on some of its specific characteristics, since slogan systems have peculiar properties and perform a variety of functions.

Slogan systems need to have three attributes if they are to be effective. First, they must have a penumbra of vagueness so that powerful groups or individuals who would otherwise disagree can fit under their umbrella. Again the example of Bruner can illuminate what I mean here. *The Process of Education*, by speaking to the importance of discipline-centered curricula, was able to integrate the interests of industry, government, and academics. At the same time, by calling for teaching the disciplines by discovery, it also enabled child-centered educators (who were losing power anyway) to find something responsive in it for them. Thus, coalitions to support a movement for curricular change could be built.

Yet successful slogan systems cannot be too vague, and here we find their second characteristic. They need to be specific enough to offer something to practitioners here and now. The large amount of money spent by the government on the development of 'teacher-proof' curriculum materials in the 1960s in, say, science, mathematics, and reading, and based on the academic disciplines, nearly guaranteed that a discipline-centered approach would at least get into classrooms. (Whether it was actually taught in the manner in which its developers wanted is another issue, of course.)[28]

Finally, and this is most difficult to specify, a slogan system seems to need to have the ability to charm. Put simply, its style must be such that it grabs us. It offers us a sense of imaginative possibility and in doing so generates a call to and a claim for action.

How does *The Paideia Proposal* stand up in regard to these three criteria? It clearly tries to meet the first. Among its sponsors are the present or past superintendents of schools of Chicago and Atlanta, the presidents of colleges and other academics, officials of several foundations, a number of professional school reformers and administrators, representatives of 'old humanist' groups, and so on. Conspicuous by their absence, though, are teachers, government officials, and, perhaps most important ideologically, capital. Because of this, I want to argue that *The Paideia Proposal* will have little impact.

One need only compare the Paideia Group's membership to that of the National Commission on Excellence in Education – whose report actually merits much more critical attention than that of the Paideia Group, and we shall turn our attention to it in the following chapter – to see the difference. The National Commission was heavily loaded with university presidents, administrators, and academics, and it also had politicians and representatives of teachers and industry on it. *The Paideia Proposal*'s impact will also be lessened considerably because of its historical roots in academic and old humanist culture – roots that limit the spread of its umbrella, as it were.[29] Working-class and rightist populist groups will *not* necessarily agree with such a definition of the basics, and historically they have often been antipathetic to the transformation of schools back into academies for what they may see as elite knowledge that has little bearing on their economic and cultural experiences.[30]

The Paideia Proposal's response to the second criterion, that of specificity, is also mixed. By calling for greater discipline and serious study, by arguing for different models of teaching ('telling,' 'coaching,' and 'asking'), it does legitimate the concerns and practices of many teachers and parents. However, it does so on such an abstract level as to provide little real guidance to the practitioner about how specifically to proceed in a very bureaucratic and complicated institution. And, it will *not* have the government and industrial sponsorship that accompanied the earlier period of discipline-centered curriculum proposals that led to the production of all that material for use in classrooms.

Finally, one must also give a mixed review of its style – its charm, so to speak. While Adler writes well, the proposal seems to lack the spark of newness, perhaps because so much of it is really a *defensive* program, a call to return to a romanticized past in which 'ideas' dominated school life and all students paid close attention to the teacher. In part, this is the result of a self-consciousness in writing, a style in which the political artifice of the volume is all too visible. It tries so hard to preserve something for everyone that the very attempt to do so can actually make the reader even more wary ideologically than might otherwise be the case.

There *are* progressive moments in its program, however, that need further discussion. Its arguments that schooling should be non-tracked, general, and liberal, and especially that education should be non-specialized and non-vocational, are important counterbalances to the intense pressure being placed on our educational system to make meeting the needs of capital into the fundamental goal of the school. Yet, on the other hand, schooling that is grounded in the connections between knowledge and labor should not be dismissed in principle, as Dewey and others realized. This creates contradictions for the proponents of *The Paideia Proposal*.

Such a situation is important in another way – what we used to call the problem of 'relevance.' Downplaying the vocational goals of the school actually flies in the face of what a large portion of high school students choose as the ideal function of schooling. We may not like this finding, but it does document the fact that for many students schools are not seen as ideally serving the purposes of 'intellectual development.' For these students – over 30 percent in Sirotnik's relatively large sample – the primary purpose of their formal education was to prepare for employment, to develop saleable skills, and to develop 'an awareness of career choices and alternatives.'[31]

Therefore, teaching students from non-elite groups may require a focus on their current lived problems, even those of a 'vocational' nature.[32] To deal only with 'academic knowledge,' with the high-status culture of the old humanists or alternatively with the technical culture of the upwardly mobile new middle class,[33] is to forget that for many working-class and minority students such knowledge represents little that is directly relevant either to their actual lives or to their future economic trajectories.[34] In fact, as a number of individuals have argued, working-class students will quite often partly reject the world of the school. These students rightly sense on what has been called a 'cultural level' that the knowledge and social relations considered legitimate by the educational system will have less objective pay-off in the end for them – given the structure of the racial, sexual, and social divisions of labor in the larger society – than school people and others promise.[35] The lack of such a structural sense – a lack to which I shall return shortly – weakens the arguments of the Paideia Group.

Thus, by de-emphasizing in the extreme the connections between the vocational and the intellectual, by arguing against any serious vocational emphasis within the common curriculum, *The Paideia Proposal* risks alienating a substantial portion of the student body. Given the probable low rates of college entrance among these students, one might anticipate a larger percentage of dropouts and/or a greater proportion of alienated students within the school.

This is a very paradoxical situation that must be faced squarely. To continue to bring the ideology of vocationalism, as we normally conceive of it, into the school in a time of both increasing rightist reaction and the increased power of industry to define what education should be about is a dangerous tendency – a tendency that is exacerbated by movements I shall discuss in the next two chapters. Yet, if one does not take vocational issues seriously one risks cutting oneself off from the sentiments of large numbers of students. Reacting to one side of this dilemma creates problems in the other. I do not think that this can necessarily be solved by schools alone. Any lasting solution requires that there be fulfilling and meaningful jobs for students to engage in after (and perhaps during) their schooling. Fruitful experiments that link academic work in schools with cooperatives, businesses, and industries that are *worker controlled* could offer interesting models here that may teach us how to deal with this complex issue honestly. We need to find ways of integrating work and education together in pedagogically interesting ways, probably for all students. But these ways must come about in a manner that does not give over the schools to the needs of the powerful.

This is a crucial point, I believe. The mere fact of a connection between education and work is not the major problem. Rather, it is the *current* form of that link that is in need of questioning.[36] Indeed, a close relationship between education and labor would lie at the heart of a truly democratic approach to schooling.[37] Much more thought needs to be given to this at the level of curricular and teaching theory and practice.

With this said, though, we should again recognize that Adler is decidedly correct elsewhere. By arguing against the privileged position of any one particular form of pedagogy, he speaks to the standardized models of human interaction that dominate classroom life. As I noted earlier, the pattern of teacher lecture or worksheet completion is all too common in our classrooms. *The Paideia Proposal* offers a rationale, though not an entirely new one, for altering these standard patterns and for challenging the dominance of the standardized textbook. It is a recognition and a rationale that is not to be scoffed at.

STRUCTURE AND CAUSES

There are other interesting arguments in *The Paideia Proposal*, of course. However, the overall case is not structural enough to make a significant difference. Crucial elements of analysis are missing – elements that weaken Adler's case for school reform. The discussion of 'laxity,' of the importance of discipline, is a case in point. There is no doubt in my mind that discipline *is* required in schools. Sometimes things do not come easily and there will be times when long and hard work inside and outside classrooms is necessary to teach and to learn the curriculum in a serious way. Yet this realization of the necessity of discipline is unlinked in the document to anything outside of the life of the mind. It merely becomes one way of blaming lax students and parents (and perhaps administrators and 'mindless' or 'unprepared' teachers) for what must be seen as a considerably larger social and ideological dilemma.

Let us look at this more closely. We should not offhandedly dismiss the claim that many schools are objectively less easy to teach in than they were before. There probably is more violence in schools and there probably is less automatic respect for teachers than in earlier periods. However, we can interpret this as mainly an internal problem to be solved by greater dependence on traditional forms of teacher authority or we can situate it in the ideological dynamics of the surrounding society. In essence, I want to claim that what we are witnessing in schools is not easily fixable, and certainly not by a return to the academy. It is in fact 'naturally' generated out of our modes of production, distribution, and consumption.

To put it all too briefly, in an economy that needs to stimulate individual consumption and a search for happiness based on the pursuit of consumable goods and services, older cultural values involving respect and the public good *need to be subverted*. Traditional cultural forms are not progressive for capital and need to be replaced by ideologies of individualism. Respect for position and 'sacred' culture will be subverted and replaced by respect for possessions.[38] What we are seeing in many ways in a huge array of our institutions from the family to the workplace to the school is this process. This is coupled with the increase throughout society of disaffection with one's job and so forth. When nearly 80 percent of the workers in the United States say they would not choose the same job again given the choice, then one can see that the level of alienation, cynicism, the sense of loss of control, the wish to be elsewhere – all of this is something that extends well beyond our educational system. It is related to a more extensive ideological, political, and economic crisis that must be met head on or we shall spin our collective wheels.[39] It is not something that is outside of schools that we can think about in our spare time. Rather, it truly constitutes what we are confronted with in the schools we work in, and throughout our society. If we do not act on the conditions outside education at the same time as we act on those inside, we will have little success.[40]

This is not to say that educators must wait for a thoroughgoing transformation of the larger social formation. There are definitely things that must be done in schools now to reestablish – if they were ever really there in a widespread manner – the conditions for serious work. It is to say, however, that without placing the problem *directly* in its social context, *The Paideia Proposal* itself acts as part of a larger ideological discourse that separates out issues into relatively non-interacting compartments. It does not give its reader sufficient space to redefine the problem as one involving a collectivity.

How does the very discourse around which the text is organized make it doubly difficult to see the relationship between structural forces and education? This requires a few

further comments. We shall want to think about the limits this proposal sets on how we think about education. These can be seen in the criticisms it marshals against existing school practices. The terms that define these criticisms are very visible throughout *The Paideia Proposal*. They signify more than they overtly say, in terms such as 'standards', 'discipline', 'the mind', and so on. All of these are important not only for what they say but for what they don't say as well. The text's language makes the current crisis in schools seem almost accidental. Its roots are psychological not structural, as I already noted. And at the same time that these terms set limits on how we think about the crisis in our schools, they either tend to silence other forms of criticism or to incorporate them into the text's own construction of 'the problem.'

To give some further examples, throughout *The Paideia Proposal*, and in the report written by the National Commission on Excellence in Education, we continually find references to a particular concept – *our*. It is 'our' country, 'our' school system, 'our' democratic society. It is in this very construction that a danger resides. For the repeated use of 'our' covers the reality of relations that are structurally unequal – relations that are not due to education and will not be solved by them.

In his discussion of how official documents and reports use language to incorporate people back into a social consensus when such a consensus is threatened by an emerging economic and political crisis, James Donald states the argument quite succinctly:

> The versatility of *our* here is remarkable. There is a hint in *our educational system* of the social democratic state providing education for 'them.' *Our country* suggests a unity of all 'citizens.' . . . *Our* must signify the imaginary communality of government and governed: and so silently confronts the materiality of class relations

of domination and subordination. *Our* incorporates the citizen [back into his or her] exploitation by capital.[41]

While Donald's points may be a bit too strident, he does allow us to see how a text might function to reassert a lost consensus. *The Paideia Proposal* does this relatively effectively when, recognizing that wide disparities exist in economic and educational opportunity in the United States, it again focuses attention away from the structures that generate these conditions. In many ways this is a conscious decision. Thus, the Paideia Group begin their discussion with a claim that we are politically a classless society.[42] If this is the case, then all institutions should be equally responsive given equal power in the political arena. However, while our political institutions are *not* reducible to mere tools of dominant classes,[43] these institutions do seem to guarantee that the top 20 percent of the population reaps 80 percent of the benefits of most of our social programs.

It is to the credit of the Paideia Group that they do recognize the existence of fundamental and widespread disparities. For example, they recognize that school reform must be accompanied by job creation – something few policy-makers seem to understand sufficiently. Yet why would job creation, especially for the many poor, working class, people of color, and others, be so continually necessary if class relations did not exist?

I do not wish to belabor this point, but I think it is essential that we educators who must work in institutions that respond to these larger social relations have a clear understanding of what the society that surrounds us looks like. Otherwise we shall latch on to bandwagons continually, even though the ride is circular and not very fulfilling at the end. A picture of the class structure of our labor force, which *The Paideia Proposal* assumes out of existence somewhat too quickly and hence cannot adequately address with its proposals, is a necessary part of this understanding.

In Erik Olin Wright's recent analysis of the class structure of the United States (though the data are similar in, say, Canada), we can begin to see the composition of the labor force. Without becoming too technical in my discussion, we can see the existence of classes even though so much of the literature would have it otherwise. After an examination of a large amount of data on occupation, salary, ownership, autonomy and control of one's job, and so on, Wright concludes that 46 percent of the current paid positions in the economy are working-class. In fact, when one looks carefully at changes in the control of labor – with a large portion of the positions in the economy actually losing autonomy and with the greatest growth of jobs being not 'high tech' but in the relatively low-paid service sector – it is possible that approximately 65 percent of the paid positions are either working-class or have significant working-class aspects.[44] Something is happening 'out there' that we need to know about.

Yet, while these figures are themselves worthy of attention, they do not speak to sex and race dynamics that are just as significant. While 39 percent of the men are in working-class locations, nearly 55 percent of all women in the labor force occupy such positions. As Wright notes, if only a small number of women engaged in paid labor outside the home, these figures would not be as consequential. However, since the rate of women's labor force participation is over 40 percent and going up, these figures are quite important. They translate into the fact I mentioned earlier, that a clear majority (54 percent) of the working class of the United States consists of women. The data on the overrepresentation of women in the working class are coupled with something else, though – the extreme underrepresentation of women in managerial and supervisory positions.[45]

When we turn to the issue of race, the inequalities in income, control, and employment are even more striking. While 44 percent of all whites are working-class, 65 percent of blacks are in such locations, a difference obviously of over 20 percent. Only 6.5 percent of blacks, but over 14 percent of whites, are in managerial positions. 'And perhaps most striking of all, only 3% of blacks are . . . employers compared to 15% of whites.'[46]

What of the interrelationships among race, sex, and class? Black women are the most exploited of all. Of the black women in the paid labor force, 69 percent are working-class. Only about 4 percent are managers. This compares to black men and white women who have about the same proportions of between 9 and 10 percent, and white men who again lead with over 17 percent.

It is worth quoting the conclusions Wright comes to after completing his analysis:

> Taking all of these data together we can make two strong conclusions. First of all, white males are, in class terms, a highly privileged category. Over 20% of all white men are either full fledged managers or capitalists (employers of ten or more workers), that is, in class locations which are either firmly part of the dominant class or within which the dominant class represents a principal element. This compares to 11% of white women, 9% of black men and only 4% of black women. If we include all . . . managers-supervisors, small employers, and capitalists, we see that nearly half (48%) of white males are in class locations either fully or partly within [dominant groups], compared to only 30.7% of white women, 24.2% of black men, and 17.4% of black women.
>
> Secondly, the American working class is predominantly composed of women and minorities. Nearly two thirds of all working class positions are filled by women and non-whites (62.2%). If we add young white males – men under 25 years of age – we find that over 70% of the U.S. working class is composed of women, minorities and youth. The traditional image of the American worker as a white, male industrial worker is thus far from representative of the working class in the United States today.[47]

These data are very important, for they challenge one of the major truth claims that underlie slogan systems such as *The Paideia Proposal.* While attempting to provide an umbrella under which 'all of us' can fit, the Paideia Group constructs a vision of education and its place in society which has less sense than it might both of the conditions of most of 'all of us' and of the realities of that society itself. Yet can we blame them for something that is widespread among so many educators? When the difficult tasks of maintaining decent educational conditions and thinking about the internal problems of the school are getting even more difficult, isn't it enough just to try to deal with that? Here I must answer as honestly as I can. I do not believe it is enough. While recognizing the hard work that so many educational actors engage in in schools and universities, it seems to me that, given the structural inequalities I portrayed above, any proposal for widespread curricular reform – be it *The Paideia Proposal* or something else – that does not have a basis in a structural appraisal of who benefits in the larger society in terms of race, class, and sex is ultimately only half a proposal. Further, I am also convinced that it will not succeed on its own terms.

I say this because of a prediction I would like to make about Adler's eloquent but in the end unsatisfactory proposal. What will its ultimate effects be? Even given its partly progressive elements – its call for a fracturing of the dominance of recitation in schools, its battle both against the current retrogressive vocationalizing of the curriculum and for a curriculum for all students, its articulate challenge to all too frequently accepted practices such as tracking – the proposal's major impact will be almost imperceptible in terms of its own goals of 'the mind.' In terms of the broader goals of industry and the current resurgence of rightist reaction, however, it will have another kind of effect. It will assist in 'exporting the crisis.' By not tying the problems we face powerfully enough to the more pervasive relations of economic, political, and cultural power outside the school, by arguing its case on the terrain of abstracted notions of knowledge, and by highlighting discipline problems as one of its most important issues in a way that discounts the reality of teachers' working conditions and the gendered specificities of so much of their labor, in the final analysis it will lend support to those forces that wish to transform the school into something the supporters of *The Paideia Proposal* might find less to their liking.[48] What will be focused on will be a return to punitive and strict control, a massive extension of testing, and an industrialization (or neglect) of our schools, especially in our inner cities. The rest by and large will simply be ignored except where it meets movements already in high gear such as the emerging emphasis on mathematics and science. But even these will be focused on not as forms for 'improving the mind'; they will be technical skills to overcome our 'disarmament.'

Thus, *The Paideia Proposal* will make a small ripple in a big pond where the waves are now being made by capital and the state. Its ripple, however, may add just a bit more to the waves of the powerful, rather than pushing the water in another direction. Meanwhile, in Washington, Mr. Ronald Reagan and his ideological allies will send their fondest regards to Mr. Mortimer Adler. I don't think he really wants to wave back.

In Washington and elsewhere, meanwhile, teachers and other educators are already discovering that the old humanists actually have less power than the conservative forces of business and the right. As we shall see in Chapter 6, the issue of who benefits and the visibility or invisibility of class, race, and gender structures will again be consequential.

CHAPTER 6

EDUCATIONAL REPORTS AND ECONOMIC REALITIES

THE POLITICS OF CONTROL

The Paideia Proposal is not the only 'text' being sent forth for our consideration. Report after report, with *A Nation at Risk* being the best-known and most powerful, has pointed a finger at 'our failing schools.' In many ways, this still seems odd. After all, for a decade or more, schools tended to languish on the sidelines of official political discourse. Then within a very short time, our formal institutions of education have come center stage, so to speak. Elementary, secondary, technical, college and university education, coupled with special attention being paid to the training and evaluation of teachers, are no longer topics that politicians, government officials, pressure groups, business, union members, newspaper columnists, academics, parents, and others talk about when 'important' things are over. Instead of being the functional equivalent of conversations about the weather, discussions about education have again become deadly serious.

The last time that so much attention was paid to education as a national issue was at the very height of the Cold War. Then, education was seen by the federal government and business as part of a larger battle with the Soviet Union and its allies over the production of technical expertise and knowledge, defense, 'manpower' planning, and industrial might. The National Defense Education Act and similar legislative mandates and policies provide examples of the government's (the 'state's') earlier concern with these issues.[1] The similarities between then and now are striking. Educators today live with the legacy of these concerns and policies through the large-scale changes they engendered in curriculum and teaching. I have discussed these alterations, including the deskilling (and partial reskilling) of teachers, the intensification of their work, the creation of an expensive and capital-intensive curriculum in our schools, and the connections between these attempts at transforming the educational system into an overt agent of state military and industrial policy and gender and class relations earlier in this book and elsewhere,[2] and shall come back to them again later on. But the fact that both the pressure education is under today and the proposed solutions do have a history, and the fact that such pressures and solutions are connected to these larger political, economic, and ideological forces, makes them quite consequential. Education talk *is* and must be serious talk, but perhaps not in the way we are used to thinking about it.

At both the local and federal levels, movements for accountability, competency-based teacher education and testing, systems management, standardized textbooks, mandated 'basics,' academic standards, and so on are clear and growing. This is occurring not only in the United States. A number of countries are experiencing similar movements, in part because similar structural problems beset their economies and in part because the United States exports both its crisis and its management techniques and procedures throughout the capitalist world.[3] (These countries often see these techniques as having the imprimatur of science and efficiency, and, hence, tend to employ them, often to the detriment of their own situations.) The many reports being produced currently did not start these movements. They themselves are in many ways products of these tendencies.

I shall not review here all of the content of the multitude of reports and reform proposals that have crossed our desks and gained so much media attention in the past two years or so. These have been described in detail in numerous places. In fact, it is quite possible that the specific content of each of these proposals is less consequential than the overall tendencies they represent and, especially, how they will be used by various groups now in contention. In a chapter of this size, I can only paint a picture of these tendencies in rather broad strokes; but, though broad, the outline of what seems to be happening in education will be quite visible.

It is important to begin with a realization that the reports are as much political as they are educational documents. I mean this in a number of ways. First, all discussions of educational policy, to the extent that they deal with the issue of changes in content, are political. The knowledge that is taught is always someone's knowledge and debates over it sponsor certain groups' visions of legitimate culture and disenfranchise others.[4] Second, the reports are attempts at rebuilding a consensus over education that has been partly fractured during the past decade. Thus, like *The Paideia Proposal*, reports such as *A Nation at Risk* will be couched in a language of the 'common good' – a language that seeks to have something in it for everybody so that as many people as possible with power can fit under their linguistic umbrella. And the documents are calls for action – calls to use scarce resources and political power for specific ends. Because of this, the language of these many reports needs to be analyzed not necessarily for its truth value (though, as we shall see later, this is not unimportant) but in its rhetorical use.

Others have noted this political nature of their discourse as well. Stedman and Smith's comments are illustrative here:

> At the outset, it should be recognized that these reports are political documents; the case they make takes the form of a polemic, not a reasoned treatise. Rather than carefully marshalling facts to prove their case, they present a litany of charges without examining the veracity of their evidence or its sources. By presenting

> their material starkly, and often eloquently, the commissions hoped to jar the public into action, and to a great extent they have been successful. Caveats and detailed analysis might have lessened the reports' impact.[5]

Lastly – and very importantly for my points about looking for the meaning of the documents in their specific uses – the various reports are decidedly political in terms of the context in which they are to be read. They do not spring out of untilled soil, and they arrive at a specific time – a time in which rightist reaction is a considerable force in the government and society at large and when Western economies are less than fully healthy. This is important in terms of the uses to which the documents may be put.

BETWEEN PROPERTY RIGHTS AND SUBSISTENCE RIGHTS

What is the nature of the crisis that the reports are responding to? It is first and foremost an economic crisis; but it is much more than that. Behind it is a crisis in authority relations and ideology as well. At the outset, let me focus primarily on economic issues.

School policies and the curricular, teaching, and evaluative practices they entail have historically had important connections with economic pressures. The various reports continue this history. It is clear that for a large majority of them it is not only the internal problems within the school that are so worrisome, but also in a major way the relationship between the school and what is happening to the country's national and international industrial 'might.' We need, of course, to be careful of being too reductive here. Like the texts I analyzed in Chapter 4, schools and educational reports and policies do have relative autonomy. As we shall see, they cannot be read off directly from the needs of the state or the economy. Educational institutions and personnel in general and curriculum and teaching policies and practices in particular have their own internal histories, their own discourses, and their own interest in protecting themselves from external forces. Yet since the reports *are* so self-consciously directed at current economic conditions, it is crucially important to place these documents within these conditions.

What are the elements of what is happening economically? In broad outline, the context is provided by the following quote from Chapter 1, which is worth restating here.

> The powers of the American state are now deployed in a massive business offensive. Its basic elements are painfully clear. Drastic cutbacks in social spending. Rampant environmental destruction. Regressive revisions of the tax system. [Looming trade wars and high unemployment now considered 'normal.'] Loosened constraints on corporate power. Ubiquitous assaults on organized labor. Sharply increased weapons spending. Escalating threats of intervention abroad.[6]

We are currently witnessing, in the words of Piven and Cloward, 'nothing less than the recurring conflict between property rights and subsistence [or person] rights, which originated with the emergence of capitalism itself.'[7] In short, the United States economy is in the midst of one of the most powerful structural crises it has experienced since the depression. In order to solve it on terms acceptable to dominant interests, as many aspects of the society as possible need to be pressured into conforming with the requirements of international competition, reindustrialization, 'rearmament' (in the words of the National Commission on Excellence in Education), and in general the needs of capital accumulation. The gains made by working men and women, minority and poor groups, and others in employment, health and safety, welfare programs, affirmative action, legal rights, and education in government, in the economy, in local communities, and elsewhere, must be rescinded since 'they are too expensive' both economically and ideologically. Both of these latter words are important. Not only are fiscal resources scarce (in part because current policies transfer them to the military), but people must be convinced that their belief that person rights come first is simply wrong or outmoded given current 'realities.' Thus, the power of the state – through legislation, persuasion, administrative, legal, and ideological pressure, and so on – must be employed to create the conditions believed necessary to meet these requirements.[8]

Though behind these assaults and pressures from capital and the right may be Theodore Roosevelt's dictum 'We must decide that it is a good deal better that some people should prosper too much than no one should prosper enough,' the reality is something else again. There is prosperity and there is prosperity. As I noted earlier, given the fact that 80 percent of the benefits of most past social programs have gone to the top 20 percent of the population, we should want to ask 'who benefits?' from any proposals coming from current government bodies and commissions and from affiliated organizations.[9] The benefits of proposed education reforms are not immune from this question.

Perhaps some figures will be helpful here in enabling us to ask this question in a more pointed way. It is estimated that, in 1985, a poor family is at least 5 percent less well off than in 1981, while a middle-class family is 14 percent better off. A rich family shows a 30 percent gain in its already large advantage. These figures, even if taken by themselves, indicate a marked redistribution of income and benefits from the poor to the rich.[10] They are made even more significant by the fact that the middle class itself is actually shrinking as the numbers at the extremes grow. We have more and more a 'double peaked' economic distribution as the numbers of well-to-do and poor increase.

These inequalities – though growing – have been around for quite some time. In the United States, the bottom 20 percent of the population receives a smaller percentage of total after tax income than the comparable group in Japan, Sweden, Australia, the Netherlands, West Germany, Norway, France, and a number of other nations. This gap is not being reduced at all within the United States. In fact, in the past three decades, the gap between the bottom 20 percent of U.S. families and the top 5 percent has nearly doubled. The percentage of families that received less than half of the median national income actually increased between 1950 to 1977. If we again take the early 1950s as our starting point, in 1951 the top 20 percent of the population received 41.6 percent of the gross national income while the bottom quintile received only 5 percent. When we look at more current figures, in 1981, for instance, the bottom 20 percent still received the very same 5 percent, but the top 20 percent had 'captured a 41.9 percent share.'[11] While these changes do not seem overwhelming, the amount of money this entails is very large and is certainly indicative of a trend favoring the top 20 percent.

Yet this is not all. One out of every seven Americans lives in poverty, as does one out of every five children under the age of six. More than one-quarter of all Hispanics and more than one-third of all Afro-Americans live below the poverty line. 'In 1981, even before the major Reagan cuts, more than 40 percent of families living below the poverty line received no food stamps, medicaid, housing subsidies, or low price school lunches.' Even the government has estimated that the diet of those living (existing?) at the official poverty level is so deficient 'that it is suitable only for "temporary or emergency use".'[12]

Gender, race, and age inequalities, as well, are so pervasive as to be almost painful to recount. Women working full-time outside the home earn less than 60 percent of what men working full-time earn. Black women working full-time earn only 53 percent and Hispanic women only 40 percent of what men earn. In 1980, one in three women working full-time outside the home earned less than $7,000 a year. In the same year, women with college degrees averaged only 56.5 percent of the income of men with equivalent education and only 81.4 percent of the income men with high school diplomas earned. In 1981, nearly 53 percent of the families headed by black women and over 27 percent of those headed by white women were officially poor. If we consider the elderly poor, 72 percent are women and, in 1980, of the elderly black women living alone, 82 percent were near or below poverty.[13]

Black and brown men earn 80 percent of the income of white men with comparable levels of education and of similar age. Access to comparable jobs is just about blocked and in fact may be worsening given current policies. Thus, 'more than 60 percent of black men and 50 percent of all Hispanic men are clustered in low-paying job classifications.'[14]

Finally, examining unemployment makes the picture of this part of our economy even more graphic. Some econometric measures indicate that the unequal cumulative impact of unemployment on minorities and women has actually doubled between 1951 and 1981. The data on unemployment rates tell a similar story. Though current figures are slightly lower than the nearly 21 percent for blacks and 9.7 percent for whites in 1982, the differential has not lessened. For white teenagers, the unemployment rate was approximately 25 percent; for black youth it was a staggering 50 percent, and even higher in many urban areas. For these and other reasons, 'the income gap between white and black families has actually widened slightly since 1970, as black median income dropped from 66 percent to 65 percent of white median family income.'[15]

I could go on here, of course. In fact, it is very tempting to do so, since many Americans are not usually brought face to face with the immense inequalities in our society, especially since it seems no longer fashionable for the media to present anything but the official statistics generated out of Washington. What is important here is to inquire into how any of the proposals take these data into account.

As we have just seen, for many of the American people, even when educational levels and 'skills' are equalized, the economy has *not* been as responsive as the theory behind the reports would have it. Education is not the solution to the bulk of these problems. Existing and quite widespread conditions of discrimination, exploitation, and inequality – that is, structural conditions generated by the economy and the dual labor market, and by governmental policies that largely reproduce these conditions – are among the root causes.[16]

To be fair, the reports do not totally ignore the problems these data signify. Most of the authors of these documents undoubtedly care about such inequalities, and they certainly care about what is happening to our economy, though perhaps not in a way that might lead to a more democratic set of economic and cultural arrangements. Yet, they construct their responses largely upon a vision of the future economy that is wrong and upon educational solutions that are largely inappropriate.

A HIGH-TECH SOLUTION?

One major response of the reports is to blame our economic problems on our educational system and on our lack of high-technology industries. For these authors, however, only the economic problems as defined by industry are significant enough to cause a crisis. Thus, a large part of the solution lies in making our schools and their curricula more responsive to industrial and technological needs. While I shall deepen this discussion considerably in the next chapter, it is important that we get a preliminary idea here of what this will mean. A sense of the effectiveness of this high-tech 'solution' can be seen from recent data on employment trends. Let us look at this a bit more closely.

The reports recognize that we are becoming what has been called a service economy. Because of this, certain kinds of jobs will be created, while others are lost. The largest number of jobs will be in relatively smaller firms. They will also be in business services, health care, and the wholesale/retail trades. This transformation readily emerges from the fact that right now the number of people working in health care is double that of those employed in construction. McDonald's employs three times as many workers as does U.S. Steel.[17] Yet these expanding positions are generally low-paying and have little autonomy. Even the expansion of business services, with its focus on a high-tech, computer-driven future, needs to be examined carefully, since it is estimated that the widespread computerization of the business world will create a net *loss* not a net gain in jobs, especially among women.[18] This last figure is quite telling, since women do constitute the fastest-growing segment of labor and already hold the largest share of working-class positions in the economy. The almost total neglect of gender specificities, the blindness to the sexual (and racial) division of labor and 'women's work' in general, when coupled with the romanticism of their high-technology vision, weakens the economic position of the reports in the extreme[19] and obscures their redefinition of legitimate knowledge as that needed by industry and the military.

As I showed in the last chapter, women, minorities, and youth – the lowest-paid and least autonomous workers – now constitute 70 percent of all working-class positions.[20] Since a high-tech solution will not have a totally beneficial impact on these groups of workers, to say the least, the reports' envisioned economic future cannot but ignore the bulk of the data I have brought together in these last two sections of my analysis.

One of the major social functions of the reports lies in the implications of this neglect. Like *The Paideia Proposal*, they will actually make it harder for us to recognize these gender, race, and class inequalities as truly structural, as long-lasting and anything but accidental and not solvable by small increments of educational reform. Because of this, a large portion of their solution may in fact exacerbate the problem. If structural conditions within a corporate society constantly generate these lamentable conditions, is giving more of the school over to the needs of capital the solution? Must we accept corporate senses of important knowledge and corporate definitions of necessary 'skills' and 'work habits' as the limits of our response?

Instead, it is quite possible to claim that the corporate sector – a sector which dominates our economy and, more and more, has enabled the logic of the commodification process to enter nearly all aspects of our cultural and personal lives – bears a significant portion of the blame for our social and educational crisis. 'Adam Smith notwithstanding, profit maximization by large, economically powerful, private corporations has not maximized the public good.' The investment and employment decisions that business has made have in large part generated 'dislocation, discrimination, declining real wages, high unemployment, pollution, poor transportation systems, and run down crime-ridden cities.' These are not costed out when the corporate sector makes these decisions, but these social costs *are* borne by the public.[21] The effects on communities, the health and welfare of the bulk of the population, and on our cultural lives and education, have been enormous.

Thus, by employing the language of the 'public good' yet bringing the educational system more closely into line with the needs of the corporate sector, what counts as the public good and what counts as the knowledge and skills that are required to be taught in schools to fulfill these needs of the 'public' are severely truncated. Such truncated discourse may help dominant groups, but it is open to question whether such benefits will be shared by the rest of us.

SHARING THE BLAME

As I mentioned at the outset, it is important that we be cautious about seeing these attempts to rationalize and standardize teaching and curricula and to create closer connections between corporate needs and the schools as stemming totally from an assault on the educational system by capital. Often, other groups are very instrumental both in sponsoring capital's requirements and in setting limits on them so that these groups' own needs are met as well. This is what is happening here. Pressure from business and industry (and the military) may have increased considerably, but the results of these pressures – when instituted into federal and state educational policy and practice – will take on a form that also meets the requirements of many existing groups who *now* have power in education within the state or are attempting to increase their control.

For example, the continuing growth in the power at local, regional, and national levels of testers and evaluators, both accountability and efficiency 'experts,' those with administrative expertise, behaviorally oriented curriculum specialists, and so on, will account for some of the reasons why such pressures will be taken up in the form they are. As holders of what I have elsewhere called technical/administrative knowledge, these groups of people will have their own relatively autonomous interests in maintaining and enhancing their positions and paths to upward mobility.[22] Added to this will be policy-oriented academics who will use the concern over standards and achievement to enhance the relative position of their own academic constituents in the debate over whose knowledge should be seen as legitimate in publicly funded schools. Therefore, the reports will signify a 'settlement' or 'accord' among these groups. The results will be a compromise, but one decidedly *within* the limits imposed by the tightening relationship between the state and the economy.

Perhaps two historical examples can help make this clear.

Let me first use the history of Taylorism and its many variants as a case in point.

Taylorism is significant not just because of its widespread application to labor in general, with the growth of time and motion studies and atomistic strategies to separate conception from execution in factories and offices in the early years of this century. It is also of considerable consequence in education. As Kliebard has demonstrated, for instance, the most widely accepted models of curriculum planning still in use have their roots originally in Taylorism.[23] Furthermore, many of the techniques now being proposed in or standing behind the reports for evaluation and testing, for standardized curricula, and for 'upgrading' and rationalizing teaching e.g., systems management and management by objectives, competency-based testing and curriculum development, reductive behavioral objectives, and so forth come from similar soil.[24] Given this, any gains in our understanding of Taylorism in general as a form of control of both the labor process and its products and of its genesis and character will be significant in pushing us toward a fuller understanding of what is happening in schools today. As I shall show, even such strategies as Taylorism – perhaps the archetypical attempt by capital to control people's work – did not come *directly* from dominant groups in an unmediated fashion. It was much more complicated than this and requires a more subtle appraisal of class dynamics both outside and inside of education.

Recent research by Peter Meiksins argues that Taylorism was not merely a tool of capitalist interests but needs also to be seen as a complicated response by engineers to changes in their own class location and labor process. That is, scientific management as ideology and technique was partly a response by engineers to their own changed conditions – conditions that led them from being largely their own entrepreneurs, or at least having a good deal of autonomy, to a situation in which they were more and more the employees of a large organization.

> In other words, large modern capitalist enterprises felt a need for significant numbers of engineers to perform the labor of conception that had become so critical to their success (and that had been performed in a more haphazard manner by other employees). The engineer, thus, was shifted from his old role as proprietor of a small machine shop to the role of employee of a large capitalist organization. He had become part of the complex, collective labor process created by the dynamics of modern capitalism.[25]

What Taylorism accomplished was not only a restructuring of the labor process so that it was more coordinated and under greater supervisory control[26] (though this *is* important to say the least). It went further. It accomplished this restructuring by substituting 'truly scientific approaches,' developed by engineers, for the older 'rule of thumb' methods of management. In so doing, it provided these once independent engineers with some semblance of the autonomy they were themselves losing, given what was happening to their own positions. 'Capitalists could see to the profits and losses, buying and selling; but, within the shop, the engineer (housed in the planning department) was to be sovereign.'[27]

Thus, techniques of control such as those associated with scientific management can often be paradoxical. They can both serve to reproduce capitalist social relations *and* be the result of class conflict at one and the same time. Caught in a contradictory position 'between' capital and labor, engineers developed ways to express their own interests and solve the problems generated by their altered location in the social division of labor and the increased concentration of capital. The conflicts over their own autonomy led in part to the development of Taylorism and its associated strategies. Odd as it may seem at first glance, scientific management hence needs to be looked at as partly *oppositional* in nature, not only as a mirror of what dominant interests want.

Because of this recent research on scientific management theory and practice, it is important that we explore the possibility that such management practices in education perform similar functions. Not only will teachers have a 'contradictory class location,' but state bureaucrats too will be in an 'intermediate' position. The proposals the latter have tried to implement may embody their own contradictory needs, not just those concerned with the extraction of more labor or with giving the school over to business and industry.

The current educational appropriation of such techniques and the ideologies that accompany them has a similar story. It is not only the history of the 'industrialization' of the school, though there is a large amount of truth in that. It is also the history of curriculum workers, administrators, and other educators – a particular segment of the new middle class – using the language of science and efficiency to enhance their own status and to provide increased positions for upward mobility within the educational system based on new definitions of educationally important knowledge.[28] Just as importantly, it is also partly the story of the *masculinization* not only of educational discourse in general but of the sexual division of labor between male administrators and women teachers that I traced out in Chapters 2 and 3.[29] The very program of rationalizing all important social relations in our major institutions is, in fact, pre-eminently a masculine discourse. As Gilligan, Ferguson, and others have shown, such a hierarchical conception is not neutral. It disenfranchises alternative concerns for human relations, connectedness, and care.[30]

Let me give one other, more current instance of what I mean – this time from outside the United States. A prime example of educational documents and policies coming from such 'intermediate' positions is one that will be familiar to those of you who have followed what happened in Australian education during the late 1970s and early 1980s when a conservative government was in power. This concerns the core curriculum proposal authored by the

Curriculum Development Centre (CDC) in Canberra. Professional educators and elements of the state bureaucracy clearly felt that they were under attack from the conservative national government and from the right and industry in general. Like many of the current reports in the United States, the aim of this attack was to redefine education so that it met corporate needs and also reduced expenses and 'frills' through a return to the 'basics.' On the other hand, to a lesser extent these educators and bureaucrats saw increasing pressure coming from less powerful, disenfranchised, and minority groups wanting to democratize the content and form of the curriculum through multiculturalism, etc. The CDC's solution was to create a national core curriculum that spoke mainly to the need to defend the jobs and cultural capital of the professional middle class – one that sought to integrate corporate claims and democratic discourse into one document.[31] It was a truly remarkable juggling act. Thus, the core curriculum proposal was not simply a reflection of the needs of capital, but a creative (though in many ways unsuccessful) response by a particular class fraction to pursue and defend its own interests and autonomy within the limits set by the conditions in which it found itself. One need not totally agree with the program that the CDC proposed or with the interests it represented, but it was clear that it was not simply a matter of imposition.

Given these examples, the very same questions must be asked of the movements that stand behind the reports. Yes, they do represent an attempt by capital to gain more influence in the educational system both directly and indirectly. But to see that as the only thing that is going on misses a good deal. Contending groups within the state, within the academy, and elsewhere have sought to incorporate their own needs within the reports. Even with the incorporation of these needs, however, it *is* the discourse of economic needs that surrounds these 'texts' and provides the context for their reading. By framing nearly all important educational questions around the logic of standardization, production, and accumulation, capital is able to accommodate these groups within its own slogan system. The vision of the economy in the reports may be unequal and wrong, but there is little doubt that they have had considerable success in moving the debate onto capital's terrain.

EXPORTING THE BLAME

If the reports in general mistake effects for causes and misconstrue the emerging tendencies in the economy, are they more accurate at the level of classroom dynamics and their proposals for curriculum and teaching? In responding to the economics and the discourse that lie behind the reports, we should not assume that everything is fine in the classrooms of America. As my discussion in the previous chapter showed, all is not fine, to say the least.

Yet like *The Paideia Proposal*, the proposals to rationalize and standardize the work of teachers and the curriculum that are now so quickly being taken up and are so evident in the reports need to be seen in the longer history of the state's attempt to control the labor process not just of its workers in general but tacitly of women workers in particular.[32]

I want to stress this point. Not only do the reports have a problematic view of the labor market outside the school, they have a seriously deficient perspective on the internal labor market as well. Only by once again linking the attempts to rationalize teaching and knowledge to the question of *who* is doing the teaching can an honest picture of the effects of such standardization and external control be gained. What is happening is actually a repetition of an older strategy: when larger economic and governmental crises erupt, export the crises outside the economy and government onto other groups.[33] Like the earlier period when schools were blamed in the 1950s and 1960s, the crisis is exported to the 'problems' of (women) teachers (though as the proposals to tighten up secondary school requirements indicate, it is not limited to women elementary school teachers). Again, the effects will be deskilling, intensification and a general loss of control. History may have a habit of repeating itself in transfigured form.

This said, though, it must be recognized that problems do exist in schools. But do they warrant the kind of 'solutions' generally advocated by the reports? Our overall answer to that question must again be no, I think. Many of the reasons why are best stated in the words of two policy analysts who engaged in a thorough examination of the educational content of the documents. Stedman and Smith, in what is perhaps one of the very best analyses of the educational strengths and weaknesses of the reports, conclude their discussion in the following way:

> The commissions used weak arguments and poor data to make their case. Neither the decline in test scores, the international comparisons, nor the growth of hi-tech employment provided a clear rationale for reform. By ignoring their background reports and carelessly handling data, their reports further lost credibility. In particular, the commissions made simplistic recommendations and failed to consider their ramifications. They proposed increasing time without altering pedagogy, instituting merit schemes without describing procedures, and adopting the 'new basics' without changing old definitions. They ignored numerous problems – teenage unemployment, teacher burnout, and high dropout rates – that must be solved before American education can be considered sound. They did not address the special needs of the poor and minorities. A blind acceptance of these recommendations could lead to little improvement. Worse, a rapid adoption in the hopes of a speedy improvement could lead to a disenchantment with reform. There is a crucial dilemma facing educational policy. On the one hand, there appears to be a legitimate desire to impose new

> and more rigorous standards on our nation's schools. On the other hand, recent studies of school effectiveness indicate the need to rest considerable responsibility for a school's instructional program on the shoulders of the staff of a school. Over and over we find that without the commitment of the school staff, topdown mandates will fail. Local school systems and state governments, therefore, should examine these reports carefully before adopting any of their recommendations.[34]

In short, the reports often misuse their data, which are technically problematic in the first place. They have an inaccurate view of the labor market and of the future of high-tech jobs, and drastically simplify what might be necessary to make lasting alterations in schools. They privilege the knowledge needed by industry and cloak it in the language of democracy,[35] ignoring in the process many persistent social problems involving the realities that poor people, people of color, and women and men workers face. Furthermore, their proposals for the most part never get to the level of the teaching act itself, except to further create the ideological conditions necessary to restructure the labor of a largely female workforce. Finally, they are tacitly elitist in major ways (though not in all others)[36] in that reform comes from the top not from the participants themselves. Their ultimate effects, then, will not necessarily be to make schools more interesting places or to change for the better the conditions of curriculum and teaching I described in Chapter 5. Instead, they will continue trends that have already had a number of negative effects. Let us examine this in somewhat more detail.

What has been called the 'commodification of education' is evident behind the logic of the proposals currently under review. An indication of this is the rapid advance of the process of rationalization – a process that is expanding to nearly all areas of the educational process. Changes in curriculum content and form bear witness to these transformations, as do major changes in what counts as good teaching.[37]

For example, at this writing thirty-eight of the fifty states now have some form of minimal competency testing for their students. 'The tests represent and reinforce a redefinition of the content of education as specific skill learning, where skills are defined narrowly.' Thus, the language of competency, performance, and effectiveness replaces broader language systems centred around knowledge, understanding, and personal development. In the process, learning and teaching are redefined. Time on task and the management of instruction become the arbiters of value.[38] Good teaching is only that which is demonstrated in competency tests for teachers. Good curricula are only those which have immediately available and easily testable results found in standardized text material. Good learning is only the accumulation of atomistic skills and facts and answering the questions in standardized achievement tests for students. All three are really aspects of what might best be thought of as deskilling,[39] and all three signify as well a restructuring of many of our cultural institutions by a technicist logic that in times of rightist resurgence can do little more than turn our schools over to the ethos and needs of that top 5 percent I pointed to at the beginning of this chapter.

In its most general terms, Wexler and Grabiner put it this way:

> Taken together, these various processes of student and teacher deskilling and expansion of methods of measurable organization and administrative surveillance constitute the commodifying aspect of a larger historic process of educational reorganization. They empty the content of curriculum and teaching of any cultural history that is not reducible to narrowly defined technical skill. The technical skill, by virtue of its method of acquisition and evaluation, is not the kind of generative capacity which engages the imagination.[40]

Thus, technique wins out over substance, and education is turned into nearly a parody of itself. Rationality is redefined to signify not thoughtfulness but meeting bureaucratic needs and conforming to the requirements of 'our' economy. In the process, the reinstitution of class and patriarchal relations is once more transformed, as our sense of the history of these commodifying tendencies is lost. Education should be something more than this in a democracy, you say? Sorry, it's too expensive.

CONCLUSION

Even if the concrete proposals made in the various commission documents are not instituted – and few of them are actually specific enough to be easily implemented at a school level – it is in the above tendencies that we shall see the reports' lasting effects. Inequalities will increase. Teachers and the curriculum will be blamed for a large portion of our social dislocations and economic and ideological problems. The knowledge needed by all of us to engage in the democratic discussion of the ends and means of our dominant institutions will be severely limited, for what will be taught in schools will be disembodied technical skills and workplace dispositions. The skills and knowledge associated with political debate and deliberation over the ends and means of our institutions, hence, will continue to atrophy. The labor process of the employees who now work in these schools will continue to look more and more similar to the rationalized, intensified, and tightly controlled labor of all too many of their colleagues in the stores, factories, and offices of America.[41] In the guise of the public good, a public consisting of the powerful will be 'rearmed.'

Profits may indeed rise for a time. Students may indeed learn a portion of our reindustrialized 'basics.' But at what cost to their own futures and those of their teachers? Surely it is a cost that is too high for those on the 'lower peak' of that double-peaked economy. Progressive educators, in concert with politically sensitive community and women's groups, labor unions, people of color, and others, have had a long history of fighting against the dominance of property rights over human needs. This fight is now occurring in our schools. To ignore our schools, to give the curriculum and teaching that goes on in them over to one limited but powerful segment of our society, would be a disaster. Obviously, schools are but a limited part of the larger society. Action in them cannot take the place of action in the economy and the state to insist that persons are more important than property. Yet fighting the battles to maintain and expand the substance of democracy in education *is* critical. It may be an essential precondition to creating a knowledgeable citizenry that will understand its own conditions. Winning some victories over the education of our children, hence, may not be sufficient, but it certainly is necessary.

The terrain of these 'battles' can be deceptive, however. Often, interventions by the state and capital, and by particular class fractions, enter the school in the guise of policies and programs that seem to most of us to genuinely be for the 'common good.' In many cases, these programs and policies for altering teachers and texts may even be proposed with what seem to be the best of intentions. The best example of such proposals currently are those surrounding the computerization of the classroom. As we shall see, the questions about teachers' lives, about the relationship between the school curriculum and the economy, and about ultimate benefits, will again be of major concern. The seemingly simple question of whether the 'computer as text' is a good idea may turn out not to be so simple after all.

CHAPTER 7

IS THE NEW TECHNOLOGY PART OF THE SOLUTION OR PART OF THE PROBLEM IN EDUCATION?

So far, I have discussed two different kinds of 'texts': those produced for the many classrooms and lecture halls throughout our school system, and those produced for the consumption of parents, educators, and others as slogan systems to convince them of the need to change what education is for. These texts take a particular form. They are printed on paper and are bound as books. However, there is a different sort of text – among the most popular today – that must be considered if our analysis is to be complete. This is one that is plugged into an electrical outlet and is marketed by IBM, Apple (no, this company is not a relative of mine), and other large corporations. Technology as text and as transformer of the labor process of both students and teachers cannot be ignored, not only because so many of the national reports make recommendations directly sponsoring 'computer literacy,' but also because a considerable number of parents and educators believe that the computer will revolutionize the classroom and their children's chances of a better life. Will it?

THE POLITICS OF TECHNOLOGY

In our society, technology is seen as an autonomous process. It is set apart and viewed as if it had a life of its own, independent of social intentions, power, and privilege. We examine technology as if it were something constantly changing, and something that is constantly changing our lives in schools and elsewhere. This is partly true, of course, and is fine as far as it goes. However, by focusing on what is changing and being changed, we may neglect to ask what relationships are remaining the same. Among the most important of these are the sets of cultural and economic inequalities that dominate even societies like our own.[1]

By thinking of technology in this way, by closely examining whether the changes associated with 'technological progress' are really changes in certain relationships after all, we can begin to ask political questions about their causes and especially their multitudinous effects. Whose idea of progress? Progress for what? And fundamentally, once again, who benefits?[2] These questions may seem rather weighty ones to be asking about schools and the curricular and teaching practices that now go on in them or are being proposed. Yet, we are in the midst of one of those many educational bandwagons that governments, industry, and others so like to ride. This wagon is pulled in the direction of a technological workplace, and carries a heavy load of computers as its cargo.

The growth of the new technology in schools is definitely not what one would call a slow movement. In one recent year, there was a 56 percent reported increase in the use of computers in schools in the United States, and even this may be a conservative estimate. Of the 25,642 schools surveyed, over 15,000 schools reported some computer usage.[3] In the United States alone, it is estimated that over 350,000 microcomputers have been introduced into the public schools in the past four years.[4] This is a trend that shows no sign of abating. Nor is this phenomenon only limited to the United

States. France, Canada, England, Australia, and many other countries have 'recognized the future.' At its center seems to sit a machine with a keyboard and a screen.

I say 'at its center' since both in industry and governmental agencies and in schools themselves the computer and the new technology have been seen as something of a savior economically and pedagogically. 'High tech' will save declining economies and will save our students and teachers in schools. In the latter, it is truly remarkable how wide a path the computer is now cutting.

The expansion of its use, the tendency to see all areas of education as a unified terrain for growth in the use of new technologies, can be seen in a two-day workshop on integrating the microcomputer into the classroom held at my own university. Among the topics covered were computer applications in writing instruction, in music education, in secondary science and mathematics, in primary language arts, for the handicapped, for teacher record keeping and management, in business education, in health occupation training programs, in art, and in social studies. To this is added a series of sessions on the 'electronic office,' how technology and automation are helping industry, and how we all can 'transcend the terror' of technology.[5]

Two things are evident from this list. First, vast areas of school life are now seen to be within the legitimate purview of technological restructuring. Second, there is a partly hidden but exceptionally close linkage between computers in schools and the needs of management for automated industries, electronic offices, and 'skilled' personnel. Thus, recognizing both what is happening inside and outside of schools and the connections between these areas is critical to any understanding of what is likely to happen with the new technologies, especially the computer, in education.

As I have argued elsewhere, educational debates are increasingly limited to technical issues. Questions of 'how to' have replaced questions of 'why.'[6] In this chapter, I shall want to reverse this tendency. Rather than dealing with what the best way might be to establish closer ties between the technological requirements of the larger society and our formal institutions of education, I want to step back and raise a different set of questions. I want us to consider a number of rather difficult political, economic, and ethical issues about some of the tendencies in schools and the larger society that may make us want to be very cautious about the current technological bandwagon in education. In so doing, a range of areas will need to be examined. Behind the slogans of technological progress and high-tech industry, what are some of the real effects of the new technology on the future labor market? What may happen to teaching and curriculum if we do not think carefully about the new technology's place in the classroom? Will the growing focus on technological expertise, particularly computer literacy, equalize or further exacerbate the lack of social opportunities for our most disadvantaged students?

At root, my claim will be that the debate about the role of the new technology in society and in schools is not and must not be just about the technical correctness of what computers can and cannot do. These may be the least important kinds of questions, in fact. Instead, at the very core of the debate, are the ideological and ethical issues concerning what schools should be about and whose interests they should serve.[7] The question of interests is very important at the moment since, because of the severe problems currently besetting economies like our own, a restructuring of what schools are *for* has reached a rather advanced stage.

Thus, while there has always been a relatively close connection between the two, as I demonstrated in the last chapter there is now an even closer relationship between the curriculum in our schools and corporate needs.[8] In a number of countries, educational officials and policy-makers, legislators, curriculum workers, and others have been subject to immense pressure to make the 'needs' of business and industry the primary goals of the school system. Economic and ideological pressures have become rather intense and often very overt. The language of efficiency, production, standards, cost-effectiveness, job skills, work discipline, and so on – all defined by powerful groups and always threatening to become the dominant way we think about schooling[9] – has begun to push aside concerns for a democratic curriculum, teacher autonomy, and class, gender, and race equality. Yet, we cannot fully understand the implications of the new technology in this restructuring unless we gain a more complete idea of what industry is now doing not only in the schools but in the economy as well.

TECHNOLOGICAL MYTHS AND ECONOMIC REALITIES

Let us look at the larger society first. It is claimed that the technological needs of the economy are such that unless we have a technologically literate labor force we will ultimately become outmoded economically. But what will this labor force actually look like?

A helpful way of thinking about this is once more to use the concepts of increasing *proletarianization* and *deskilling* of jobs. As I noted in Chapter 2, these concepts signify a complex historical process in which the control of labor has altered – one in which the skills workers have developed over many years are broken down and reduced to their atomistic units, automated, and redefined by management to enhance profit levels, efficiency, and control. In the process, the employee's control of timing, over defining the most appropriate way to do a task, and over criteria that establish acceptable performance, are slowly taken over as the prerogatives of management personnel who are usually divorced from the place where the actual labor is carried out. Loss of control by the worker is almost always the result. Pay is often lowered. And the job itself becomes routinized, boring, and alienating as conception is separated from execution and more and more aspects of jobs are rationalized to bring them into line with management's need for a tighter economic and ideological ship.[10] Finally, and very importantly, many of these jobs may simply disappear.

There is no doubt that the rapid developments in, say, micro-electronics, genetic engineering, and associated 'biological technologies,' and other high-tech areas, are in fact partly transforming work in a large number of sectors in the economy. This may lead to economic prosperity in certain sections of our population, but its other effects may be devastating. Thus, as the authors of a recent study that examined the impact of new technologies on the future labor market demonstrate:

> This transformation . . . may stimulate economic growth and competition in the world marketplace, but it will displace thousands of workers and could sustain high unemployment for many years. It may provide increased job opportunities for engineers, computer operators, and robot technicians, but it also promises to generate an even greater number of low level, service jobs such as those of janitors, cashiers, clericals, and food service workers. And while many more workers will be using computers, automated office equipment, and other sophisticated technical devices in their jobs, the increased use of technology may actually reduce the skills and discretion required to perform many jobs.[11]

This scenario requires further elaboration.

Rumberger and Levin make a distinction that is very useful to this discussion. They differentiate between high-tech industries and high-tech occupations – in essence between what is made and the kinds of jobs these goods require. High-tech industries that manufacture technical devices such as computers, electronic components, and the like currently employ less than 15 percent of the paid workforce in the United States and other industrialized nations. Just as importantly, a substantial knowledge of technology is required by *less than one-fourth* of all occupations within these industries. On the contrary, the largest share of jobs created by high-tech industries are in areas such as clerical and office work or in production and assembly. These actually pay below average wages.[12] Yet this is not all. High-tech occupations that do require considerable skill – such as computer specialists and engineers – may indeed expand. However, most of these occupations actually 'employ relatively few workers compared to many traditional clerical and service fields.'[13] Rumberger and Levin summarize a number of these points by stating that 'although the percentage growth rate of occupational employment in such high technology fields as engineering and computer programming was higher than the overall growth rate of jobs, far more jobs would be created in low-skilled clerical and service occupations than in high technology ones.'[14]

Some of these claims are supported by the following data. It is estimated that even being generous in one's projections, only 17 percent of new jobs that will be created between now and 1995 will be in high-tech industries. (Less generous and more restrictive projections argue that only 3 to 8 percent of future jobs will be in such industries.)[15] As I noted, though, such jobs will not be all equal. Clerical workers, secretaries, assemblers, warehouse personnel, etc. – these will be the largest occupations within the industry. If we take the electronic components industry as an example here, this is made much clearer. Engineering, science, and computing occupations constituted approximately 15 percent of all workers in this industry. The majority of the rest of the workers were engaged in low-wage assembly work. Thus, in the late 1970s, nearly two-thirds of all workers in the electronic components industry took home hourly wages 'that placed them in the bottom third of the national distribution.'[16] If we take the archetypical high-tech industry – computers and data processing – and decompose its labor market, we get similar results. In 1980, technologically oriented and skilled jobs accounted for only 26 percent of the total.[17]

These figures have considerable weight, but they are made even more significant by the fact that many of that 26 percent may themselves experience a deskilling process in the near future. That is, the reduction of jobs down into simpler and atomistic components, the separation of conception from execution, and so on – processes that have had such a major impact on the labor process of blue-, pink-, and white-collar workers in so many other areas – are now advancing into high-technology jobs as well. Computer programming provides an excellent example. New developments in software packages and machine language and design have meant that a considerable portion of the job of programming now requires little more than performing 'standard, routine, machine-like tasks that require little in-depth knowledge.'[18]

What does this mean for the schooling process and the seemingly widespread belief that the future world of work will require increasing technical competence on the part of all students? Consider the occupations that will contribute the most number of jobs not just in high-tech industries but throughout the society by 1995. Economic forecasts indicate that these will include building custodians, cashiers, secretaries, office clerks, nurses, waiters and waitresses, elementary school teachers, truck drivers, and other health workers such as nurses' aides and orderlies.[19] None of these are directly related to high technology. Excluding teachers and nurses, none of them require any post-secondary education. (Their earnings will be approximately 30 percent below the current average earnings of workers, as well.)[20] If we go further than this and examine an even larger segment of expected new jobs by including the forty job categories that will probably account for about half of all the jobs that will be created, it is estimated that only about 25 percent will require people with a college degree.[21]

In many ways, this is strongly related to the effects of the new technology on the job market and the labor process in general. Skill levels will be raised in some areas, but will decline in many others, as will jobs themselves decline. For instance, 'a recent study of robotics in the United States suggests that robots will eliminate 100,000 to 200,000 jobs by 1990, while creating 32,000 to 64,000 jobs.'[22] My point about declining skill requirements is made nicely by Rumberger and Levin. As they suggest, while it is usually assumed that workers will need computer programming and other sophisticated skills because of the greater use of technology such as computers in their jobs, the ultimate effect of such technology may be somewhat different. 'A variety of evidence suggests just the opposite: as machines become more sophisticated, with expanded memories, more computational ability, and sensory capabilities, the knowledge required to use the devices declines.'[23] The effect of these trends on the division of labor will be felt for decades. But it will be in the sexual division of labor that it will be even more extreme. As I argued, since historically *women's work* has been subject to these processes in very powerful ways, we shall see increased proletarianization and deskilling of women's labor and, undoubtedly, a further increase in the feminization of poverty.[24]

These points clearly have implications for our educational programs. We need to think much more rigorously about what they mean for our transition from school to work programs, especially since many of the 'skills' that schools are currently teaching are transitory because the jobs themselves are being transformed (or lost) by new technological developments and new management offensives.

Take office work, for example. In offices, the bulk of the new technology has not been designed to enhance the quality of the job for the largest portion of the employees (usually women clerical workers). Rather it has usually been designed and implemented in such a way that exactly the opposite will result. Instead of accommodating stimulating and satisfying work, the technology is there to make managers' jobs 'easier,' to eliminate jobs and cut costs, to divide work into routine and atomized tasks, and to make administrative control more easily accomplished.[25] The vision of the future society seen in the microcosm of the office is inherently undemocratic and perhaps increasingly authoritarian. Is this what we wish to prepare our students for? Surely, our task as educators is neither to accept such a future labor market and labor process uncritically nor to have our students accept such practices uncritically either. To do so is simply to allow the values of a limited but powerful segment of the population to work through us. It may be good business but I have my doubts about whether it is ethically correct educational policy.

In summary, then, what we will witness is the creation of enhanced jobs for a relative minority and deskilled and boring work for the majority. Furthermore, even those boring and deskilled jobs will be increasingly hard to find. Take office work again, an area that is rapidly being transformed by the new technology. It is estimated that between one and five jobs will be lost for every new computer terminal that is introduced.[26] Yet this situation will not be limited to office work. Even those low-paying assembly positions noted earlier will not necessarily be found in the industrialized nations with their increasingly service-oriented economies. Given the international division of labor, and what is called 'capital flight,' a large portion of these jobs will be moved to countries such as Korea, the Philippines and Indonesia.[27]

This is exacerbated considerably by the fact that many governments now find 'acceptable' those levels of unemployment that would have been considered a crisis a decade ago. 'Full employment' in the United States is now often seen as between 7 and 8 percent *measured* unemployment. (The actual figures are much higher, of course, especially among minority groups and workers who can only get part-time jobs or who have given up looking for paid work after so many disappointments.) This is a figure that is *double* that of previous economic periods. Even higher rates are now seen as 'normal' in other countries. The trend is clear. The future will see fewer jobs. Most of those that are created will not necessarily be fulfilling, nor will they pay well. Finally, the level of technical skill will continue to be lowered for a large portion of them.[28]

Because of this, we need convincing answers to some very important questions about our future society and the economy before we turn our schools into 'production plants' for creating new workers. *Where* will these new jobs be? *How many* will be created? Will they *equal* the number of positions lost in offices and factories, and service jobs in retailing, banks, telecommunications, and elsewhere? Are the bulk of the jobs that will be created relatively unskilled, less than meaningful, and themselves subject to the 'inexorable' logics of management so that they too will be likely to be automated out of existence?[29]

These are not inconsequential questions. Before we give the schools over to the requirements of the new technology and the corporation, we must be very certain that it will benefit all of us, not primarily those who already possess economic and cultural power. This requires continued democratic discussion, not a quick decision based on the economic and political pressure now being placed on schools.

Much more could be said about the future labor market. I urge the interested reader to pursue it in greater depth, since it will have a profound impact on our school policies and programs, especially in vocational areas, in working-class schools, and among programs for young women. The difficulties with the high-tech vision that permeates the beliefs of the proponents of a technological solution will not remain outside the school door, however. Similar disproportionate benefits and dangers await us inside our educational institutions as well, and it is to this that we now turn.

INEQUALITY AND THE TECHNOLOGICAL CLASSROOM

Once we go inside the school, a set of questions concerning 'who benefits?' also arises. We shall need to ask about what may be happening to teachers and students given the emphasis now being placed on computers in schools. I shall not talk about the individual teacher or student here. Obviously, some teachers will find their jobs enriched by the new technology and some students will find hidden talents and will excel in a computer-oriented classroom. What we need to ask instead (or at least before we deal with the individual) is what may happen to classrooms, teachers, and students differentially. Once again, I shall seek to raise a set of issues that may not be easy to solve, but cannot be ignored if we are to have a truly democratic educational system not just in name only.

Though I have dealt with this in greater detail in *Ideology and Curriculum* and *Education and Power*,[30] let me briefly situate the growth of the technologized classroom into what seems to be occurring to teaching and curriculum in general. Currently, considerable pressure is building to have teaching and school curricula be totally prespecified and tightly controlled for the purposes of 'efficiency,' 'cost effectiveness,' and 'accountability.' In many ways, the deskilling that is affecting jobs in general is now having an impact on teachers as more and more decisions are moving out of their hands and as their jobs become even more difficult to do. This process is more advanced in some countries than others, but it is clear that the movement to rationalize and control the act of teaching and the content and evaluation of the curriculum is very real.[31] Even in those countries that have made strides away from centralized examination systems, powerful inspectorates and supervisors, and tightly controlled curricula, there is an identifiable tendency to move back toward state control. Many reforms have only a very tenuous hold at the present time. This is in part due to economic difficulties and partly due as well to the importing of American styles and techniques of educational management – styles and techniques that have their roots in industrial bureaucracies and have almost never had democratic aims.[32] Even though a number of teachers may support computer-oriented curricula, an emphasis on the new technology needs to be seen in this context of the rationalization of teaching and curricula in general.

Given these pressures, what will happen to teachers if the new technology is accepted uncritically? One of the major effects of the current (over)emphasis on computers in the classroom may again be the deskilling and depowering of a considerable number of teachers. Given the already heavy workload of planning, teaching, meetings, and paperwork for most teachers, and given the expense, it is probably wise to assume that the largest portion of teachers will not be given more than a very small amount of training in computers, their social effects, programming, and so on. This will be especially the case at the primary and elementary school level, where most teachers are already teaching a wide array of subject areas. Research indicates in fact that few teachers in any district are actually given substantial information before computer curricula are implemented. Often only one or two teachers are the 'resident experts.'[33] Because of this, most teachers have to rely on pre-packaged sets of material, existing software, and specially purchased material from any of the scores of software manufacturing firms that are springing up in a largely unregulated way. This will be heightened by the contradictory sense of professionalism and technical expertise many teachers already have.

The impact of this can be striking. What is happening is the exacerbation of trends we have begun to see in a number of nations. Instead of teachers having the time and the skill to do their own curriculum planning and deliberation, they become isolated executors of someone else's plans, procedures, and evaluative mechanisms. In industrial terms, this is very close to what I noted in my previous discussion of the labor process – the separation of conception from execution.[34]

The reliance on pre-packaged software can have a number of long-term effects. First, it can cause a decided loss of important skills and dispositions on the part of teachers. When the skills of local curriculum planning, individual evaluation, and so on are not used, they atrophy. The tendency to look outside of one's own or one's colleagues' historical experience about curriculum and teaching is lessened as considerably more of the curriculum, and the teaching and evaluative practices that surround it, is viewed as something one purchases. In the process – and this is very important – the school itself is transformed into a lucrative market. The industrialization of the school I talked of previously is complemented, then, by further opening up the classroom to the mass-produced commodities of industry. The technological 'text' joins the existing textbook in the political economy of commodified culture. And once again, financial capital will dominate. In many ways, it will be a publisher's and salesperson's delight. Whether students' educational experiences will markedly improve is open to question.

The issue of the relationship of purchased software and hardware to the possible deskilling and depowering of teachers does not end here, though. The problem is made even more difficult by the rapidity with which software developers have constructed and marketed their products. There is no guarantee that the mass of such material has any major educational value. Exactly the opposite is often the case. One of the most knowledgeable government officials has put it this way: 'High quality educational software is almost non-existent in our elementary and secondary schools.'[35] While perhaps overstating his case to emphasize his points, the director of software evaluation for one of the largest school systems in the United States has concluded that of the more than 10,000 programs currently available, approximately 200 are educationally significant.[36]

To their credit, the fact that this is a serious problem is recognized by most computer enthusiasts, and reviews and journals have attempted to deal with it. However, the sheer volume of material, the massive amounts of money spent on advertising software in professional publications, at teachers' and administrators' meetings, and so on, the utter 'puffery' of the claims made about much of this material, and the constant pressure by industry, government, parents, some school personnel, and others to institute computer programs in schools *immediately* – all of this makes it nearly impossible to do more than make a small dent in the problem. As one educator put it, 'There's a lot of junk out there.'[37] The situation is not made any easier by the fact that teachers simply do not now have the time to thoroughly evaluate the educational strengths and weaknesses of a considerable portion of the *existing* curricular material and texts before they are used. Adding one more element, and a sizable one at that, to be evaluated only increases the load. As we saw in Chapter 2, teachers' work is increasingly becoming what students of the labor process call *intensified*. More and more needs to be done; less and less time is available to do it.[38] Thus, one has little choice but to buy ready-made material, in this way continuing a trend in which all of the important curricular elements are not locally produced but purchased from commercial sources whose major aim may be profit, not necessarily educational merit.[39]

A significant consideration here, besides the loss of skill and control, is expense. This is at least a three-pronged issue. First, we must recognize that we may be dealing with something of a 'zero-sum game.' While dropping, the cost of computers is still comparatively high, though some manufacturers may keep purchase costs relatively low, knowing that a good deal of their profits may come from the purchase of software later on or through a home–school connection, something I shall discuss shortly. This money for the new technology *must come from somewhere*. This is an obvious point, but one that is very consequential. In a time of fiscal crisis, where funds are already spread too thinly and necessary programs are being starved in many areas, the addition of computer curricula most often means that money must be drained from one area and given to another. What will be sacrificed? If history is any indication, it may be programs that have benefited the least advantaged. Little serious attention has been paid to this, but it will become an increasingly serious dilemma.

A second issue of expense concerns staffing patterns, for it is not just the content of teachers' work and the growth of purchased materials that are at stake. Teachers' jobs themselves are on the line here. At a secondary school level in many nations, for example, layoffs of teachers have not been unusual as funding for education is cut. Declining enrollment in some regions has meant a loss of positions as well. This has caused intense competition over students within the school itself. Social studies, art, music, and other subjects must fight it out with newer, more 'glamorous' subject areas. To lose the student numbers game for too long is to lose a job. The effect of the computer in this situation has been to increase competitiveness among staff, often to replace substance with both gloss and attractive packaging of courses, and to threaten many teachers with the loss of their livelihood.[40] Is it really an educationally or socially wise decision to tacitly eliminate a good deal of the choices in these other fields so that we can support the 'glamor' of a computer future? These are not only financial decisions, but are ethical decisions about teachers' lives and about what our students are to be educated in. Given the future labor market, do we really want to claim that computers will be more important than further work in humanities and social sciences or, perhaps even more significantly in working-class and ethnically diverse areas, in the students' own cultural, historical, and political heritage and struggles? Such decisions must not be made by only looking at the accountant's bottom line. These too need to be arrived at by the lengthy democratic deliberation of all parties, including the teachers who will be most affected.

Third, given the expense of microcomputers and software in schools, the pressure to introduce such technology may increase the already wide social imbalances that now exist. Private schools to which the affluent send their children and publicly funded schools in more affluent areas will have more ready access to the technology itself.[41] Schools in inner-city, rural, and poor areas will be largely priced out of the market, even if the cost of 'hardware' continues to decline. After all, in these poorer areas, and in many public school systems in general in a number of countries, it is already difficult to generate enough money to purchase new textbooks and to cover the costs of teachers' salaries. Thus, the computer and literacy over it will 'naturally' generate further inequalities. Since, by and large, it will be the top 20 percent of the population who will have computers in their homes[42] and many of the jobs and institutions of higher education their children will be applying for will either ask for or assume 'computer skills' as keys of entry or advancement, the impact can be enormous in the long run.

The role of the relatively affluent parent in this situation does not go unrecognized by computer manufacturers.

> Computer companies . . . gear much of their advertising to the educational possibilities of computers. The drive to link particular computers to schools is a frantic competition. Apple, for example, in a highly touted scheme proposed to 'donate' an Apple to every school in America. Issues of philanthropy and intent aside, the clear market strategy is to couple particular computer usages to schools where parents – especially middle class parents with the economic wherewithal and keen motivation [to insure mobility] – purchase machines compatible with those in schools. The potentially most lucrative part of such a scheme, however, is not in the

purchase of hardware (although this is also substantial) but in the sale of proprietary software.[43]

This very coupling of school and home markets, then, cannot fail to further disadvantage large groups of students. Those students who already have computer backgrounds – be it because of their schools or their homes or both – will proceed more rapidly. The social stratification of life chances will increase. These students' original advantage – one *not* due to 'natural ability,' but to *wealth* – will be heightened.[44]

We should not be surprised by this, nor should we think it odd that many parents, especially middle-class parents, will pursue a computer future. The knowledge itself is part of the technical-administrative 'cultural capital' of the new middle class. Computer skills and 'literacy,' however, is partly a strategy for the maintenance of middle-class mobility patterns.[45] Having such expertise, in a time of fiscal and economic crisis, is like having an insurance policy. It partly guarantees that certain doors remain open in a rapidly changing labor market. In a time of credential inflation, more credentials mean fewer closed doors.[46] (This also works within the school. Some teachers will support computerization because it offers a real sense of competence and control that may be missing in their jobs now *and* perhaps because it offers paths to upward mobility within the school bureaucracy as well.)

The credential factor here is of considerable moment. In the past, as gains were made by ethnically different people, working-class groups, women, and others in schooling, one of the latent effects was to raise the credentials required by entire sectors of jobs. Thus, class, race, and gender barriers were partly maintained by an ever-increasing credential inflation. Though this was more of a structural than a conscious process, the effect over time has often been to again disqualify entire segments of a population from jobs, resources and power. This too may be a latent outcome of the computerization of the school curriculum. Even though, as I have shown, the bulk of new jobs will not require 'computer literacy,' the establishment of computer requirements and mandated programs in schools will condemn many people to even greater economic disenfranchisement. Since the requirements are in many ways artificial – computer knowledge will not be so very necessary and the number of jobs requiring high levels of expertise will be relatively small – we will simply be affixing one more label to these students. 'Functional illiteracy' will simply be broadened to include computers.[47]

Thus, rather than blaming an unequal economy and a situation in which meaningful and fulfilling work is not made available, rather than seeing how the new technology for all its benefits is 'creating a growing underclass of displaced and marginal workers,' the lack is personalized. It becomes the students' or workers' fault for not being computer literate. One significant social and ideological outcome of computer requirements in schools, then, is that they can serve as a means 'to justify those lost lives by a process of mass disqualification, which throws the blame for disenfranchisement in education and employment back on the victims themselves.'[48]

Of course, this process may not be visible to many parents of individual children. However, the point does not revolve around the question of individual mobility, but around large-scale effects. Parents may see such programs as offering important paths to advancement and some will be correct. However, in a time of severe economic problems, parents tend to overestimate what schools can do for their children.[49] As I documented earlier, there simply will not be sufficient jobs, and competition will be intense. The uncritical introduction of and investment in hardware and software will by and large hide the reality of the transformation of the labor market and will support those who are already advantaged unless thought is given to these implications now.

Let us suppose, however, that it was important that everyone become computer literate and that these large investments in time, money, and personnel were indeed so necessary for our economic and educational future. Given all this, what is currently happening in schools? Is inequality in access and outcome now being produced? While many educators are continually struggling against these effects, we are already seeing signs of this disadvantagement being created.

There is evidence of class-, race-, and gender-based differences in computer use. In middle-class schools, for example, the number of computers is considerably more than in working-class or inner-city schools populated by children of color. The ratio of computers to children is also much higher. This in itself is an unfortunate finding. However, something else must be added here. These more economically advantaged schools not only have more contact hours and more technical and teacher support, but the very manner in which the computer is used is often different than what would be generally found in schools in less advantaged areas. Programming skills, generalizability, a sense of the multitudinous things one can do with computers both within and across academic areas – these tend to be stressed more[50] (though simply drill and practice uses are still widespread even here).[51] Compare this to the rote, mechanistic, and relatively low-level uses that tend to dominate the working-class school.[52] These differences are not unimportant, for they signify a ratification of class divisions.

Further evidence to support these claims is now becoming more readily available as researchers dig beneath the glowing claims of a computer future for all children. The differential impact is made clearer in the following figures. In the United States, while over two-thirds of the schools in affluent areas have computers, only approximately 41 percent of the poorer public schools have them. What one does with the machine is just as important as having one, of course, and here the differences are again very real. One study of poorer elementary schools found that white children were four times more likely than black children to use computers for programming. Another found that the children of professionals employed computers for programming and for other 'creative' uses. Non-professional children were more apt to use them for drill and practice in mathematics and reading, and for 'vocational' work. In general, in fact, 'programming has been seen as the purview of the gifted and talented' and of those students who are more affluent. Less affluent students seem to find that the computer is only a tool for drill and practice sessions.[53]

Gender differences are also very visible. Two out of every three students currently learning about computers are boys. Even here these data are deceptive, since girls 'tend to be clustered in the general introductory courses,' not the advanced level ones.[54] One current analyst summarizes the situation in a very clear manner:

> While stories abound about students who will do just about anything to increase their access to computers, most youngsters working with school computers are [economically advantaged], white and male. The ever-growing number of private computer camps, after-school and weekend programs serve middle class white boys. Most minority [and poor] parents just can't afford to send their children to participate in these programs.[55]

This class, race, and gendered impact will also occur because of traditional school practices such as tracking or streaming. Thus, vocational and business tracks will learn operating skills for word processing and will be primarily filled with (working-class) young women.[56] Academic tracks will stress more general programming abilities and uses and will be disproportionately male.[57] Since computer programs usually have their home bases in mathematics and science in most schools, gender differences can be heightened even more given the often differential treatment of girls in these classes and the ways in which mathematics and science curricula already fulfill 'the selective function of the school and contribute to the reproduction of gender differences.'[58] While many teachers and curriculum workers have devoted considerable time and effort to equalizing both the opportunities and outcomes of female students in mathematics and science (and such efforts are important), the problem still remains a substantive one. It can be worsened by the computerization of these subjects.

TOWARD SOCIAL LITERACY

We have seen some of the possible negative consequences of the new technology in education, including the deskilling and depowering of teachers and the creation of inequalities through expense, credential inflation, and limitations on access. Yet it is important to realize that the issues surrounding the deskilling process are not limited to teachers. They include the very ways students themselves are taught to think about their education, their future roles in society, and the place of technology in that society. Let me explain what I mean by this.

The new technology is not just an assemblage of machines and their accompanying software. It embodies a *form of thinking* that orients a person to approach the world in a particular way. Computers involve ways of thinking that are primarily *technical*.[59] The more the new technology transforms the classroom in its own image, the more a technical logic will replace critical political and ethical understanding. The discourse of the classroom will center on technique, and less on substance. Once again 'how to' will replace 'why,' but this time at the level of the student. This situation requires what I shall call social, not technical, literacy for all students.

Even if computers make sense technically in all curricular areas and even if all students, not mainly affluent white males, become technically proficient in their use, critical questions of politics and ethics remain to be dealt with in the curriculum. Thus, it is crucial that whenever the new technology is introduced into schools, students have a serious understanding of the issues surrounding their larger social effects, many of which I raised earlier.

Unfortunately, this is not often the case. When the social and ethical impacts of computers are dealt with, they are usually addressed in a manner that is less than powerful. One example is provided by a recent proposal for a statewide computer curriculum in one of the larger states in the United States. The objectives that dealt with social questions in the curriculum centered around one particular set of issues. The curriculum states that 'the student will be aware of some of the major uses of computers in modern society . . . and the student will be aware of career opportunities related to computers.'[60] In most curricula the technical components of the new technology are stressed. Brief glances are given to the history of computers (occasionally mentioning the role of women in their development, which is at least one positive sign). Yet in this history, the close relationship between military use and computer development is largely absent. 'Benign' uses are pointed to, coupled with a less than realistic description of the content and possibility of computer careers and what Douglas Noble has called 'a gee-whiz glance at the marvels of the future.' What is almost never mentioned is job loss or social disenfranchisement. The very real destruction of the lives of unemployed autoworkers, assemblers or clerical workers is marginalized.[61] The political, economic, and ethical dilemmas involved when we choose between, say, 'efficiency' and the quality of the work people experience, between profit and someone's job – these too are made invisible.

How would we counterbalance this? By making it clear from the outset that knowledge about the new technology that it is necessary for students to have goes well beyond what we now too easily take for granted. A considerable portion of the curriculum would be organized around questions concerned with social literacy: 'Where are computers used? What are they used to do? What do people *actually* need to know in order to use them? Does the computer enhance anyone's life? Whose? Does it hurt anyone's life? Whose? Who decides when and where computers will be used?'[62] Unless these are *fully* integrated in a school program at *all* levels, I would hesitate to advocate the use of the new technology in the curriculum. To do less makes it much more difficult for students to think critically and independently about the place the new technology does and should have in the lives of the majority of people in our society. Our job as educators involves skilling, not deskilling. Unless students are able to deal honestly and critically with these complex ethical and social issues, only those now with the power to control technology's uses will have the capacity to act. We cannot afford to let this happen.

CONCLUSION

I realize that a number of my points in this chapter may prove to be rather contentious. But stressing the negative side can serve to highlight many of the critical issues that are too easy to put off given the immense amount of work that school personnel are already responsible for. Decisions often get made too quickly, only to be regretted later on when forces are set in motion that could have been avoided if the implications of one's actions had been thought through more fully.

As I noted at the outset of this discussion, there is now something of a mad scramble to employ the computer in every content area. In fact, it is nearly impossible to find a subject that is not being 'computerized.' Though mathematics and science (and some parts of vocational education) remain the home base for a large portion of proposed computer curricula, other areas are not far behind. If it can be packaged to fit computerized instruction, it will be, even if this is inappropriate, less effective than the methods that teachers have developed after years of hard practical work, or less than sound educationally or economically. Rather than the machine fitting the educational needs and visions of the teacher, students, and community, all too often these needs and visions are made to fit the technology itself.

Yet, as I have shown, the new technology does not stand alone. It is linked to transformations in real groups of people's lives, jobs, hopes, and dreams. For some of these groups, their lives will be enhanced. For others, their dreams will be shattered. Wise choices about the appropriate place of the new technology in education, then, are not only educational decisions. They are fundamentally choices about the kind of society we shall have, about the social and ethical responsiveness of our institutions to the majority of our future citizens. Here educators can be guided by the critical positions on the introduction and use of the new technology that have been taken by some of the more progressive unions in a number of countries.

My discussion here has not been aimed at making us all neo-Luddites, people who go out and smash the machines that threaten our jobs or our children. The new technology is here. It will not go away. Our task as educators is to make sure that when it enters the classroom it is there for politically, economically, and educationally wise reasons, not because powerful groups may be redefining our major educational goals in their own image. We should be very clear about whether or not the future it promises our students is real, not fictitious. We need to be certain that it is a future *all* of our students can share in, not just a select few. After all, the new technology is expensive and will take up a good deal of our time and that of our teachers, administrators, and students. It is more than a little important that we question whether the wagon we have been asked to ride on is going in the right direction. It's a long walk back.

CONCLUSION

CHAPTER 8

SUPPORTING DEMOCRACY IN EDUCATION

EDUCATING THE EDUCATORS

In this volume, I have traced a number of historical and current tendencies out of which teachers and texts have been and are being constructed. Each chapter has sought to place educational issues back in their social context, to situate what is happening to teachers, textbooks, curriculum, and technology in the larger social movements of which they are a part.

Stanley Aronowitz and Henry Giroux have rightly urged critical educators to develop not only a 'language of critique' but also a 'language of possibility.' Absent a serious analysis of 'the degree to which popular forces might appropriate the democratic ideology of schools, elements of school knowledge, and on the basis of these, find the possibility of accumulating power within the schools,' the possibility of a critical democratic educational practice is lessened considerably. We need to recognize the positive, not just the negative, relationship between knowledge and power.[1] Only then can a political and educational program around which people can organize be developed. These are very important points, and ones I fully agree with. Yet a language of possibility needs to be grounded in a sense of history. We need to recapture our past to see what is possible. For this reason, I have given considerable attention here to the history of teaching as a classed and, especially, gendered occupation. By seeing how teachers *helped make their own history* (contradictory though it may be), by once again restoring their (and our) collective memory of the range and success of particular political and cultural struggles, we take a large step toward making such struggles legitimate once again in a time of conservative restoration. A democratic future is enchanced by the very sense of our own previous, even partial, victories.

Possibilities must also be grounded in an unromantic appraisal of the circumstances in which we find ourselves. This is not meant to create cynicism or to lead to quiescence. Rather, it is intended to show that these conditions cannot simply be wished away. Organized action is required, not romantic dreams – though such utopian dreams provide the imaginative resources for picturing difference and should not be neglected. Our first task as educators in these circumstances is to educate ourselves about these conditions. For the institutions of our society to be reconstructed around the principles not of privatization and greed but of the common good,[2] people – including educators – need to be convinced that the current and emerging organization of a large part of our economic, political, and cultural institutions is neither equal nor just. I hope that by bringing together data on class, gender, and race inequalities inside and outside of our formal institutions of education and by providing criticisms of some of the major proposals to reconstruct teaching and curricula I have helped demonstrate the seriousness of these issues.

Of course, the long history of the action not only of teachers but of what Vincent Harding has called that vast river of struggles of people of color, women, and others,[3] will be less known to us as textbooks become increasingly organized around the needs of financial capital, as schools become increasingly industrialized, and as teachers lose the autonomy it has taken years to win. Our ability as educators to educate ourselves – and, hence, the later education of our students at all levels – is thus more than a little dependent on protecting the possibility of more democratic curricular and teaching practice. Our having knowledge may not guarantee power or a more democratic future; but one can be certain that without it that future will be harder than ever to see as a possibility.

We need to remember that there are *educational and cultural preconditions* for large-scale, or even small-scale, movements and challenges to the conservative restoration. Unless we 'school' ourselves about the unequal realities of this society, how can we make it possible for the students, teachers, and others with whom we work to have the resources for recognizing and acting on these realities as well?

Oddly, all too many educators and academics suffer from a peculiar form of self-hatred. They all 'know' that the educational system won't change the world, that education makes little difference in the long run to macro-social relations. (Perhaps they should listen more to the comments about literacy made by the peasants and workers of Nicaragua?) Yet, these same individuals have largely come to these conclusions through discussions, reading, and study. Why deny education's place for others as well? Obviously such educational activity is only a part of what is necessary for collective action. But for such action to be mindful, and for such action to grow out of the lived experiences of people in the manner documented by Freire in Latin America and by Shor and others in the United States, it cannot be ignored.[4]

Of course, as educators we need to realize that to assume that reforming schools by itself can have a major impact on the structures of the economy and the larger society is rather naive. However, as Ken Jones reminds us, 'It is not impossible to encourage an education that resists the continual pressure to prepare students for [less than powerful] political and economic roles, and that, in the process, can stimulate a criticism of the system that makes such demands.'[5] Nor is it impossible to work closely with teachers on this and to tap the roots of so many teachers' feelings that they too are losing control of their own labor process. Combining their personal analysis with one's own structural sense of what is happening, listening and learning from each other, is a first step.

It was a group of feminist teachers who first showed me the power of thinking about teaching as women's work. Their willingness to listen to my largely class analysis and our continuing joint efforts to blend the two positions together has mutually reinforced and altered what were seemingly separate positions at the outset. In the process, not only have we built a stronger analysis, but a foundation of political and educational trust has been laid. Unless we work with progressive teachers – many of whose intuitions about what is occurring to their own jobs and to the lives of others in the larger society are more than a little insightful – both our own actions in education and the analyses connected to them will simply be incomplete and perhaps doomed to failure.

FACING COMPLEXITY

The critical power of any social analysis does not arise from some alleged disinterestedness. That is often illusory in many ways in the first place. Rather it stems from the ability of such an investigation to help us pass judgment upon social realities that seem unjust.[6] This has been one of my primary aims in this book – to provide us both with tools and with applications of their use that would assist all of us in asking critical questions about the nature of 'teachers' and 'texts' and their relations to larger ideological, political, and economic dynamics. While I pointed to arenas of conflict and to specific tendencies that have been, are now, and must be contested, I have preferred to be honest about what is happening right now, rather than be superficially optimistic. I tend to believe that honesty about the difficulties we may face in creating the conditions for the democratization of teaching, texts, and technology is something of a virtue.

Insight into these social realities is not only the product of analysis. It is profoundly shaped by our political actions in the real world. (Certainly mine has been.) Even in the face of what seem, in one's political/economic analysis, to be overwhelming odds, real women and men have constantly shown that, given half a chance, it is possible to build and protect the substance of democracy in their cultural, political, and economic lives. Perhaps Gramsci said it best in his phrase 'Pessimism of the intellect, optimism of the will.' Of course, it is the combination of these two that is so important: not 'reason' detached from emotion, value, and action, but these qualities intimately interconnected, each one informing the other about how we create the common good and act against the impediments to that goal.

In this society, however, it is so hard to make that organic connection. This is the case in part because our modern concept of social reason seems more and more to be characterized as a form of something like cost-benefit analysis. (It is always coded as profit vs. people – what I earlier called property vs. person rights – and in this calculus of values the latter are only useful if they enhance the former.) Just as important is the very difficulty of engaging in disciplined critical reflection at a time when significant portions of our universities are being reconstructed around the needs of capital[7] and when social criticism in general is once again seen as being somehow 'un-American' in the climate of unbridled boosterism that pervades the current right-wing resurgence.

Yet what kind of society is it that we live in, when serious critical analyses repeatedly arise either from our own and others' phenomenological experiences or from the pens of scholars and are placed on the shelf as instances of 'doom and gloom' that can be ignored? What kind of society is it that makes a virtue of distraction, so much so that the sustained discussion of the lives and futures (and in a nuclear age, of the very survival) of our children and their teachers as other than economic beings who do their part in the profit machine, is made to seem odd? One is left, even in the midst of the current crisis, with an image that materializes 'of a cluttered room in which someone is trying to think, while there is a fan-dance going on in one corner and a military band is blasting away in the other.'[8] The band is not playing union songs or songs of solidarity and protest. It is playing music written to keep 'standards,' productivity, and profits up so we can help in rearming and reindustrializing 'our nation.' And the music is played on the keyboard of a computer.

The music is loud; the dance is seductive. But the people on that line near the school in Washington still hurt. And the growing numbers of increasingly poor women and people of color still struggle to make ends meet. And essential programs in education, nutrition, legal aid, safety, health and welfare, and so on are cut. And the jobs of so many women and men leave the country to be replaced by low-skilled, low-paid, often part-time, alienating labor (or not replaced at all). And the jobs that remain – even those that have had some measure of autonomy – are restructured to make them 'more efficient' and more controlled. And economic power is centralized. And the band plays on.

Other people, though, including many like those on that line and like those who are losing their programs, jobs, and autonomy, are attempting to silence that band and stop the dance. It is hard work to think with all that noise; but the thinking does go on, often in important ways. Sometimes, just thinking seriously can be a form of resistance in itself.

Actually, it has become something of a commonplace to recognize that wherever there is power, there is resistance. They are two parts of a social couplet. However, these forms of resistance take on a political character only in certain cases. Only under specific conditions do they become 'struggles directed toward putting an end to relations of domination as such.' Given this, one of our most pressing theoretical and political problems is to identify those conditions that lead to collective action.[9] That was one of the central tasks I set out to accomplish in *Education and Power*, the volume that preceded this one. There, I began the examination of the impact of the ideological and economic crisis on our social lives, changes in the labor process and our lived culture, conflicts over economic, political, and cultural policies within the state, and the growing importance of technical/administrative knowledge in the economy and the school in an attempt to show the limits on and possibilities of a more democratic set of social and cultural arrangements within our society in general and within our educational system in particular. At the same time, in a preliminary manner, I pointed out the importance of taking gender and race relations as seriously as those of class if we were to act in more progressive ways.[10] This non-reductive program has provided much of the emphasis behind the analysis I have done in this book, where I have sought to take these arguments further, and just as importantly to apply them and make them clearer.

Obviously, giving more parallel status to gender and race dynamics complicates matters considerably. The recognition that culture and the state are both linked to and relatively autonomous from the economy does little to lessen that complexity. These involved relations – conflicts between (*and* within) race, class, and gender formations, over cultural, political, and economic power, over social and educational goals within the state – are real. Why pretend, because of some odd commitment to orthodoxy, that they do not exist?

Unfortunately, too often the search within the critical educational community for the conditions that could lead to collective action has focused almost exclusively on class, thereby in effect denying one of the primary realities experienced by so many elementary teachers, for example. Hence, it makes it that much more difficult to uncover some of the most powerful bases for effective action.

I have argued here that class relations constitute but one pole – an important one, to be sure, as I have also pointed out – around which these collective actions have arisen and might arise. Throughout this volume, I have asked us to pay particular attention to race and, especially, gender struggles.

At the same time, I have shown some of the ways in which cultural, political, and, especially, economic relations act in defining teachers and texts in education.

While stressing some elements more than others, I have tried to stay away from dichotomous views of these phenomena. While I have argued that gender, race, and class are relatively autonomous and are not reducible to each other, it is next to impossible to completely understand each of them through a 'discrete mode of analysis.' That is, we live in a class *and* gender *and* racially structured society. Gender has a concrete impact on race and class consciousness and organization. But class in turn is reciprocally related to gender and race. It is the articulation among the three that needs to be understood, not just their separate tendencies.[11] The point is decidedly not to devalue class, but to show its emerging relational qualities, to show its embodiment in gendered and raced subjects. Hence my discussions throughout the book of the changing place of women and people of color in the class composition of advanced capitalist countries.

Teachers and Texts has turned most of its attention to gender and class, demonstrating their articulation over time in the construction of the labor process of teaching and of the political economy of texts for both students and the wider public. To complete this analysis would require just as serious an interrogation of the construction of teaching and curricula in terms of the racial structuring of our social formation, the beginnings of which have already been done in England and the United States.[12] In demonstrating this articulation, I have situated it within certain emerging tendencies in the economy and their dialectical connections with the current attempts to restructure education.

Some may argue that I have gone too far in highlighting gender relations. (I, on the other hand, know that I have probably still not gone far enough.) Others may conclude that not enough emphasis has been given to the simple and straightforward control of education by the state, and the control of both of these by the economy. After all, isn't education simply one tool among many within capital's arsenal for getting its own way in teaching and curriculum and in the reproduction of a labor force? As my chapters on women teachers, on the internal 'political economy' of textbooks, and on documents such as *The Paideia Proposal* and *A Nation at Risk* demonstrate, economically and sexually dominant groups have a good deal of power (and it *is* increasing in some areas). However, this power is highly mediated and altered by the self-formative actions of teachers, by class fractions within the state, and by the very fact that schools are very much part of the political, not just the economic, arena. Because of this latter point in particular, they will be pressured to act according to democratic norms.[13] Even when the reproduction of hegemonic conditions is the outcome, it is never simple, never a result of unmediated imposition, but always the result of conflicts and compromises.

Here I must admit that I find the arguments advanced by Stuart Hall, one of the most insightful writers on the politics of culture, to be essential. As he states:

> The task of critical theory is to produce as accurate a knowledge of complex social processes as the complexity of their functioning requires. It is not its task to console the left by producing simple but satisfying myths, distinguished only by their super-left wing credentials. (If the laws and tendencies of [for example] the capitalist mode of production can be stated in a simplified form because they are essentially simple and reducible, why on earth did Marx go on about them for so long – three incompleted volumes, no less?) Most important of all, these differences and complexities have real *effects*, which ought to enter into any serious calculations about how their tendencies might be resisted or turned.[14]

It is these effects which should concern us, since they are

the result of and may offer possibilities for social action. Thus, I have argued that to neglect the politics of patriarchy is to ignore one of the most significant arenas in which these effects are produced.

In much of this analysis, I have taken my examples primarily from the United States and I am 'sometimes arguing close up to its specific circumstances. But the point is to move on from these to much more general situations,'[15] to the politics of teaching and texts in similar (and different) locations. I have confidence that the issues I have pointed to – the connections among education, state, and economy, among class, gender, and race – are not limited to the American experience. If anything, having worked with groups from and in other countries, I believe that these dynamic interconnections are essential as building blocks to any complete understanding of education, even where their articulations to each other may be different due to historically distinct developments.

The way teaching is dealt with provides an interesting example here. I have used the United States, and in part England, to demonstrate the close connections between gender and class relations in the very constitution and control of teaching and have pointed out how the current proposals to alter teaching and curricula might impact on education given these connections. I am perfectly well aware that altered demographic and political circumstances will create conditions for a distinctly different articulation between the two. But the key point is to combine the two to use as a lens to see more clearly some of the most significant forces making teaching as we know it.

Thus, not just in the United States, but elsewhere as well, we need at all times to situate the work of teaching in its material conditions and especially in its history. As I have demonstrated throughout this volume, the current 'reforms' proposed to rationalize and standardize teaching and texts can only be fully comprehended if they are seen as historical extensions of how women's paid labor has been dealt with and in the context of the political/economic history of publishing. To lose the sense of this past is both to misrecognize the patterns of disproportionate benefits that will result and to ignore the long history of concrete struggles by real teachers to gain even the limited autonomy they now possess. These overt and covert struggles occurred on a variety of levels, over control of content, time, skills, and even over one's bodily presentation. They did not end, but continue in transformed context and discourse today. Only by focusing on this past can we see how far we have actually come. And only by keeping this past in sight can we see how much we have to lose, what the stakes actually are, in the current attempt to restructure education.

All this is made clearer if we think about the idea of teacher skills. The concept of skill not only denotes a technical relation to a particular labor process. It also, and fundamentally, is a social concept. It speaks to the successful or unsuccessful struggle to gain control over one's workplace and job content.[16] It implies a connection between conception and execution that is a relationship of both technique and power. In schools, it is also profoundly constructed around the history of gender politics. The continuing attempt by administrators and state bureaucrats to define the skills of teaching as a set of objectively determined competencies and to rationalize the job itself through such competencies and through the overly standardized textbook, standardized teacher and student testing, and the computer, documents exactly this continuing connection between skill and power. The external specification of the 'competencies' of teaching is a rearticulation of that struggle – one in which the gender specificities remain hidden under the rhetorical artifice of technique and accountability.[17]

Of course, all this is not to say that one should uncritically accept teachers' positions on everything of importance simply because it is a group of people whose work is being restructured and intensified who hold such beliefs. Given teachers' contradictory class position, there *will* be times when they will take less than democratic stances. Rather, it is to say that without a thoroughgoing analysis of the long history of gender as well as class struggles and strategies in teaching, we would not know what stance is progressive in what specific arena in the first place. Too often we have assumed that once you know the class position of teachers, or their sentiments about class politics, you know everything of importance in figuring out what your position should be on their stances. It would be comforting if that were the case; but it is simply wrong. It is by showing the sometimes complementary and sometimes contradictory interconnections between class and gender, between paid and unpaid work, between home and school, that the real positions of teachers can be found. And it is by showing how these are embodied not in structures, but in agents, in real teachers with real hopes, dreams, fears, and material circumstances – as R. W. Connell and Sara Freedman have begun to do, for example[18] – that possibilities for democratic action can be known. Only here can we truly identify what is progressive or not about any particular stance.

RESTRUCTURING EDUCATION

Democratic action (in goals *and* process) is the aim, of course. What is required is agreement on a set of positions that takes into account the lived experiences of teachers and the inequalities that are being built in our cultural, political, and economic lives. This will inevitably be a compromise, but arguing out such a set of positions can enable coalitions like those established by the Boston Women's Teachers' Group and others to build a movement for defending and extending the democratizing tendencies now extant in schools.

There *are* alternative sets of positions to proposals attempting to standardize and rationalize our educational institutions, and the curricular and teaching practices that go on within them, that may enable such coalitions to be formed. Let me briefly note one significant example that has been hammered out by an international group of educators concerned with the negative effects the conservative restoration is having on curricular, teaching, and evaluative policies and practices. In most instances, this example runs directly counter to the tendencies toward the industrialization of the school, the tight control of teachers' work, the standardization of texts and curricula, and the technologization of student and teacher meanings that are now increasingly dominant.

The Public Education Information Network (an outgrowth of the International Committee of Correspondence for Democratic Schools) has prepared an 'agenda for school reform,' *Education for a Democratic Future: Equity and Excellence*. They propose changes in five areas: (1) reform of the curriculum; (2) school structure and governance; (3) increasing teacher effectiveness; (4) testing and evaluation; and (5) pedagogy and school discipline. In each of these areas, the Network members are expressly responding to the arguments set forth in *The Paideia Proposal*, *A Nation at Risk*, and other such documents. What sets this group apart from others is its consistent attempt at organizing educators at all levels – administrators, teachers, writers, academics, and others, including members of minority and feminist groups – to support and work for the principles they espouse in both national and local arenas. While still in the formative stage, the Network's basic goals are worth stating.

For the Network, there are three constitutive elements of a truly democratic curriculum. The first is 'critical literacy.' The emphasis here is on both of these terms. Not just the ability to read and write, but particular kinds of dispositions are important – e.g., 'the motivation and capacity to be critical of what one reads, sees, and hears; to probe and go beyond the surface appearances and question the common wisdom.' The second element includes 'knowledge and understanding of the diverse intellectual, cultural and scientific traditions.' This is not limited to the traditions of high or elite culture and the academic disciplines. It needs to go beyond these to 'the histories and cultural perspectives of those people, including women and minorities, traditionally excluded from formal study.' Finally, a democratic curriculum must include the 'ability to use knowledge and skill' in particular ways to create and 'pursue one's own interests; to make informed personal and political decisions; and to work for the welfare of the community.'[19]

The Network members' proposals for school structure and governance are of considerable interest. Rather than top down styles, they advocate a distinct shift toward more democratic forms of governance. For instance, they argue that hierarchical models could begin to be replaced through working on the following proximate goals:

> Institute district policies which establish school site-management and fiscal control, and various forms of school community governance;
>
> Influence state and local officials to introduce more responsive forms of assessment that encourage greater involvement and collective responsibility at the school level by administrators and teachers;
>
> Revise discretionary federal and state regulations to eliminate provisions that impose prescribed procedures (e.g. mandated use of standardized test scores for determining eligibility and evaluating outcomes). These should be replaced with more flexible and permissive guidelines that encourage more creativity and responsibility by teachers, local districts and individual schools;
>
> Abolish or significantly modify the practice of centralized state and/or district wide textbook adoptions.[20]

The proposals for increasing teacher effectiveness also carry a democratic intent and a recognition that school reforms must be grounded in the day-to-day labor of teachers, not in hierarchically organized and overly bureaucratic models. The document argues for much greater teacher autonomy, and material and ideological support for it – support that will counter the deskilling, intensification, and rationalization of teachers' work. The key here is collective responsibility. In this regard, three elements are proposed: (1) More informal time to be spent with students and parents and for observing and discussing curriculum and teaching practices with other teachers, writers, artists, and experts in a variety of fields. This would also include increased time for planning and evaluating their own and their colleagues' actions. (2) Provisions for periodic sabbaticals for all teachers so that they have time for 'sustained study, writing, and keeping current in their chosen areas.' (3) Making more easily available curricular materials, films, books, computer software, and so forth, with provision of physical facilities for teachers to create and develop their own curricular and teaching strategies. Yet this latter element is less than powerful, if the conditions specified in number 1 – the time (and financial resources, of course) to jointly evaluate and produce – are not seriously acted on. All of this is to be coupled with across-the-board increases in salaries (not merit plans, which foster competition), peer review procedures, and closer working relationships between reformed and more democratic teacher education programs and schools.[21]

In the areas of testing and evaluation, the Network recognizes the critical importance that the availability of information about how schools are performing has for a democratic culture. However, they reject as making teachers 'mere functionaries,' and as taking decisions out of educators', parents', and others' hands, the all too prevalent overreliance on standardized tests produced by testing agencies and publishers. Those, they believe, can actually lead to 'the deterioration of educational standards, teacher passivity, and a lack of student involvement.' Thus, the use of the usual paper-and-pencil measures should be drastically curtailed and as much as possible should be used as a supplement to more 'subtle, sensitive, and educationally useful forms of assessment' which place more emphasis on self-evaluations of schools and classrooms by teachers, administrators, parents, and the local community. These assessments would require the creation of a systematic yet nuanced plan for collecting a range of documentary evidence about student performance. The plan would not be based only on standardized tests and lists of competencies, behavioral objectives, and so on, as is too often the case now. It would be democratically developed and would be carried out by a 'school site evaluation team' made up of selected teachers, parents, subject-matter specialists, and consultants in curriculum and pedagogy from area colleges. The evaluation would be the result of interviews with all concerned parties, systematic observations, and the 'recording and analysis of curriculum, pedagogy' and the entire educational environment.[22]

Finally, *Education for a Democratic Future* raises serious questions about the prevailing forms of pedagogy and school discipline. It argues that both 'an engaging pedagogy' (one that builds on students' cultural forms and employs student initiative as much as possible) and 'democratic class discipline' must be at the heart of any serious school reform. Drawing upon the experiences of teachers' successes in some of our most difficult classrooms, they point out that

> Close monitoring, ubiquitous boredom and the resistance and antagonism they engender are neither necessary nor inevitable.
>
> Many teachers have developed pedagogy that builds upon students' own knowledge and interests, and leads them to incorporate realms of public knowledge; that teaches students to look critically at taken-for-granted perspectives as well as to respect traditions and democratic values; that stimulates intrinsic interests as well as requires students to master skills and ideas they do not see as immediately useful.[23]

These proposals are obviously still broad, and they are still in the process of being refined and argued over. Yet they are not meant to be utopian. They are meant to establish the irreducible principles around which a democratic coalition can form to defend public education and make it more equal both in access and in outcome. The 'text' itself is insistent on not giving up on teachers, but instead recognizing the degenerating conditions of their labor. Unlike documents such as *A Nation at Risk*, it highlights rather than ignores the experiences not only of teachers but of minority groups and other oppressed peoples. Further, even where it criticizes existing modes of controlling curriculum, teaching, and school organization (in its rejection of state textbook adoption policies, centralized governance, administratively defined testing and teaching practices, and so forth), it recognizes the democratizing potential of the school. Even where the Network's position is too vague (and, hence, as a slogan system can suffer the fate of *The Paideia Proposal* in this regard), what stands behind it has been used to generate successful practice. It can provide a 'language of possibility.'

For example, in England, Philip Cohen and his colleagues have demonstrated how it is possible to use the state school as a site for building a popular and more democratic educational practice for many of those students who will suffer most from the current economic crisis. Alternative curricular and teaching practices drawing on the students' own cultural and economic experiences of work and family, and grounded in their class, race, and gender realities, have successfully focused on the problems of the transition from secondary school to work in ways that empower students politically.[24] Similar models are being developed in Australia, Canada, and in many other places.

The Australian situation is particularly instructive here. 'Counter hegemonic' practices have been created by linking trade union and leftist groups together to engage in policy formation for unemployed youth in New South Wales. John Freeland's work on the 'Community Youth Support Scheme Campaign' is notable here.[25] Bob Connell and his colleagues have also demonstrated how their own research on the role of schooling in the creation of inequality can be used to generate democratic discussions of such issues among teacher and community groups.[26] These are but a few of the instances one could point to.

These examples are less isolated than one might imagine. They have had and will continue to have an impact, especially since they provide models out of which others can generate their own politically aware curricula and pedagogy.

It is of vital importance that we remember that even with the role schools have been shown to play in the reproduction of race, gender, and class relations of this society, historically the educational system and its internal policies and practices have been built out of conflicts. Many of the results of these conflicts have been compromises that signify victories, not losses, for the majority of people. The fact that struggles over education have been at least partly successful in the past is documented by the fact that schooling itself tends to be more equally distributed than, say, economic capital, income, or employment status. 'Schooling produces relatively more equal outcomes than the workplace and other institutions of the larger society.' Even though our formal institutions of elementary and secondary education bear some very real organizational resemblance to paid workplaces such as offices and factories, and even though they do engage in 'screening and preparing youth for inequality,' when compared to these other workplaces schools are clearly more equal and participatory.[27] As I noted earlier, since schools *are* part of the state, of the political sphere, and the state has been a site of conflict between property rights and person rights, we should *expect* that schools will be more democratic than these other institutions.[28]

This is perhaps best summed up by Carnoy and Levin:

> Educational institutions are not just producers of dominant class conceptions of what and how much schooling should be provided; public schools also reflect social demands. Attempts by the capitalist State to

> reproduce the relations of production and the class division of labor confront social movements that demand more public resources for their needs and more say in how these resources are to be used. The capitalist State and its educational system are therefore more than just a means for co-opting social demands, or for simply manipulating them to satisfy dominant class needs. Social demands shape the State and education.[29]

Echoing a number of themes which I argued in *Education and Power*, they conclude that

> The educational system is not an instrument of the capitalist class. It is the product of conflict between the dominant and the dominated. The struggle in the production sector, for example, affects schools, just as it conditions all state apparatuses. Furthermore, because the State, including the educational system, is itself the political arena, schools are part of social conflict. Education is at once the result of contradictions and the source of new contradictions. It is an arena of conflict over the production of knowledge, ideology, and employment, a place where social movements try to meet their needs and business attempts to reproduce its hegemony.[30]

There are contradictory tendencies within a number of these spheres that we can identify and this should give us hope. Since I have focused a good deal of my attention in this book on the relationship between education and the economy, some possible emerging contradictory tendencies in the economy and the labor process are worth further comment.

Four negative and one positive factor are among the forces that may lead to a greater democratization of schooling. Each of the four negative aspects has been mentioned earlier in this book: the transformation of women's paid and unpaid labor; the 'normalization' of high unemployment; the utter neglect of people of color and the poor; and the real, rather than romanticized, impact of the new technology. The positive factor is the increasing tendency toward greater participation in the paid workplace.[31] Each of these will foster the growth of new social movements and coalitions that will bring pressure on the school for greater equality. The high unemployment and underemployment rate among minority youth, the proletarianization of women's work and the feminization of poverty, the growing minority population of the school systems in many cities (a population that will require education and jobs) – these conditions and more will create pressures to both defend and extend the more democratic elements of schooling.[32]

Speaking specifically about the paid workplace, Carnoy and Levin point out how some of these pressures may impact on education and may lead to conditions more favorable to the position taken by the Network, for instance. They argue that as a shift occurs in some areas of the paid workplace from individualized labor to the use of work teams that will stress group decisions, there will be a corresponding shift in education. There, too, instead of the competitive individualism (what I have elsewhere called the possessive individual)[33] that dominates schooling today, we may witness the slow growth of an education that gives more emphasis on working together cooperatively. Cooperative problem-solving and small group work on projects could be given much greater attention.[34] They also make the interesting claim that other workplace alterations – particularly the movement toward a team assembly approach where individual workers often have to perform a 'wider range of potential tasks' and make their own decisions – may have a concomitant effect on the internal dynamics of classrooms. Teachers and curricula will at least partly move from their overreliance on 'memorization and routinization of learning to individual decision making and problem solving.'[35] (Here, given the rearticulation of patriarchal relations in teachers' work, we would need a thoroughgoing *feminist* analysis of teachers' labor to complement Carnoy and Levin's primarily class and economic analysis to make any assessment of such a prediction. I am inclined to be less sanguine here.)

Finally, in line with their prediction that many workplaces will shift to team production, Carnoy and Levin also predict that this change will help create the social conditions that will make it easier for programs of peer tutoring to be established in schools.[36] All of these are part of a democratic dynamic that is emerging even under conditions of the conservative restoration. These changes may help counterbalance the intensification and proletarianization of teachers' work, the standardization of goals, procedures, texts, and technology, and other conditions that are emerging simultaneously with these other tendencies. At the very least, they provide the grounds for considerable conflict over the policies and practices of our educational institutions.

RECONSTRUCTING OUR DISCOURSE

In the previous section of this concluding chapter, I focused on the importance of continuing the history of the struggle for democracy in our educational institutions – for a democratic culture, labor process, and governance. This position is grounded in an emerging set of arguments now being confronted within the leftist community. It is a set of arguments that are important not just for education, but for our political thought in general. Not only must we reject the class reductionism still so pervasive in democratic socialist thought, but we also need to question the notion that only economic struggles 'really' count in the long run. To stress only the latter is to ignore the fact that – if I may speak technically for a moment – people are constructed by a variety of discourses, in a multitude of institutions from the paid workplace to the family, the school, the media, and so forth. In *political* terms, none of these has a *necessarily* privileged place. It is the effect of all of these together that matters. Thus, interventions and struggles in each are significant. Laclau and Mouffe summarize these points theoretically in the following way: 'Judicial institutions, the educational system, labour relations, the discourses of resistances of marginal populations, [of women and people of color], construct original and irreducible forms of social protest, and thereby contribute all of the discursive complexity and richness on which the programme of a radical democracy should be founded.'[37] Our task is to make concrete linkages between our own actions in the educational arena and those of these other arenas. From this, a shared, yet pluralist, 'discourse' of democracy can grow.

In this regard, it is just as important to identify the kinds of discourse that *impede* the formation of collective action.[38] As I have documented here, economic discourse and the accompanying discourse of rationalization, standardization, technique, and technology – when coupled with the contradictory language of professionalism – have increasingly defined the class and gender terrain on which action takes place in education. There are, however, linguistic resources already available which, when reconstructed, can help us counter these tendencies. The languages of a genuine populism, of democratic faith, and, within education, of the progressive tradition, can be reappropriated, reconstructed, and made more politically astute (this last factor being an essential point, of course).[39] The right has been immensely successful in appropriating the language of 'the people' for its own purposes, thereby leaving the left pictured as 'democratic socialist' with none of the former and with the latter seen as a code word for state control. One of the fundamental challenges facing us is to reestablish such discourse as our own.

However, this 'linguistic task' is not limited to rejecting both the class and economic reductionism of the left or, just as critically, the economic discourse of the dominant. It goes well beyond this to a recognition of the importance of the way critical scholarship itself has used language in education.

In the final section of this chapter, I want to make an argument against some trends in recent radical work in education about such language use – an argument that some of you will realize is partly a form of auto-criticism as well.

I am wary of pushing this argument with my friends and colleagues too far; after all, at a time when greed and profit are now replacing a sense of the common good in so much of our public lives, one should build up, not criticize, one's allies. Furthermore, progressive people do have a history of killing each other off. I am reminded of the joke about how many leftists it takes to go fishing. (One hundred, of course: one to hold the pole and ninety-nine to argue about the correct line.) Even with these dangers, however, there are things that need to be said – perhaps even more so today, because, as I have noted throughout this book, this is a time when we are witnessing (perhaps 'living' *is* a better word) a serious set of losses for women, people of color, workers, and others in education, welfare, 'defense,' health care, the environment, and elsewhere.

Just as all of our action is relational (remember my example in Chapter 4 about the fact that turning on a light when I walk into a room is not merely using an object; it is having an anonymous but very real social relationship with the miners who worked to dig the coal to produce the electricity, many of whom were killed or injured in the process), so too is our language. The way we talk to others in education and the language we use to describe and criticize the workings of educational institutions constitute our audience as subjects. The language we use embodies a politics in and of itself – not just in the fact that it advances positions about gender, race, and class dynamics from a generally leftist point of view, but in another way. It has a vision of the reader already built in, a set of social relationships between author and reader. And too often that relationship is a bit too elitist.

Too many educational critics 'focus on their theoretical paraphernalia,' in the end writing articles or books *about* this or that rather than actually applying these tools.[40] Because of this, we have a relatively highly developed body of meta-theory, but a seriously underdeveloped tradition of applied, middle-range work. To the extent that critical work in education remains at such an abstract level, we risk cutting ourselves off from the largest part of the educational community. Thus, my focus in this volume has been on using the tools we have developed to look not only at theoretical matters but at the current and past conditions that help structure teachers and texts.

We must take much more seriously the question 'Who is our audience?' We have seemingly taken it for granted that our audience consists of academic theorists or of social and cultural theorists on the left in general. While this may have increased the academic respectability of the program of critical scholarship (and this *is* important, given the increasing difficulty of gaining tenure in a time of rightist resurgence), it has latently had a number of negative effects. First, it has often led to an isolation of this work on the borders of scholarship. Second, its marginalization has grown because of the increasingly arcane quality of its very discourse. In a field that has historically shunted theoretical work to the sidelines (sometimes for very good reasons, since educational theory has usually involved male academics theorizing about what is largely women's labor – i.e., teaching), the nearly mystical quality of some critical work, its tendency *not* to take sufficient time to clarify its basic concepts or to write clearly, cannot help but limit its impact.

We must go beyond the tacit belief that analytic and political clarity is something of a sideshow or, worse, a tool of dominant interests.[41] If our job is pedagogic (as I think it is), if our role is to help teach our colleagues at universities and elementary and secondary schools (and enable them to teach us) what kind of society it is that we live in and how schooling now reproduces *and* contradicts the relations of inequality that now exist (for there are some very good things going on now as well that need to be defended), then such pedagogic work needs to be held accountable to particular norms. The 'student' or reader isn't the only one who should be required to do all the work.

Do not misconstrue my arguments. My point is not to deny the importance of critical theoretical work. All educational practice is theory-laden and has a political consequence, and it is better to uncover what those theories and politics now are or should be than to let values work through us unconsciously. Nor is my point that it is possible to say everything of significance in everyday language. As Adorno and Benjamin demonstrate, sometimes aphorisms and metaphors, even when damnedly difficult to understand, can be powerful disclosure models. They can illuminate relations between, say, culture and economy (and isn't that what critical scholarship in education is primarily about?) in ways that would otherwise be missed.

Thus, abstract theory is of crucial importance. Speaking of the critical place intellectual work has played in the politics of gender relations, R. W. Connell makes the general point well:

> Abstract theory can often be a diversion from practice, in sexual politics as elsewhere. Yet theory matters. Intellectuals have been of particular importance in women's liberation and gay liberation compared with other social movements; and the subversion of oppressive gender relations in part *is* intellectual work. (It is not an accident that a key technique of early second-wave feminism was 'consciousness raising.') The importance of theory is sensed by the ideological opponents of feminism and gay liberation. You have only to notice how much airplay has been given in the conservative media to the supposed 'recantations' by Betty Friedan and Germaine Greer.[42]

The same 'consciousness raising' is necessary (but not sufficient) in education, even when it is done in ways that are sometimes initially difficult to grasp.

Sometimes seeing the connections between our curricular,

pedagogical, and evaluative actions and the inequalities in the larger society does require something of a wrenching experience, a conscious attempt to step outside our everyday language and commonsense thought. And often this requires hard and disciplined work. Examining our institutions relationally, seeing them as being constructed in a context that has clear relations of domination and exploitation, is a labor process itself. *It must be worked at* since so many other messages in the media and in our everyday political, economic, and cultural discourse deny the reality of such relations. Those involved in critical educational scholarship do have a right to ask that the reader take seriously the complexity of these connections between education and class, gender and race inequalities and, hence, the possible complexity of the analysis that uncovering such relations may require.

Pierre Bourdieu makes a point that is worth noting in this regard. Complexity in both style and argument is often necessary to reconstitute 'the complexity of the social world in a language capable of holding together the most diverse things while setting them in rigorous perspective.' It prevents the reader 'from slipping back into . . . simplicities' and helps fight the tendency to exclude important elements of one's arguments.[43]

One is tempted in fact to ask 'Why, if it takes no small effort to master the traditions associated with empirical and statistical work – to know when to use beta weights instead of an r^2 – why should we assume that critical theoretical and political work will be any easier?' Therefore, we need to be careful that our criticisms of, say, neo-marxist scholarship – for its difficulty, for its use of unfamiliar terms and the density of its writing – is not in large part due to our own misperceptions of the kind of discipline that is required to rethink our dominant institutions.

Recognizing these issues, however, does not serve to lessen the burden. It simply postpones the questions 'For whom are we writing?' and 'What are the purposes of these analyses?' Even though we have made major progress in reconstructing the neo-marxist tradition so that it is more open and less reductive, and in taking much more seriously feminist as well as class issues in studying curriculum and teaching (and I believe these are real conceptual and political gains),[44] we have still been less aware of other political issues surrounding our work.

In his own discussion of the dangers of overly theorized work, the well-known historian of popular movements Raphael Samuel shows the contradictory tendencies that evolve here:

> On the one hand by treating Marxism [and other critical traditions] as unfinished – i.e. as a continuous and cumulative model of understanding the world rather than as an unquestioning set of dogmas – [current work] has undoubtedly released an enormous amount of theoretical energy on the left, and helped to produce a greater diffusion of [classical critical] texts and a greater readiness to use them, quite explicitly, in current intellectual work. On the other hand, it has created a climate of anxiety around the very notion of theory, and has had the effect, however unintended, of suggesting that it was the close preserve of an esoteric sect of initiates. However fruitful the questions, the discourse itself is imprisoning. Much of the recent work . . . is disfigured by a mannered prose, a talismanic use of reference, and by a defensive recourse to a limited number of well thumbed, mostly recent texts . . . Like other academic fashions . . . it involves a good deal of posturing, and insofar as it has a discernible political purpose it is that of keeping an uncomfortable world at bay.[45]

Now this is a rather biting comment, to say the least, but it is worth taking seriously since it relates directly to the cautions I have raised. Critical scholarship in education is not merely a commodity, to be 'bought' and 'sold' in the academic marketplace. It is – if I may borrow from Wittgenstein – a language game that is a *form of life*. It involves action in the real world, on real relations of power. It is not just contemplative, but should lead to, and stem from, political action in real institutions such as universities, schools, cultural and social movements, and so on. To the extent that it isn't, to the extent that the writing of it is one's only political act, and to the extent that it is written in such a way that only the 'initiates' can cope with it in a meaningful way, then it should give us cause to worry.

In fact, I would like to claim that, in not just a metaphorical way, unless it takes its democratic politics seriously such work can tend to reproduce on an ideological level the separation of conception from execution that lies at the heart of the division of labor in our economy. 'We' will generate the 'correct' criticisms; 'you' will be 'taught' how to operate in educational institutions. This is why it is so very important that those who engage in critical scholarship in education should have constant and close ties to the real world of teachers, students, and parents, and why they need to be closely connected to feminist groups, people of color, unions, and to those teachers and curriculum workers who are now struggling so hard in very difficult circumstances to defend from rightist attacks the gains that have been made in democratizing education and to make certain that our schools and the curricular and teaching practices within them are responsive in race, gender, and class terms. After all, teaching is a two-way street and academics can use some political education as well.

The constant struggle to be clear is just that, then – a struggle. It is hard work to be understandable. Yet to construct one's audience in the way too many of us have done in the past is to reproduce in transfigured form some of the relations we are supposedly against. Sophisticated critical work must go on, of course, but the constant attempt to take seriously the politics of our own discourse is as much a part of the larger political struggle as the content of what we talk about. Clarity begins at home.

Teachers and Texts has been a particular kind of labor for me in this regard. I had wanted to demonstrate how the attempt to privilege economic conditions and class, gender, and race relations enables us to see more clearly what is happening to education, to our curricula, students, and teachers. Yet at the same time, it became increasingly obvious to me that part of the struggle was over making these arguments more accessible. In parts of this volume I have been considerably more successful in doing this than in others. Yet, the very recognition of the importance of this by many individuals in the United States, England, Australia, and elsewhere is a significant step in the development of a more organic connection among progressive academics, teachers, labor, women's groups, people of color, and others. Building these organic connections is of no small moment on the long road toward a more democratic reality. Solutions to the social ills that beset us may not come easily, but we can be certain that working collectively on them can only enhance their development.

In his usual eloquent way, Raymond Williams states the position thus:

> It is only in a shared belief and insistence that there are practical alternatives that the balance of forces and chances begins to alter. Once the inevitabilities are challenged, we begin gathering our resources for a journey of hope. If there are no easy answers there are still available discoverable hard answers, and it is these that we can now learn to make and share. This has been, from the beginning, the sense and the impulse of the long revolution.[46]

Education, and educators, can have a valued place in this long revolution, in the creative impulse toward a democratized culture, a democratized polity, and a democratized economy. Will we accept it?

NOTES

1 THE POLITICS OF TEACHERS AND TEXTS

1 Joshua Cohen and Joel Rogers, *On Democracy: Toward a Transformation of American Society* (New York: Penguin Books, 1983), p. 15.

2 *Ibid.*

3 I take this phrase from Ira Shor's forthcoming political history of the recent struggle over the goals and means of American schooling. See his *Culture Wars* (Boston and London: Routledge & Kegan Paul, 1986).

4 These points are discussed in greater detail in Michael W. Apple and Lois Weis (eds.), *Ideology and Practice in Schooling* (Philadelphia: Temple University Press, 1983) and Michael W. Apple (ed.), *Cultural and Economic Reproduction in Education* (Boston and London: Routledge & Kegan Paul, 1982).

5 See R. W. Connell *et al.*, *Making the Difference* (Boston and London: George Allen & Unwin, 1982).

6 For further discussion, see Apple and Weis (eds.), *Ideology and Practice in Schooling*, especially chapter 1. On the dual nature of our usual use of 'subject,' see Goran Therborn, *The Ideology of Power and the Power of Ideology* (London: New Left Books, 1980), pp. 15–28.

7 An interesting treatment of a number of these issues can be found in Robert G. Hollands, 'Working for the Best Ethnography,' unpublished paper, Centre for Contemporary Cultural Studies, University of Birmingham.

8 Paul Willis, *Learning to Labour* (Westmead: Saxon House, 1977), R. W. Connell *et al.*, *Making The Difference*, Robert Everhart, *Reading, Writing and Resistance* (Boston and London: Routledge & Kegan Paul, 1983), Linda Valli, *Becoming Clerical Workers* (Boston and London:

Routledge & Kegan Paul, 1985), and Lois Weis, *Between Two Worlds* (Boston and London: Routledge & Kegan Paul, 1985).

9 Michael W. Apple, *Ideology and Curriculum* (Boston and London: Routledge & Kegan Paul, 1979), and Michael W. Apple, *Education and Power* (Boston and London: Routledge & Kegan Paul, 1982).

10 Gerald Grace, 'Judging Teachers: The Social and Political Contexts of Teacher Evaluation,' *British Journal of Sociology of Education* 6 (No. 1, 1985), 4.

11 Mortimer Adler, *The Paideia Proposal* (New York: Macmillan, 1982).

12 National Commission on Excellence in Education, 'A Nation at Risk: An Imperative for Educational Reform,' *Education Week*, April 27, 1983, 12–16.

13 Richard Johnson, 'What Is Cultural Studies Anyway?,' Occasional Paper SP No. 74, Centre for Contemporary Cultural Studies, University of Birmingham, September, 1983, p. 17.

14 This is discussed in more detail in Apple, *Ideology and Curriculum*.

15 For further elaboration of these points, see Daniel Liston, 'Are Critical Analyses of Curriculum Correct? Functional Explanation and Ethical Justification in Recent Curriculum Studies,' unpublished doctoral dissertation, University of Wisconsin, Madison, 1985.

16 Apple, *Education and Power*. See also Apple and Weis (eds.), *Ideology and Practice in Schooling*, especially chapter 1.

17 Many of these arguments are analyzed in Apple (ed.), *Cultural and Economic Reproduction in Education*. See also Michael W. Apple, 'Against Reductionism,' *History of Education Quarterly* 24 (Summer 1984), 247–56.

18 This evidence is summarized in Cohen and Rogers, *On Democracy*.

19 Apple, *Education and Power*, chapter 4.

20 For a provocative analysis of the attack on women by the new right and of the politics of 'the family' in this discourse, see Allen Hunter, 'Virtue with a Vengeance: The Pro-Family Politics of the New Right,' unpublished doctoral dissertation, Brandeis University, 1984.

21 Johnson, 'What Is Cultural Studies Anyway?' p. 3.

22 See especially, Apple, *Education and Power*; Apple (ed.), *Cultural and Economic Reproduction in Education*; and Henry Giroux, *Theory and Resistance in Education* (South Hadley, Mass.: Bergin & Garvey, 1983).

23 See Samuel Bowles and Herbert Gintis, *Schooling in Capitalist America* (New York: Basic Books, 1976); Basil Bernstein, *Class,*

Codes and Control, Vol. 3 (Boston and London: Routledge & Kegan Paul, 1977); Giroux, *Theory and Resistance in Education*; Apple, *Ideology and Curriculum*; and Apple, *Education and Power*.

24 Apple and Weis (eds.), *Ideology and Practice in Schooling*, chapter 1. For a brief overview of this history, see also Martin Carnoy, 'Marxism and Education,' in Bertell Ollman and Edward Vernoff (eds.), *The Left Academy: Marxist Scholarship on American Campuses*, Vol. 2, (New York: Praeger, 1984), pp. 79–97.

25 Michael Omi and Howard Winant, 'By the Rivers of Babylon: Race in the United States,' *Socialist Review* 13 (September–October 1983), 40.

26 *Ibid.*, 39.

27 Lise Vogel, *Marxism and the Oppression of Women* (New Brunswick: Rutgers University Press, 1983), pp. 30–1.

28 Alice Kessler-Harris, *Out to Work: A History of Wage-Earning Women in the United States* (New York: Oxford University Press, 1982), p. 148.

29 This is treated in more detail in William Leach, 'Transformations in the Culture of Consumption: Women in Department Stores, 1865–1900,' *Journal of American History* 71 (September 1984), 319–42.

30 Heidi Hartmann, 'The Unhappy Marriage of Marxism and Feminism: Towards a More Progressive Union,' in Roger Dale, Geoff Esland, Ross Fergusson and Madeleine MacDonald (eds.), *Education and the State Vol. 2: Politics, Patriarchy and Practice*, (Barcombe, Sussex: Falmer Press, 1981), p. 191.

31 For some of the debates over these issues, see Michele Barrett, *Women's Oppression Today* (London: New Left Books, 1980); Vogel, *Marxism and the Oppression of Women*; and Apple, *Education and Power*.

32 See Apple (ed.), *Cultural Economic Reproduction in Education*, and Giroux, *Theory and Resistance in Education*.

33 See Harry Braverman, *Labor and Monopoly Capital* (New York: Monthly Review Press, 1974); Richard Edwards, *Contested Terrain: The Transformation of the Workplace in the Twentieth Century* (New York: Basic Books, 1979); Stephen Wood (ed.), *The Degradation of Work?* (London: Hutchinson, 1982); and Apple, *Education and Power*.

34 An overview of this material can be found in Apple, *Education and Power*. See also a number of the chapters in Apple and Weis (eds.), *Ideology and Practice in Schooling*.

35 Much of this work can be found in Apple, *Education and Power*; Kevin Harris, *Teachers and Classes* (Boston and London: Routledge &

Kegan Paul, 1982); and Carol Buswell, 'Pedagogic Change and Social Change,' *British Journal of Sociology of Education* 1 (No. 3, 1980), 293–306.

36 These novels and the changes in class, race, and gender relations they signify have been analyzed in an exceptional study by Linda Christian, 'Becoming a Woman Through Romance,' unpublished doctoral dissertation, University of Wisconsin, Madison, 1984.

2 CONTROLLING THE WORK OF TEACHERS

1 Erik Olin Wright and Joachim Singelmann, 'The Proletarianization of Work in American Capitalism,' University of Wisconsin-Madison Institute for Research on Poverty, Discussion Paper No. 647–81, 1981, p. 38.

2 *Ibid.*, p. 43. See also Michael W. Apple, 'State, Bureaucracy and Curriculum Control,' *Curriculum Inquiry* 11 (Winter 1981), 379–88. For a discussion that rejects part of the argument about proletarianization, see Michael Kelly, *White Collar Proletariat* (Boston and London: Routledge & Kegan Paul, 1980).

3 Deskilling, technical control and proletarianization are both technical and political concepts. They signify a complex historical process in which the control of labor has altered – one in which the skills employees have developed over many years on the job are broken down into atomistic units, redefined, and then appropriated by management to enhance both efficiency and control of the labor process. In the process, workers' control over timing, over defining appropriate ways to do a task, and over criteria that establish acceptable performance are all slowly taken on as the prerogatives of management personnel who are usually divorced from the actual place in which the work is carried out. Deskilling, then, often leads to the atrophy of valuable skills that workers possessed, since there is no longer any 'need' for them in the redefined labor process. The loss of control or proletarianization of a job is hence part of a larger dynamic in the separation of conception from execution and the continuing attempts by management in the state and industry to rationalize as many aspects of one's labor as possible. I have discussed this in considerably more detail in Michael W. Apple, *Education and Power* (Boston and London: Routledge & Kegan Paul, 1982). See also Richard Edwards, *Contested Terrain* (New York: Basic Books, 1979), and Michael Burawoy, *Manufacturing Consent* (Chicago: University of Chicago Press, 1979).

4 Erik Olin Wright, 'Class and Occupation,' *Theory and Society* 9 (No. 2, 1980), 182–3.

5 Apple, *Education and Power.*

6 Wright, 'Class and Occupation,' 188. Clearly race plays an important part here too. See Michael Reich, *Racial Inequality* (Princeton: Princeton University Press, 1981), and Mario Barrera, *Race and Class in the Southwest: A Theory of Racial Inequality* (Notre Dame: Notre Dame University Press, 1979).

7 Janet Holland, 'Women's Occupational Choice: The Impact of Sexual Divisions in Society,' Stockholm Institute of Education, Department of Educational Research, Reports on Education and Psychology, 1980, p. 7.

8 *Ibid.*, p. 27.

9 *Ibid.*, p. 45.

10 Gail Kelly and Ann Nihlen, 'Schooling and the Reproduction of Patriarchy,' in Michael W. Apple (ed.), *Cultural and Economic Reproduction in Education: Essays on Class, Ideology and the State* (Boston and London: Routledge & Kegan Paul, 1982), pp. 167–8. One cannot fully understand the history of the relationship between women and teaching without tracing out the complex connections among the family, domesticity, child care, and the policies of and employment within the state. See especially, Miriam David, *The State, the Family and Education* (Boston and London: Routledge & Kegan Paul, 1980).

11 For an interesting history of the relationship among class, gender and teaching, see June Purvis, 'Women and Teaching in the Nineteenth Century,' in Roger Dale, Geoff Esland, Ross Fergusson, and Madeleine MacDonald (eds.), *Education and the State, Vol. 2: Politics, Patriarchy and Practice* (Barcombe, Sussex: Falmer Press, 1981), pp. 359–75. I am wary of using a concept such as patriarchy, since its very status is problematic. As Rowbotham notes, 'Patriarchy suggests a fatalistic submission which allows no space for the complexities of women's defiance' (quoted in Tricia Davis, 'Stand by Your Men? Feminism and Socialism in the Eighties,') in George Bridges and Rosalind Brunt (eds.), *Silver Linings: Some Strategies for the Eighties* (London: Lawrence & Wishart, 1981), p. 14. A history of women's day-to-day struggles falsifies any such theory of 'fatalistic submission.'

12 Jane Barker and Hazel Downing, 'Word Processing and the Transformation of the Patriarchal Relations of Control in the Office,' in Dale, Esland, Fergusson and MacDonald (eds.), *Education and the*

State, Vol. 2, pp. 229–56. See also the discussion of deskilling in Edwards, *Contested Terrain*.

13 For an analysis of how such language has been employed by the state, see Michael W. Apple, 'Common Curriculum and State Control,' *Discourse* 2 (No. 4, 1982), 1–10, and James Donald, 'Green Paper: Noise of a Crisis,' *Screen Education* 30 (Spring 1979), 13–49.

14 See, for example, Seymour Sarason, *The Culture of the School and the Problem of Change* (Boston: Allyn & Bacon, 1971).

15 Apple, *Education and Power*, and Susan Porter Benson, 'The Clerking Sisterhood: Rationalization and the Work Culture of Sales Women in American Department Stores,' *Radical America* 12 (March/April 1978), 41–55.

16 Roger Dale's discussion of contradictions between elements within the state is very interesting in this regard. See Roger Dale, 'The State and Education: Some Theoretical Approaches,' in *The State and Politics of Education* (Milton Keynes: The Open University Press, E353, Block 1, Part 2, Units 3–4, 1981), and Roger Dale, 'Education and the Capitalist State: Contributions and Contradictions,' in Apple (ed.), *Cultural and Economic Reproduction in Education*, pp. 127–61.

17 Dale, 'The State and Education,' p. 13.

18 I have examined this in greater detail in Apple, *Education and Power*. See as well Edwards, *Contested Terrain*, and Daniel Clawson, *Bureaucracy and the Labor Process* (New York: Monthly Review Press, 1980).

19 Magali Larson, 'Proletarianization and Educated Labor,' *Theory and Society* 9 (No. 2, 1980), 166.

20 *Ibid.*, 167.

21 *Ibid.* Larson points out that these problems related to intensification are often central grievances even among doctors.

22 *Ibid.*, 168.

23 *Ibid.*, 169.

24 *Ibid.*, 167.

25 Apple, *Education and Power*. See also Carol Buswell, 'Pedagogic Change and Social Change,' *British Journal of Sociology of Education* 1 (No. 3, 1980), 293–306.

26 The question of just how seriously schools take this, the variability of their response, is not unimportant. As Popkewitz, Tabachnick and Wehlage demonstrate in their interesting ethnographic study of school reform, not all schools use materials of this sort alike. See Thomas Popkewitz, B. Robert Tabachnick, and Gary Wehlage, *The*

Myth of Educational Reform (Madison: University of Wisconsin Press, 1982).

27 This section of my analysis is based largely on research carried out by Andrew Gitlin. See Andrew Gitlin, 'Understanding the Work of Teachers,' unpublished Ph.D. dissertation, University of Wisconsin, Madison, 1980.

28 *Ibid.*, 208.

29 *Ibid.*

30 *Ibid.*, 197.

31 *Ibid.*, 237.

32 *Ibid.*, 125.

33 *Ibid.*, 197.

34 This is similar to the use of liberal discourse by popular classes to struggle for person rights against established property rights over the past one hundred years. See Herbert Gintis, 'Communication and Politics,' *Socialist Review* 10 (March/June 1980), 189–232. The process is partly paradoxical, however. Attempts to professionalize do give women a weapon against some aspects of patriarchal relations; yet, there is a clear connection between being counted as a profession and being populated largely by men. In fact, one of the things that are very visible historically is the relationship between the sexual division of labor and professionalization. There has been a decided tendency for full professional status to be granted only when an activity is 'dominated by men – in both management and the ranks.' Jeff Hearn, 'Notes on Patriarchy: Professionalization and the Semi-Professions,' *Sociology* 16 (May 1982), 195.

35 Magali Larson, 'Monopolies of Competence and Bourgeois Ideology,' in Dale, Esland, Fergusson, and MacDonald (eds.), *Education and the State, Vol. 2*, p. 332.

36 Larson, 'Proletarianization and Educated Labor,' p. 152. Historically, class as well as gender dynamics have been quite important here, and recent research documents this clearly. As Barry Bergen has shown in his recent study of the growth of the relationship between class and gender in the professionalization of elementary school teaching in England, a large portion of elementary school teachers were both women and of the working class. As he puts it:

> Teaching, except at the university level, was not highly regarded by the middle class to begin with, and teaching in the elementary schools was the lowest rung on the teaching ladder. The middle

> class did not view elementary teaching as a means of upward mobility. But the elementary school teachers seemed to view themselves as having risen above the working class, if not having reached the middle class. . . . Clearly, the varied attempts of elementary teachers to professionalize constitute an attempt to raise their class position from an interstitial one between the working class and middle class to the solidly middle class position of a profession.

See Barry H. Bergen, 'Only a Schoolmaster: Gender, Class, and the Effort to Professionalize Elementary Teaching in England, 1870–1910,' *History of Education Quarterly* 22 (Spring 1982), 10.

37 Gitlin, 'Understanding the Work of Teachers,' p. 128.

38 *Ibid.*

39 Martin Lawn and Jenny Ozga, 'Teachers: Professionalism, Class and Proletarianization,' unpublished paper, The Open University, Milton Keynes, 1981, p. 15 in mimeo.

40 Jenny Ozga, 'The Politics of the Teaching Profession,' in *The Politics of Schools and Teaching* (Milton Keynes: The Open University Press, E353, Block 6, Units 14–15, 1981), p. 24.

41 We need to be very careful here, of course. Certainly, not all teachers will respond in this way. That some will not points to the partial and important fracturing of dominant gender and class ideologies in ways that signal significant alterations in the consciousness of teachers. Whether these alterations are always progressive is an interesting question. Also, as Connell has shown, such 'feminine' approaches are often important counterbalances to masculinist forms of authority in schools. See R. W. Connell, *Teachers' Work* (Boston and London: George Allen & Unwin, 1985).

42 See Henry Giroux, 'Theories of Reproduction and Resistance in the New Sociology of Education: A critical Analysis,' *Harvard Educational Review* 53 (August 1983), 257–93, even though he is not specifically interested in gender relations.

43 While I have focused here on the possible impacts in the school and the home on women teachers, a similar analysis needs to be done on men. We need to ask how masculinist ideologies work through male teachers and administrators. Furthermore, what changes, conflicts, and tensions will evolve, say, in the patriarchal authority structures of the home given the intensification of men's labor? I would like to thank Sandra Acker for raising this critically important point. For an analysis of changes in women's labor in the home, see Susan Strasser,

Never Done: A History of American Housework (New York: Pantheon, 1982).

44 Clawson, *Bureaucracy and the Labor Process*, pp. 152–3.

45 In addition, Connell makes the interesting point that since teachers' work has no identifiable object that it 'produces,' it can be intensified nearly indefinitely. See Connell, *Teachers' Work*, p. 86.

46 Apple, *Education and Power*, and Manuel Castells, *The Economic Crisis and American Society* (Princeton: Princeton University Press, 1980).

3 TEACHING AND 'WOMEN'S WORK'

1 Barbara Melosh, *The Physician's Hand: Work Culture and Conflict in American Nursing* (Philadelphia: Temple University Press, 1982), p. 8.

2 Michele Barrett, *Women's Oppression Today* (London: New Left Books, 1980), pp. 154–5.

3 Alice H. Cook, *The Working Mother: A Survey of Problems and Programs in Nine Countries* (Ithaca: New York State School of Industrial and Labor Relations, Cornell University, 1978), p. 11.

4 Barrett, *Women's Oppression Today*, p. 155. This is of course reproduced in education, where substitute teachers in the elementary school are largely women.

5 Linda Murgatroyd, 'Gender and Occupational Stratification,' *Sociological Review* 30 (November 1982), 582.

6 Nancy S. Barrett, 'Women in the Job Market: Occupations, Earnings, and Career Opportunities,' in Ralph E. Smith (ed.), *The Subtle Revolution: Women at Work* (Washington, D.C.: The Urban Institute, 1979), p. 49. Similar but slightly different figures can be found in Cook, *The Working Mother*, p. 12.

7 Barrett, *Women's Oppression Today*, pp. 156–7.

8 This is quite a complicated process – one that includes changes not only in the division of labor in capitalism, but in the family/household system as well. See Johanna Brenner and Maria Ramas, 'Rethinking Women's Oppression,' *New Left Review* 144 (March/April 1984), 33–71.

9 Erik Olin Wright *et al.*, 'The American Class Structure,' *American Sociological Review* 47 (December 1982), 723.

10 See for example, Jane Barker and Hazel Downing, 'Word Processing and the Transformation of Patriarchal Relations of Control in the Office,' in Roger Dale *et al.* (eds.), *Education and the State, Vol. 2:*

Politics, Patriarchy and Practice (Barcombe, Sussex: Falmer Press, 1981), pp. 229–56, and Rosemary Crompton and Stuart Reid, 'The Deskilling of Clerical Work,' in Stephen Wood (ed.), *The Degradation of Work?* (London: Hutchinson, 1982), pp. 163–78.

11 Murgatroyd, 'Gender and Occupational Stratification,' 591.

12 *Ibid.*, 575.

13 *Ibid.*, 588.

14 *Ibid.*, 595.

15 *Ibid.*, 581.

16 Barrett, *Women's Oppression Today*, pp. 166–8. Barrett goes on to say here that the extent to which any job is seen as requiring a high level of skill is often dependent on the ability of the people who do it to have the power to establish that definition over competing ones.

17 Veronica Beechey, 'The Sexual Division of Labour and the Labour Process: A Critical Assessment of Braverman,' in Wood (ed.), *The Degradation of Work?*, p. 67. See also Margery Davies, *Woman's Place Is at the Typewriter* (Philadelphia: Temple University Press, 1982).

18 Barry H. Bergen, 'Only a Schoolmaster: Gender, Class, and the Effort to Professionalize Elementary Teaching in England, 1870–1910,' *History of Education Quarterly* 22 (Spring 1982), 12.

19 *Ibid.*

20 *Ibid.*, 5.

21 Myra Strober, 'Segregation by Gender in Public School Teaching: Toward a General Theory of Occupational Segregation in the Labor Market,' unpublished manuscript, Stanford University, 1982, p. 16. Figures for the eastern cities of Canada are similar (though individual cities – such as Toronto and Montreal – do differ, often for ethnic and religious reasons). See Marta Danylewycz and Alison Prentice, 'Teachers, Gender, and Bureaucratizing School Systems in Nineteenth Century Montreal and Toronto,' *History of Education Quarterly* 24 (Spring 1984), 75–100.

22 See, for example, Sheila Rothman, *Women's Proper Place* (New York: Basic Books, 1978), and Barrett, *Women's Oppression Today*. The role women were meant to play in upholding the religious and moral 'fiber' of the nation should not go unnoticed here either. Native-born Protestant women were often recruited by the National Board of Popular Education to teach on, say, the American frontier to 'redeem' the West. Many women themselves combined this vision with a clear sense of economic necessity and the possibilities of independence and adventure. These women were as a rule somewhat

older than beginning teachers and were looking for both personal and professional autonomy in conjunction with their 'moral mission.' Attempts at controlling the religious and other content of the curriculum were also visible in these western schools. However, many of these women teachers were successful in resisting such pressures on their teaching practices. See Polly Welts Kaufman, *Women Teachers on the Frontier* (New Haven: Yale University Press, 1984), especially part I.

23 John Richardson and Brenda Wooden Hatcher, 'The Feminization of Public School Teaching, 1870–1920,' *Work and Occupations* 10 (February 1983), 84. Following Douglas and others, Richardson and Hatcher also associate this with the relationship between middle-class women and religion.

24 Bergen, 'Only a Schoolmaster,' 13.

25 *Ibid.*, 14.

26 Nancy Hoffman, *Women's 'True' Profession: Voices from the History of Teaching* (Old Westbury: The Feminist Press, 1981), p. xix. Conditions in Canada were very similar. See Danylewycz and Prentice, 'Teachers, Gender, and Bureaucratizing School Systems,' 88.

27 Strober, 'Segregation by Gender in Public School Teaching,' p. 18. On the difficulties schools had in keeping male teachers, even in earlier periods, see Joan M. Jensen, 'Not Only Ours But Others: The Quaker Teaching Daughters of the Mid-Atlantic, 1790–1850,' *History of Education Quarterly* 24 (Spring 1984), 3–19.

28 See the discussion in Frances Widdowson, *Going Up into the Next Class: Women and Elementary Teacher Training, 1840–1914* (London: Hutchinson, 1983).

29 David Gordon, Richard Edwards, and Michael Reich, *Segmented Work, Divided Workers: The Historical Transformation of Labor in the United States* (New York: Cambridge University Press, 1982), p. 68. Many 'native-born' women, however, fled the factories for other reasons. Not only had working conditions deteriorated, but a significant portion of these women preferred not to work alongside the immigrant women who were being hired to work in the mills. For further analysis of the changing conditions of women's labor and the tension between immigrant and native-born women workers, see Alice Kessler-Harris, *Out to Work: A History of Wage-Earning Women in the United States* (New York: Oxford University Press, 1982), pp. 108–41.

30 Strober, 'Segregation by Gender in Public School Teaching,' p. 19.

See also Keith E. Melder, 'Mask of Oppression: The Female Seminary Movement in the United States,' *New York History* 55 (July 1974), 261–79.

31 Strober, 'Segregation by Gender in Public School Teaching.' This 'willingness' often had *religious* roots. Thus evangelical religious imperatives, and the history of Protestant denominationalism, may have led to 'moral' reasons for women to teach. See Joan Jacobs Brumberg, 'The Feminization of Teaching: "Romantic Sexism" and American Protestant Denominationalism,' *History of Education Quarterly* 23 (Fall 1983), 383.

32 Lanford, quoted in Strober, 'Segregation by Gender in Public School Teaching,' p. 21.

33 Richardson and Hatcher, 'The Feminization of Public School Teaching,' 82.

34 Myra Strober and David Tyack, 'Why Do Women Teach and Men Manage?: A Report on Research on Schools,' *Signs* 5 (Spring 1980), 499.

35 *Ibid.*, 500. The authors also note that men made it to the top in school systems in part because of the advantages they had over women in linking schools to the surrounding community. Maleness was an asset in meeting with the mostly male power structure of organizations such as the Kiwanis, Lions clubs, etc. This point was also made much earlier by Willard S. Elsbree in *The American Teacher* (New York: American Book Co., 1939), p. 555.

36 Hoffman, *Women's 'True' Profession*, pp. xvii–xviii. For a general discussion of related points, see Keith E. Melder, 'Women's High Calling: The Teaching Profession in America, 1830–1860.' *American Studies* 12 (Fall 1972), 19–32.

37 Angela V. John, 'Foreword' to Widdowson, *Going Up into the Next Class*, p. 9.

38 *Ibid.*

39 See, for example, Danylewycz and Prentice, 'Teachers, Gender, and Bureaucratizing School Systems.'

40 Richardson and Hatcher, 'The Feminization of Public School Teaching,' 87–8.

41 On the importance of thinking about the United States in class terms, see David Hogan, 'Education and Class Formation: The Peculiarities of the Americans,' in Michael W. Apple (ed.), *Cultural and Economic Reproduction in Education: Essays on Class, Ideology and the State* (Boston and London: Routledge & Kegan Paul, 1982),

pp. 32–78, and Erik Olin Wright, *Class, Crisis and the State* (London: New Left Books, 1978).

42 June Purvis, 'Women and Teaching in the Nineteenth Century,' in Dale *et al.* (eds.), *Education and the State, Vol. 2*, p. 372. See also Widdowson, *Going Up into the Next Class.*

43 See the interesting historical analysis of the place of socialist women here in Mari Jo Buhle, *Women and American Socialism, 1870–1920* (Urbana: University of Illinois Press, 1981).

44 Purvis, 'Women and Teaching in the Nineteenth Century,' pp. 361–3. See also Rothman, *Women's Proper Place.* We should not assume that such educational and political struggles by middle-class women meant that these gains simply reproduced a 'safe liberalism' and bourgeois hegemony. For an argument that liberal discourse can be progressive at times, see Apple, *Education and Power* (Boston and London: Routledge & Kegan Paul, 1982), pp. 123–5, and Herbert Gintis, 'Communication and Politics,' *Socialist Review* 10 (March/June 1980), 189–232.

45 Carl Degler, *At Odds: Women and the Family in America from the Revolution to the Present* (New York: Oxford University Press, 1980), p. 381.

46 Purvis, 'Women and Teaching in the Nineteenth Century,' p. 372. I stress *paid* teaching here, since Purvis also argues that middle- and upper-class women often worked as voluntary teachers in working-class literacy programs. Philanthropy and voluntary teaching could solve the problem brought about by the dominance of bourgeois ideals of femininity. A women *could* work, but only for the highest ideals and without remuneration.

47 Strober and Tyack, 'Why Do Women Teach and Men Manage?' 496. See also Mary Roth Walsh, *Doctors Wanted, No Women Need Apply: Sexual Barriers in the Medical Profession, 1835–1975* (New Haven: Yale University Press, 1977). For England, see Jane Lewis, *The Politics of Motherhood* (London: Croom Helm, 1980), and Sheila Rowbotham, *Hidden from History* (New York: Random House, 1974).

48 Sandra Acker, 'Women and Teaching: A Semi-Detached Sociology of a Semi-Detached Profession,' in Stephen Walker and Len Barton (eds.), *Gender, Class and Education* (Barcombe, Sussex: Falmer Press, 1983), p. 134.

49 Degler, *At Odds*, p. 380. Paul Mattingly, too, argues that by the 1890s even many normal schools had become almost exclusively female and had directed their attention to a 'lower-class' student body. See Paul Mattingly, *The Classless Profession* (New York: New York

University Press, 1975), p. 149. The significant portion of teachers who came from working-class families in Canada, as well, is documented in Danylewycz and Prentice, 'Teachers, Gender, and Bureaucratizing School Systems,' 91–3.

50 Interestingly enough, some believed that upper-middle-class young women were at an academic disadvantage compared to working-class young women in teacher training institutions in England. See Widdowson, *Going Up into the Next Class*.

51 Purvis, 'Women and Teaching in the Nineteenth Century,' p. 364. Widdowson claims, however, that in general by the first decade of the twentieth century 'the early education of the nation's children was predominantly in the hands of aspiring ladies recruited mainly from the lower-middle classes' (*Going Up into the Next Class*, p. 79). She also makes the interesting point that the ultimate entry of significant numbers of lower-middle-class young women into such positions contributed a good deal to the 'professionalization' and increase in status of teaching.

52 Purvis, 'Women and Teaching in the Nineteenth Century,' p. 364.

53 *Ibid.*, p. 366. For further discussion of the effect of such needlework on the women teachers of working-class girls, see the interesting treatment in Dina Copelman, 'We Do Not Want to Turn Men and Women into Mere Toiling Machines: Teachers, Teaching, and the Taught,' unpublished paper, University of Missouri, Department of History, Columbia, 1985.

54 I wish to thank Rima D. Apple for this point.

55 Purvis, 'Women and Teaching in the Nineteenth Century,' p. 366.

56 Rothman, *Women's Proper Place*, p. 58. For a discussion of how secondary schools grew as 'training grounds' for preparing women for clerical work, see John L. Rury, 'Vocationalism for Home and Work: Women's Education in the United States, 1880–1930,' *History of Education Quarterly* 24 (Spring 1984), 21–44.

57 Purvis, 'Women and Teaching in the Nineteenth Century,' p. 367.

58 *Ibid.* See also William Edward Eaton, *The American Federation of Teachers, 1916–1961* (Carbondale: Southern Illinois University Press, 1975). The problem of a lack of connection between working-class parents and teachers in England is still a serious one. See, e.g., C.C.C.S. Education Group, *Unpopular Education: Schooling and Social Democracy in England Since 1944* (London: Hutchinson, 1981).

59 See Barrett, *Women's Oppression Today*, pp. 187–226. See also her discussion of class differences in this section.

60 See Ann Marie Wolpe, 'The Official Ideology of Education for

Girls,' in Michael Flude and John Ahier (eds.), *Educability, Schools and Ideology* (London: Halsted Press, 1974), pp. 138–59.

61 Degler, *At Odds*, pp. 413–14. Degler does point out, however, that the Depression did not ultimately drive women out of the paid workforce. Their rates of participation continued to increase. See p. 415. Similar policies were put into effect elsewhere as well. In New South Wales, Australia, married women were dismissed from their teaching jobs during the Depression to protect men's positions. See R. W. Connell, *Teachers' Work* (Boston and London: George Allen & Unwin, 1985), p. 154.

62 Eaton, *The American Federation of Teachers*, pp. 5–8. In his nicely written study of the history of teachers' organizations in the United States, Wayne Urban argues, however, that most of the members of these early teachers' organizations were significantly less radical than many of their leaders. Economic, not political, demands were more important for the bulk of the teachers. This, though, needs to be situated within the history of women's struggles over disparities in income, since in terms of this history economic issues may be less conservative than at first glance. See Wayne J. Urban, *Why Teachers Organized* (Detroit: Wayne State University Press, 1982).

63 The leadership of the CTF believed that teachers might be lost in an amalgam of other unions and, to be taken seriously nationally, had to form their own national union. The attempt was first made in 1899, and again in 1902 by Haley and Goggin. The National Teachers Federation, an early precursor of the AFT, limited membership to grade school teachers and, while it did attract some national membership, it ultimately failed. See Eaton, *The American Federation of Teachers*, p. 10.

64 See Giraldine Clifford, 'The Female Teacher and the Feminist Movement,' unpublished paper, University of California, Berkeley, 1981. Similar struggles occurred in Canada, as well. See, e.g., Danylewycz and Prentice, 'Teachers, Gender, and Bureaucratizing School Systems,' 93–4. For England, see Copelman, 'We Do Not Want to Turn Men and Women into Mere Toiling Machines.' Copelman has also analyzed the relationship between women teachers, feminism, and professional struggles in England in her interesting paper, 'The Politics of Professionalism: Women Teachers, 1904–1914,' unpublished paper, University of Missouri, Department of History, Columbia, 1985.

65 Craig Littler, 'Deskilling and Changing Structures of Control,' in Wood (ed.), *The Degradation of Work?*, p. 141. The importance of class as well as gender dynamics is made visible in Gerald Grace's

argument that external control of teaching and curriculum by the state in England was lessened in the 1920s because of fears that a Labour government would use its power over teachers and curriculum to instill socialist ideas. Though Grace could have made more of gender issues, his points are provocative. See Gerald Grace, 'Judging Teachers: The Social and Political Contexts of Teacher Evaluation,' *British Journal of Sociology of Education* 6 (No. 1, 1985), 3–16.

66 For a current statistical portrait of American Teachers, see C. Emily Feistritzer (ed.), *The American Teacher* (Washington, D.C.: Feistritzer Publications, 1983).

4 THE CULTURE AND COMMERCE OF THE TEXTBOOK

1 Raymond Williams, *Marxism and Literature* (New York: Oxford University Press, 1977), p. 19. See also, Michael W. Apple and Lois Weis (eds.), *Ideology and Practice in Schooling* (Philadelphia: Temple University Press, 1983), especially chapter 1.

2 Janet Wolff, *The Social Production of Art* (London: Macmillan, 1981), p. 47.

3 I have described this in more detail in Michael W. Apple (ed.), *Cultural and Economic Reproduction in Education: Essays on Class, Ideology and the State* (Boston and London: Routledge & Kegan Paul, 1982). For further analysis of this, see Williams, *Marxism and Literature*, Colin Sumner, *Reading Ideologies* (New York: Macmillan, 1979), G. A. Cohen, *Karl Marx's Theory of History: A Defense* (Princeton: Princeton University Press, 1978), and Paul Hirst, *On Law and Ideology* (London: Macmillan, 1979).

4 See Todd Gitlin, 'Television's Screens: Hegemony in Transition,' in Apple (ed.), *Cultural and Economic Reproduction in Education*. The British journal *Screen* has been in the forefront of such analyses. See also Will Wright, *Sixguns and Society* (Berkeley: University of California Press, 1975). An even greater number of investigations of literature exist, of course. For representative approaches, see Terry Eagleton, *Marxism and Literary Criticism* (Berkeley: University of California Press, 1976).

5 Michael W. Apple, *Ideology and Curriculum* (Boston and London: Routledge & Kegan Paul, 1979). It is important to realize, however, that educational institutions are *not* merely engaged in transmission or distribution. They are also primary sites for the *production* of technical/administrative knowledge. The contradiction between

distribution and production is one of the constitutive tensions educational institutions must try to solve, usually unsuccessfully. For arguments about the school's role in the production of cultural capital, see Michael W. Apple, *Education and Power* (Boston and London: Routledge & Kegan Paul, 1982), especially chapter 2.

6 Pierre Bourdieu and Jean-Claude Passeron, *Reproduction in Education, Society and Culture* (Beverly Hills: Sage, 1977), and Basil Bernstein, *Class, Codes and Control, Vol. 3* (Boston and London: Routledge & Kegan Paul, 1977).

7 For an analysis of recent theoretical and empirical work on the connections between education and cultural, economic, and political power, see Apple, *Education and Power*.

8 Paul Goldstein, *Changing the American Schoolbook* (Lexington, Mass.: D. C. Heath, 1978), p. 1. On which subjects are taught the most, see John I. Goodlad, *A Place Called School* (New York: McGraw-Hill, 1983).

9 I do not want to ignore the importance of the massive number of textbook analyses that concern themselves with, say, racism and sexism. These are significant, but are usually limited to the question of balance in content, not the relationship between economic and cultural power. Some of the best analyses of the content and form of educational materials can be found in Apple and Weis (eds.), *Ideology and Practice in Schooling*. See also Sherry Keith, 'Politics of Textbook Selection,' Institute for Research on Educational Finance and Governance, Stanford University, April 1981.

10 Lewis Coser, Charles Kadushin, and Walter Powell, *Books: The Culture and Commerce of Publishing* (New York: Basic Books, 1982), p. 3.

11 *Ibid.*, p. 7.

12 Lucien Febvre and Henri-Jean Martin, *The Coming of the Book* (London: New Left Books, 1976), p. 109. As Febvre and Martin make clear, however, in the fifteenth and sixteenth centuries printers and publishers did act as well as 'the protectors of literary men,' published daring books, and frequently sheltered authors accused of heresy. See p. 150.

13 *Ibid.*

14 *Ibid.*, p. 44.

15 *Ibid.*, p. 54.

16 Wendy Griswold, 'American Character and the American Novel: An Expansion of Reflection Theory in the Sociology of Literature,' *American Journal of Sociology* 86 (January 1981), 742.

17 *Ibid.*, 748. For a thorough historical treatment of the politics of the copyright controversy, see James J. Barnes, *Authors, Publishers and Politicians: The Quest for an Anglo-American Copyright Agreement 1815–1854* (Boston and London: Routledge & Kegan Paul, 1974).

18 *Ibid.*, pp. 748–9.

19 See Ian Watt, *The Rise of the Novel* (Berkeley: University of California Press, 1974), and Raymond Williams, *The Long Revolution* (London: Chatto & Windus, 1961).

20 Griswold, 'American Character and the American Novel,' 743.

21 Leonard Shatzkin, *In Cold Type* (Boston: Houghton Mifflin, 1982), pp. 1–2. For estimated figures for years beyond 1980, see John P. Dessauer, *Book Industry Trends, 1982* (New York: Book Industry Study Group, 1982).

22 Coser, Kadushin and Powell, *Books*, p. 273. While I shall be focusing on text production here, we should not assume that texts are the only books used in elementary, secondary, and college markets. The expanding market of other material can have a strong influence in publishing decisions. In fact, some mass-market paperbacks are clearly prepared with both school and college sales in the forefront of the decision. Thus, it is not unusual for publishers to produce a volume with very different covers depending on the audience for which it is aimed. See Benjamin M. Compaine, *The Book Industry in Transition: An Economic Study of Book Distribution and Marketing* (White Plains, N.Y.: Knowledge Industry Publications, 1978), p. 95.

23 Shatzkin, *In Cold Type*, p. 63.

24 Coser, Kadushin and Powell, *Books*, p. 273.

25 Goldstein, *Changing the American Schoolbook*, p. 61.

26 Coser, Kadushin, and Powell, *Books*, p. 100.

27 *Ibid.*, pp. 154–5.

28 *Ibid.*, p. 101.

29 Coser, Kadushin, and Powell, however, do report that most editors, no matter what kind of house they work for, tend to be overwhelmingly liberal. *Ibid.*, p. 113.

30 *Ibid.*, p. 30.

31 *Ibid.*, p. 56.

32 *Ibid.*, p. 135.

33 *Ibid.*, pp. 56–7.

34 Goldstein, *Changing the American Schoolbook*, p. 56.

35 Coser, Kadushin, and Powell, *Books*, p. 123.

36 *Ibid.*, p. 190.

37 Keith, 'Politics of Textbook Selection,' p. 12.

38 Coser, Kadushin, and Powell, *Books*, p. 366.

39 I have discussed this at greater length in Michael W. Apple, 'Curriculum in the Year 2000: Tensions and Possibilities,' *Phi Delta Kappan* 64 (January 1983), 321–6.

40 Coser, Kadushin, and Powell, *Books*, p. 181.

41 Compaine, *The Book Industry in Transition*, p. 20.

42 *Ibid.*, pp. 33–4.

43 Keith, 'Politics of Textbook Selection,' p. 8.

44 Goldstein, *Changing the American Schoolbook*, p. 47. Further discussion of the internal politics of state adoption policies can be found in Michael W. Kirst's personal reflections on textbook policies. See Michael W. Kirst, 'Choosing Textbooks: Reflections of a State Board President,' *American Educator* 8 (Summer 1984), 18–23.

45 Goldstein, *Changing the American Schoolbook*, pp. 48–9.

46 For an interesting discussion of how economic needs help determine what counts as the public for which a specific cultural product is aimed, see the treatment of changes in the radio sponsorship of country music in Richard A. Peterson, 'The Production of Cultural Change: The Case of Contemporary Country Music,' *Social Research* 45 (Summer 1978), 292–314. See also Paul DiMaggio and Michael Useem, 'The Arts in Class Reproduction,' in Apple (ed.), *Cultural and Economic Reproduction in Education*, pp. 181–201.

47 I have discussed the relationship between the commodification process and the dynamics of cultural capital at greater length in Apple, *Education and Power*. Of course, these questions should not only be asked of those conditions that exist in the public sector. One of the largest-growing areas is publishing for private, especially religious, schools. Christian fundamentalist schools, for example, have close links with their own publishers. It is now possible, in fact, for those interested in starting their own fundamentalist academy to purchase *everything* they will need for the school in kit form. The growth of publishing for such religious schools is worth considerable attention. What is the political economy of this kind of publishing? Whose knowledge dominates? How are class, race, and gender treated? How and why are decisions on this made? Given the increasing numbers of students now attending such schools, these are not unimportant issues, to say the least.

48 *Ibid.*, especially chapter 5.

49 A related argument is made in Douglas Kellner, 'Network Television and American Society,' *Theory and Society* 10 (January 1981), 31–62. See also Philip Wexler, 'Structure, Text and Subject: A Critical Sociology of School Knowledge,' in Apple (ed.), *Cultural and Economic Reproduction in Education*, pp. 275–303.

50 This is discussed in greater detail in Apple (ed.), *Cultural and Economic Reproduction in Education.*

51 Coser, Kadushin, and Powell, *Books*, p. 185.

52 Wexler's argument that texts need to be seen as the result of a long process of transformative activity is clearly related here. In essence, what I have been attempting to demonstrate is part of the structure in which such transformations occur and which makes some more likely to occur than others. See Wexler, 'Structure, Text and Subject.'

53 Wolff, *The Social Production of Art*, p. 36.

54 The relationship among deskilling, reskilling, and the sexual division of labor is treated in more depth in Alice Kessler-Harris, *Out to Work: A History of Wage-Earning Women in the United States* (New York: Oxford University Press, 1982). See also David Gordon, Richard Edwards, and Michael Reich, *Segmented Work, Divided Workers: The Historical Transformation of Labor in the United States* (New York: Cambridge University Press, 1982).

55 See, for example, Apple, *Education and Power*, Roger Dale, Geoff Esland, Ross Fergusson, and Madeleine MacDonald (eds.), *Education and the State, Vol. 1* (Barcombe, Sussex: Falmer Press, 1981), and Michael W. Apple, 'Common Curriculum and State Control,' *Discourse* 2 (No. 4, 1982), 1–10.

56 I am indebted to Dan Liston for documenting the possible power of Offe's work. See Daniel Liston, 'Have We Explained the Relationship Between Curriculum and Capitalism?' *Educational Theory* 34 (Summer 1984), 234–53, Martin Carnoy, 'Education, Economy and the State,' in Apple (ed.), *Cultural and Economic Reproduction in Education*, pp. 79–126, and Roger Dale, 'Education and the Capitalist State: Contributions and Contradictions,' in Apple (ed.), *Cultural and Economic Reproduction in Education*, pp. 127–61.

57 I do not want to imply that what is 'transmitted' in schools is necessarily what is in the text. Nor do I want to claim at all that what is taught is wholly 'taken in' by students. For analyses of teacher and student rejection, mediation, or transformation of the form and/or content of curriculum, see Paul Willis, *Learning to Labour* (Westmead, England: Saxon House, 1977); Robert Everhart, *Reading, Writing and Resistance* (Boston and London: Routledge & Kegan Paul, 1983),

Apple, *Education and Power*, the chapters by Linda McNeil, Andrew Gitlin, and Lois Weis, in Apple and Weis (eds.), *Ideology and Practice in Schooling*, and Carmen Luke, Suzanne Castell, and Alan Luke, 'Beyond Criticism: The Authority of the School Text,' *Curriculum Inquiry* 13 (Summer 1983), 111–27.

5 OLD HUMANISTS AND NEW CURRICULA

1 National Commission on Excellence in Education, 'A Nation at Risk: An Imperative for Educational Reform,' *Education Week*, April 27, 1983, 12–16.

2 *Ibid.*

3 *Ibid.*

4 Mortimer Adler, *The Paideia Proposal* (New York: Macmillan, 1982).

5 *Ibid.*, pp. xi-xii.

6 *Ibid.*, p. 15.

7 *Ibid.*, p. 16.

8 *Ibid.*, p. 17.

9 *Ibid.*

10 I have discussed this in greater length in Michael W. Apple, 'Power and Culture in the Report of the Committee of Ten,' *New York University Education Quarterly* 14 (Winter 1983), 28–32. See also Herbert Kliebard, *The Struggle for the American Curriculum* (Boston and London: Routledge & Kegan Paul, 1986).

11 Adler, *The Paideia Proposal*, p. 20.

12 See, for example, Jonas Soltis, *An Introduction to the Analysis of Educational Concepts* (Reading, Mass.: Addison-Wesley, 1978).

13 See Walter Kolesnik, *Mental Discipline in Modern Education* (Madison: University of Wisconsin Press, 1958).

14 Herbert Kliebard, 'Education at the Turn of the Century: A Crucible for Curriculum Change,' *Educational Researcher* 11 (January 1982), 16–24.

15 Adler, *The Paideia Proposal*, p. 24.

16 *Ibid.*, p. 31.

17 *Ibid.*, p. 33.

18 Kenneth A. Sirotnik, 'What You See is What You Get: Consistency, Persistency, and Mediocrity in Classrooms,' *Harvard Educational Review* 53 (February 1983), 29.

19 *Ibid.*, 23.

20 See Michael W. Apple, *Education and Power* (Boston and London: Routledge & Kegan Paul, 1982); Andrew Gitlin, 'School Structure and Teachers' Work,' in Michael W. Apple and Lois Weis (eds.), *Ideology and Practice in Schooling* (Philadelphia: Temple University Press, 1983), pp. 193–212; Thomas Popkewitz, B. Robert Tabachnick, and Gary Wehlage, *The Myth of Educational Reform* (Madison: University of Wisconsin Press, 1982); and Landon Beyer, 'Aesthetic Curriculum and Cultural Reproduction,' in Apple and Weis (eds.), *Ideology and Practice in Schooling*, pp. 89–113.

21 Linda McNeil, 'Defensive Teaching and Classroom Control,' in Apple and Weis (eds.), *Ideology and Practice in Schooling*, p. 116.

22 It is unfortunate that phrases such as 'burn-out' have such currency. They tend to reduce the phenomenon to the level of the individual, thereby removing the structural issues concerning the control of one's labor and skills from serious scrutiny. See Michael W. Apple, 'Curriculum in the Year 2000: Tensions and Possibilities,' *Phi Delta Kappan* 64 (January 1983), 321–6.

23 Marilyn Frankenstein and Louis Kampf, 'Preface to "The Other End of the Corridor,"' *Radical Teacher* 23 (Spring 1983), 1.

24 Boston Women's Teachers' Group, 'The Other End of the Corridor: The Effects of Teaching on Teachers,' *Radical Teacher* 23 (Spring 1983), 3.

25 B. Paul Komisar and James E. McClellan, 'The Logic of Slogans,' in B. Othanel Smith and Robert H. Ennis (eds.), *Language and Concepts in Education* (Chicago: Rand McNally, 1961), pp. 195–214.

26 Ralph Tyler, *Basic Principles of Curriculum and Instruction* (Chicago: University of Chicago Press, 1949).

27 Jerome Bruner, *The Process of Education* (New York: Vintage Books, 1960).

28 See Seymour Sarason, *The Culture of the School and the Problem of Change* (Boston: Allyn & Bacon, 1971).

29 For a discussion of how elite culture is sometimes reappropriated in interesting ways, compare this to some of the contradictory uses of particular class cultures by working-class and peasant groups in George Rude, *Ideology and Popular Protest* (New York: Pantheon, 1980).

30 On working-class culture and responses to education, see David Hogan, 'Education and Class Formation: The Peculiarities of the Americans,' in Michael W. Apple (ed.), *Cultural and Economic Reproduction in Education* (Boston and London: Routledge & Kegan Paul, 1982), pp. 32–78; Education Group of the Centre for Contemporary

Cultural Studies, *Unpopular Education* (London: Hutchinson, 1981); and John Clarke, Chas Critcher, and Richard Johnson (eds.), *Working Class Culture: Studies in History and Theory* (London: Hutchinson, 1979).

This very issue of the relationship between class and political persuasion on the one hand and definitions of legitimate knowledge on the other naturally arises here, though it is unfortunately rather muted in most professional curriculum debate. James Donald puts the case quite clearly: 'The separation of questions of *knowledge* from those of *power* is deeply ingrained. It is a habit that needs to be broken, though, because there is a relationship between the two which is neither accidental nor simply instrumental.' See James Donald, 'Green Paper: Noise of a Crisis,' *Screen Education* 30 (Spring 1979), 14.

31 Sirotnik, 'What You See is What You Get,' 27.

32 See Ira Shor, *Critical Teaching and Everyday Life* (Boston: South End Press, 1980).

33 For discussions of the technical culture of the 'new middle class,' see Basil Bernstein, *Class, Codes and Control, Vol. 3* (Boston and London: Routledge & Kegan Paul, 1977), and Apple, *Education and Power.*

34 For an analysis of the differential economic benefits and trajectories that compares black with white students and economically advantaged with economically disadvantaged, see Christopher Jencks *et al., Who Gets Ahead?* (New York: Basic Books, 1979). See also Erik Olin Wright, *Class Structure and Income Determination* (New York: Academic Press, 1979).

35 See Apple, *Education and Power*; Robert Everhart, *Reading, Writing and Resistance* (Boston and London: Routledge & Kegan Paul, 1983), and Paul Willis, *Learning to Labour* (Westmead: Saxon House, 1977). For analytic criticisms of this position, see Jim Walker's work on materialistic pragmatism. See James C. Walker, 'Romanticising Resistance; Romanticising Culture,' unpublished paper, Department of Education, University of Sydney, n.d., and James C. Walker, 'Materialist Pragmatism and Sociology of Education,' *British Journal of Sociology of Education* 6 (No. 1, 1985), 55–74.

36 For an exceptionally fine examination of the ideological, economic, and educational problems with some of the current programs that link education to the workplace, see Linda Valli, *Becoming Clerical Workers* (Boston and London: Routledge & Kegan Paul, 1986).

37 Donald, 'Green Paper,' 15. Martin Carnoy has also argued that the way the issue of work is handled in *The Paideia Proposal* is inherently

undemocratic. See Martin Carnoy, 'Education, Democracy and Social Conflict,' *Harvard Educational Review* 53 (November 1983), 398–402.

38 Basil Bernstein's discussion of the effects of changes from mechanical to organic solidarity is helpful here, as are Will Wright's and Todd Gitlin's analyses of changes in the ideological content of popular culture. See Bernstein, *Class Codes and Control, Vol. 3*, Will Wright, *Sixguns and Society* (Berkeley: University of California Press, 1975), and Todd Gitlin, 'Television's Screens: Hegemony in Transition,' in Apple (ed.), *Cultural and Economic Reproduction in Education*, pp. 202–46. For an outstanding investigation of alterations in gender and class relations and their effects on popular cultural forms specifically produced for young women, see Linda Christian, 'Becoming a Woman Through Romance,' unpublished doctoral dissertation, University of Wisconsin, Madison, 1984.

39 Manuel Castells, *The Economic Crisis and American Society* (Princeton: Princeton University Press, 1980).

40 For further discussion of these points, see Apple, *Education and Power.*

41 Donald, 'Green Paper,' 23.

42 Adler, *The Paideia Proposal*, p. 5.

43 Apple, *Education and Power*, especially chapter 2. See also the analysis in Martin Carnoy, *The State and Political Theory* (Princeton: Princeton University Press, 1984).

44 Erik Olin Wright *et al.*, 'The American Class Structure,' *American Sociological Review* 47 (December 1982), 718.

45 *Ibid.*, 723.

46 *Ibid.*, 724.

47 *Ibid.*, 722–3.

48 In many ways, the Paideia Group's position will founder on shoals similar to that experienced by Charles Eliot and others who supported the 'Committee of Ten Report.' The similarities of their respective positions are often striking, as will be their final effect. See Apple, 'Power and Culture in the Report of the Committee of Ten.'

6 EDUCATIONAL REPORTS AND ECONOMIC REALITIES

1 See Joel Spring, *The Sorting Machine* (New York: David McKay, 1976), for a history of such federal policies and some of the conditions out of which they arose.

2 Michael W. Apple, *Education and Power* (Boston and London: Routledge & Kegan Paul, 1982), and Michael W. Apple and Kenneth Teitelbaum, 'Are Teachers Losing Control of Their Skills and Curriculum?' *Journal of Curriculum Studies* 18 (April–June 1986), 177–84.

3 See Michael W. Apple, 'Common Curriculum and State Control,' *Discourse* 2 (No. 2, 1982), 1–10.

4 For further discussion of these issues, see Michael W. Apple, *Ideology and Curriculum* (Boston and London: Routledge & Kegan Paul, 1979), and Michael W. Apple and Lois Weis (eds.), *Ideology and Practice in Schooling* (Philadelphia: Temple University Press, 1983).

5 Lawrence C. Stedman and Marshall S. Smith, 'Recent Reform Proposals for American Education,' *Contemporary Education Review* 2 (Fall 1983), 87. Along with Stedman and Smith, I shall focus largely on committee reports, not on, say, the work of Sizer and Boyer. The latter two are interesting but may actually have little power other than 'moral suasion.'

6 Joshua Cohen and Joel Rogers, *On Democracy: Toward a Transformation of American Society* (New York: Penguin Books, 1983), p. 15.

7 Frances Fox Piven and Richard A. Cloward, *The New Class War* (New York: Pantheon Books, 1982), p. 41.

8 The role of the state in times of economic crisis is discussed further in Manuel Castells, *The Economic Crisis and American Society* (Princeton: Princeton University Press, 1980). See also Erik Olin Wright, *Class, Crisis and the State* (London: New Left Books, 1978). For a more general overview of theories of the state, see the nicely written volume by Martin Carnoy, *The State and Political Theory* (Princeton: Princeton University Press, 1984). On the destruction of our sense of 'common good' and person rights and for very interesting proposals on what we can do in health, education, military, and other policy areas, see Marcus Raskin, *The Common Good* (New York and London: Routledge & Kegan Paul, 1986).

9 I have reviewed these data at greater length in Apple, *Education and Power*, especially chapter 1.

10 Martin Carnoy, Derek Shearer, and Russell Rumberger, *A New Social Contract* (New York: Harper & Row, 1983), pp. 22–3.

11 Cohen and Rogers, *On Democracy*, p. 30.

12 *Ibid.*, p. 31. The official poverty income level and rate fluctuate, of course, and are manipulated for political purposes. For a family of four, the official level is currently $10,178. Recent figures show an increase

in the percentage of people living in poverty from 14 percent to over 15 percent of the total U.S. population.

13 *Ibid.*, pp. 31–2.

14 *Ibid.*, p. 32.

15 Ibid.

16 For a clear historical treatment of the growth of dual labor markets and segmented work in the United States, see David M. Gordon, Richard Edwards, and Michael Reich, *Segmented Work, Divided Workers* (New York: Cambridge University Press, 1982).

17 Carnoy, Shearer, and Rumberger, *A New Social Contract*, p. 71.

18 *Ibid.*, p. 88.

19 This neglect of women's labor is a serious problem in most educational proposals. It often nearly destroys the credibility of their economic claims and of the educational policies that emerge from them.

20 See Erik Olin Wright *et. al.*, 'The American Class Structure,' *American Sociological Review* 47 (December 1982), 709–26.

21 Carnoy, Shearer, and Rumberger, *A New Social Contract*, p. 61.

22 Apple, *Education and Power.*

23 Herbert Kliebard, 'Bureaucracy and Curriculum Theory,' in Vernon Haubrich (ed.), *Freedom, Bureaucracy and Schooling* (Washington: Association for Supervision and Curriculum Development, 1971), pp. 74–93.

24 Apple, *Ideology and Curriculum*, chapter 4.

25 Peter Meiksins, 'Scientific Management and Class Relations,' *Theory and Society* 13 (March 1984), 188.

26 It is possible, however, to argue that Taylorism was never fully successful on its own terms. See, for example, the discussion in Richard Edwards, *Contested Terrain* (New York: Basic Books, 1979), and Daniel Clawson, *Bureaucracy and the Labor Process* (New York: Monthly Review Press, 1980).

27 Meiksins, 'Scientific Management and Class Relations,' 188.

28 I have discussed this in greater detail in Apple, *Ideology and Curriculum.* See also Basil Bernstein, *Class Codes and Control, Vol. 3* (Boston and London: Routledge & Kegan Paul, 1977).

29 Many women, however, embraced scientific management for a variety of class- and gender-based reasons. See the treatment of this in Alice Kessler-Harris, *Out to Work* (New York: Oxford University Press, 1982).

30 See Kathy E. Ferguson, *The Feminist Case Against Bureaucracy* (Philadelphia: Temple University Press, 1984), pp. 158–60, and Carol Gilligan, *In a Different Voice: Psychological Theory and Women's Development* (Cambridge, Mass.: Harvard University Press, 1982).

31 For further analysis of this, see Michael W. Apple, 'Common Curriculum and State Control.'

32 For further discussion of these points and for criticisms of the reports' proposals for merit pay plans and the like, see Sara Freedman, 'Master Teacher/Merit Pay – Weeding Out Women from "Women's True Profession": A Critique of the Commissions on Education,' *Radical Teacher* 25 (November 1983), 24–8.

33 I have discussed how powerful elements within the state and economy export their crises in Apple, *Education and Power*, especially chapter 4.

34 Stedman and Smith, 'Recent Reform Proposals for American Education,' 102–3.

35 Technically speaking, the writers of the reports actually attempt to create a *compromise* between the cultural capital of what could be called the 'academy' – with its academic standards and visions of high status culture centered around the disciplines of knowledge – and the needs of industry. Thus, we should not see the authors of the reports or the reports themselves as being mere 'tools' of industry. In the present political and economic context, however, what will be seized upon and highlighted within the reports will not be the requirements of the academy, especially since universities themselves are currently faced with declining revenues – a situation which forces them to increasingly act in the interests of business and industry. For further discussion of this, see Apple, *Education and Power*, chapter 2, and David Dickson, *The New Politics of Science* (New York: Pantheon Books, 1984).

36 The various reports could have overtly proposed 'extensive adoption of gifted and talented programs, the resurrection of systematic tracking by early test scores, or the introduction of specialized math and science programs for the academic high achievers.' Instead most of them chose to focus on 'the basics' and had as their overt goal raising the achievement of the 'average student.' See Stedman and Smith, 'Recent Reform Proposals for American Education,' 94.

37 Philip Wexler and Gene Grabiner, 'The Education Question: America During the Crisis,' unpublished paper, School of Education and Human Development, University of Rochester, p. 31.

38 For an excellent analysis of problems with the time on task

orientation of the reports, see Henry M. Levin, 'About Time for Education Reform,' *Educational Evaluation and Policy Analysis* 6 (Summer 1984), 151–63.

39 Wexler and Grabiner, 'The Education Question.' I have discussed the transformation of learning and the process of deskilling in much greater detail in Apple, *Education and Power.*

40 Wexler and Grabiner, 'The Education Question.' For further analysis of the restructuring of education, see Henry Giroux, 'Public Philosophy and the Crisis in Education,' *Harvard Educational Review* 54 (May 1984), 186–94.

41 Compare here Richard Edwards, *Contested Terrain* (New York: Basic Books, 1979).

7 THE NEW TECHNOLOGY – SOLUTION OR PROBLEM?

1 David Noble, *Forces of Production: A Social History of Industrial Automation* (New York: Alfred A. Knopf, 1984), pp. xi-xii. For a more general argument about the relationship between technology and human progress, see Nicholas Rescher, *Unpopular Essays on Technological Progress* (Pittsburgh: University of Pittsburgh Press, 1980).

2 Noble, *Forces of Production*, p. xv.

3 Paul Olson, 'Who Computes? The Politics of Literacy,' unpublished paper, Ontario Institute for Studies in Education, Toronto, 1985, p. 6.

4 Patricia B. Campbell, 'The Computer Revolution: Guess Who's Left Out?' *Interracial Books for Children Bulletin* 15 (No. 3, 1984), 3.

5 'Instructional Strategies for Integrating the Microcomputer into the Classroom,' The Vocational Studies Center, University of Wisconsin, Madison, 1985.

6 Michael W. Apple, *Ideology and Curriculum* (Boston and London: Routledge & Kegan Paul, 1979).

7 Olson, 'Who Computes?' p. 5.

8 See Michael W. Apple, *Education and Power* (Boston and London: Routledge & Kegan Paul, 1982).

9 For further discussion of this, see Apple, *Ideology and Curriculum*, Apple, *Education and Power*, and Ira Shor, *Culture Wars* (Boston and London: Routledge & Kegan Paul, 1986).

10 This is treated in greater detail in Richard Edwards, *Contested Terrain*

(New York: Basic Books, 1979). See also the more extensive discussion of the effect these tendencies are having in education in Apple, *Education and Power.*

11 Russell W. Rumberger and Henry M. Levin, 'Forecasting the Impact of New Technologies on the Future Job Market,' Project Report No. 84–A4, Institute for Research on Educational Finance and Government, School of Education, Stanford University, February, 1984, p. 1.

12 *Ibid.*, p. 2.

13 *Ibid.*, p. 3.

14 *Ibid.*, p. 4.

15 *Ibid.*, p. 18

16 *Ibid.*

17 *Ibid.*, p. 19.

18 *Ibid.*, pp. 19–20.

19 *Ibid.*, p. 31.

20 *Ibid.*, p. 21.

21 *Ibid.*

22 *Ibid.*, p. 25.

23 *Ibid.*

24 On the history of women's struggles against proletarianization, see Alice Kessler-Harris, *Out to Work* (New York: Oxford University Press, 1982).

25 Ian Reinecke, *Electronic Illusions* (New York: Penguin Books, 1984), p. 156.

26 See the further discussion of the loss of office jobs and the deskilling of many of those that remain in *ibid.*, pp. 136–58. The very same process could be a threat to middle- and low-level management positions as well. After all, if control is further automated, why does one need as many supervisory positions? The implications of this latter point need to be given much more consideration by many middle-class proponents of technology since their jobs may soon be at risk too.

27 Peter Dwyer, Bruce Wilson, and Roger Woock, *Confronting School and Work* (Boston and London: George Allen & Unwin, 1984), pp. 105–6.

28 The paradigm case is given by the fact that, as I mentioned in the previous chapter, three times as many people now work in low-paying positions for McDonald's as for U.S. Steel. See Martin Carnoy,

Derek Shearer, and Russell Rumberger, *A New Social Contract* (New York: Harper & Row, 1983), p. 71. As I have argued at greater length elsewhere, however, it may not be important to our economy if all students and workers are made technically knowledgeable by schools. What is just as important is the production of economically useful knowledge (technical/administrative knowledge) that can be used by corporations to enhance profits, control labor, and increase efficiency. See Apple, *Education and Power*, especially chapter 2.

29 Reinecke, *Electronic Illusions*, p. 234. For further analysis of the economic data and the effects on education, see W. Norton Grubb, 'The Bandwagon Once More: Vocational Preparation for High-Tech Occupations,' *Harvard Educational Review* 54 (November 1984), 429–51.

30 Apple, *Ideology and Curriculum*, and Apple, *Education and Power*. See also Michael W. Apple and Lois Weis (eds.), *Ideology and Practice in Schooling* (Philadelphia: Temple University Press, 1983).

31 Apple, *Ideology and Curriculum*, Apple, *Education and Power*, Apple and Weis (eds.), *Ideology and Practice in Schooling*. See also Arthur Wise, *Legislated Learning: The Bureaucratization of the American Classroom* (Berkeley: University of California Press, 1979).

32 Apple, *Ideology and Curriculum*, and Apple, *Education and Power*. On the general history of the growth of management techniques, see Richard Edwards, *Contested Terrain*.

33 Douglas Noble, 'The Underside of Computer Literacy,' *Raritan* 3 (Spring 1984), 45.

34 See the discussion of this in Apple, *Education and Power*, especially chapter 5.

35 Douglas Noble, 'Jumping Off the Computer Bandwagon,' *Education Week*, October 3, 1984, 24.

36 *Ibid.*

37 *Ibid.* See also, Noble, 'The Underside of Computer Literacy,' 45.

38 For further general discussion of the intensification and transformation of other kinds of work, see Robert Thomas, 'Citizenship and Gender in Work Organization: Some Considerations for Theories of the Labor Process,' in Michael Burawoy and Theda Skocpol (eds.), *Marxist Inquiries: Studies of Labor, Class, and States* (Chicago: University of Chicago Press, 1982), pp. 86–112.

39 Apple, *Education and Power*. For further analysis of the textbook publishing industry, see Michael W. Apple, 'Curriculum Conflict in the United States,' in Anthony Hartnett and Michael Naish (eds.),

Education and Society Today (Barcombe, Sussex: Falmer Press, in press).

40 I am endebted to Susan Jungck for this point. See her excellent dissertation, 'Doing Computer Literacy,' unpublished Ph.D. dissertation, University of Wisconsin, Madison, 1985.

41 Reinecke, *Electronic Illusions*, p. 176.

42 *Ibid.*, p. 169.

43 Olson, 'Who Computes?' p. 23.

44 *Ibid.*, p. 31. Thus, students' familiarity and comfort with computers becomes a form of what has been called the 'cultural capital' of advantaged groups. For further analysis of the dynamics of cultural capital, see Apple, *Education and Power*, and Pierre Bourdieu and Jean-Claude Passeron, *Reproduction in Education, Society and Culture* (Beverly Hills: Sage, 1977).

45 Olson, 'Who Computes?' p. 23. See also the discussion of interclass competition over academic qualifications in Pierre Bourdieu, *Distinction: A Social Critique of the Judgement of Taste* (Cambridge, Mass.: Harvard University Press, 1984), pp. 133–68.

46 Once again, I am endebted to Susan Jungck for this argument.

47 Noble, 'The Underside of Computer Literacy,' 54.

48 Douglas Noble, 'Computer Literacy and Ideology,' *Teachers College Record* 85 (Summer 1984), 611. This process of 'blaming the victim' has a long history in education. See Apple, *Ideology and Curriculum*, especially chapter 7.

49 R. W. Connell, *Teachers' Work* (Boston and London: George Allen & Unwin, 1985), p. 142.

50 Olson, 'Who Computes?' p. 22.

51 For an analysis of the emphasis on and pedagogic problems with such limited uses of computers, see Michael J. Streibel, 'A Critical Analysis of the Use of Computers in Education,' unpublished paper, Department of Curriculum and Instruction, University of Wisconsin, Madison, 1984.

52 Olson, 'Who Computes?' p. 22.

53 Campbell, 'The Computer Revolution: Guess Who's Left Out?' 3. Many computer experts, however, are highly critical of the fact that students are primarily taught to program in BASIC, a less than appropriate language for later advanced computer work. Michael Streibel, personal communication.

54 Campbell, 'The Computer Revolution.'

55 *Ibid.*

56 An interesting analysis of what happens to young women in such business programs and how they respond to both the curricula and their later work experiences can be found in Linda Valli, 'Becoming Clerical Workers: Business Education and the Culture of Femininity,' in Apple and Weis (eds.), *Ideology and Practice in Schooling*, pp. 213–34. See also her more extensive treatment in Linda Valli, *Becoming Clerical Workers* (Boston and London: Routledge & Kegan Paul, 1986).

57 Jane Gaskell in Olson, 'Who Computes?' p. 33.

58 Feodora Fomin, 'The Best and the Brightest: The Selective Function of Mathematics in the School Curriculum,' in Lesley Johnson and Deborah Tyler (eds.), *Cultural Politics: Papers in Contemporary Australian Education, Culture and Politics* (Melbourne: University of Melbourne Sociology Research Group in Cultural and Educational Studies, 1984), p. 220.

59 Michael Streibel's work on the models of thinking usually incorporated within computers in education is helpful in this regard. See Streibel, 'A Critical Analysis of the Use of Computers in Education.' The more general issue of the relationship between technology and the control of culture is important here. A useful overview of this can be found in Kathleen Woodward (ed.), *The Myths of Information: Technology and Postindustrial Culture* (Madison: Coda Press, 1980).

60 Quoted in Noble, 'The Underside of Computer Literacy,' 56.

61 *Ibid.*, 57. An interesting but little-known fact is that the largest proportion of computer programmers actually work for the military. See Joseph Weizenbaum, 'The Computer in Your Future,' *New York Review of Books* 30 (October 27, 1983), 58–62.

62 Noble, 'The Underside of Computer Literacy,' 40. For students in vocational curricula especially, these questions would be given more power if they were developed within a larger program that would seek to provide these young men and women with extensive experience in and understanding of *all* aspects of operating an entire industry or enterprise, not simply those 'skills' that reproduce workplace stratification. See Center for Law and Education, 'Key Provision in New Law Reforms Vocational Education: Focus is on Broader Knowledge and Experience for Students/Workers,' *Center for Law and Education, Inc. D. C. Report*, December 28, 1984, 1–6.

8 SUPPORTING DEMOCRACY IN EDUCATION

1 Stanley Aronowitz and Henry Giroux, *Education under Siege* (South Hadley, Mass.: Bergin & Garvey 1985), pp. 6–7.

2 For a brilliant discussion of the principles surrounding the common good, see Marcus Raskin, *The Common Good* (New York and London: Routledge & Kegan Paul, 1986).

3 Vincent Harding, *There Is a River: The Black Struggle for Freedom in America* (New York: Vintage, 1981).

4 See Paulo Freire, *The Politics of Education* (South Hadley, Mass.: Bergin & Garvey, 1985), and Ira Shor, *Critical Teaching and Everyday Life* (Boston: South End Press, 1980). See also the discussion in Aronowitz and Giroux, *Education under Seige* and in the final chapter of Ira Shor, *Culture Wars* (New York and London: Routledge & Kegan Paul, 1986).

5 Ken Jones, *Beyond Progressive Education* (London: Macmillan, 1983), p. 12.

6 Jorge Larrain, *Marxism and Ideology* (Atlantic Highlands, N.J.: Humanities Press, 1983), p. 5.

7 See, for example, David Dickson, *The New Politics of Science* (New York: Pantheon Books, 1984).

8 Raymond Williams, *The Year 2000* (New York: Pantheon Books, 1983), p. 18.

9 Ernesto Laclau and Chantal Mouffe, *Hegemony and Socialist Strategy: Towards a Radical Democratic Politics* (London: Verso, 1985), pp. 152–3.

10 See Michael W. Apple, *Education and Power* (Boston and London: Routledge & Kegan Paul, 1982), and, as well, Michael W. Apple and Lois Weis (eds.), *Ideology and Practice in Schooling* (Philadelphia: Temple University Press, 1983).

11 John Solomos, 'Varieties of Marxist Conceptions of Race, Class and the State: A Critical Analysis,' in John Rex and David Mason (eds.), *Theories of Race and Ethnic Relations* (Cambridge: Cambridge University Press, in press), p. 8.

12 See, e.g., Centre for Contemporary Cultural Studies, *The Empire Strikes Back* (London: Hutchinson, 1982), and Michael Omi and Howard Winant, *Racial Formation in the United States* (New York and London: Routledge & Kegan Paul, 1986). Cameron McCarthy has been particularly helpful in my understanding of this point.

13 See my discussion of the need for schools to act on democratic

norms and for the state in general to partly support 'person rights' because of the need to maintain legitimacy, in Apple, *Education and Power*.

14 Stuart Hall, 'The Whites of Their Eyes: Racist Ideologies and the Media,' in George Bridges and Rosalind Brunt (eds.), *Silver Linings: Some Strategies for the Eighties* (London: Lawrence & Wishart, 1981), p. 36.

15 Williams, *The Year 2000*, p. 21.

16 Martin Lawn and Jenny Ozga, 'Teachers: Professionalism, Class and Proletarianization,' unpublished paper, The Open University, 1981, p. 10.

17 We have to be cautious here. The arguments used to justify defining elementary school teaching as women's work and, hence, in need of external control, can change over time and be different in different national contexts. Just as importantly, they may differ among various groups with their own distinct ideological and material interests. Finally, the arguments may have contradictory results. See Linda Murgatroyd, 'Gender and Occupational Stratification,' *Sociological Review* 30 (November 1982), 589.

18 See R. W. Connell, *Teachers' Work* (Boston and London: George Allen & Unwin, 1985), and Sara Freedman's work with the Boston Women's Teachers' Group on the concrete experiences of teachers.

19 The Public Education Information Network, *Education For a Democratic Future: Equity and Excellence* (St. Louis: Public Education Information Network, 1985), p. 7.

20 *Ibid.*, p. 9.

21 *Ibid.*, pp. 10–12.

22 *Ibid.*, pp. 13–14.

23 *Ibid.*, pp. 15–16.

24 See Cohen's description of the model project he helped establish in Philip Cohen, 'Against the New Vocationalism,' in Inge Bates *et al.* (eds.), *Schooling for the Dole?* (London: Macmillan, 1984), pp. 104–69.

25 For further discussion of this, see Geoff Whitty, 'Recent American and Australian Approaches to the Sociology and Politics of Education,' *Educational Theory*, in press. See also Peter Dwyer, Bruce Wilson, and Roger Woock, *Confronting School and Work* (Boston and London: George Allen & Unwin, 1984).

26 See Whitty, 'Recent American and Australian Approaches to the Sociology and Politics of Education,' and R. W. Connell *et al.*, *Making the Difference* (Boston and London: George Allen & Unwin, 1982).

27 Martin Carnoy and Henry Levin, *Schooling and Work in the Democratic State* (Stanford: Stanford University Press, 1985), p. 2. See also pp. 12–13.

28 *Ibid.*, p. 24. See also the extensive discussion of this in Apple, *Education and Power*. The historical range of these conflicts can be seen in William J. Reese, *Power and the Promise of School Reform: Grass-roots Movements during the Progressive Era* (New York and London: Routledge & Kegan Paul, 1986).

29 Carnoy and Levin, *Schooling and Work in the Democratic State*, p. 47.

30 *Ibid.*, p. 50.

31 *Ibid.*, p. 263.

32 *Ibid.*, p. 266.

33 Apple, *Education and Power*, chapter 5.

34 Carnoy and Levin, *Schooling and Work in the Democratic State*, pp. 242–3.

35 *Ibid.*, p. 243.

36 *Ibid.*, p. 245.

37 Laclau and Mouffe, *Hegemony and Socialist Strategy*, p. 192.

38 *Ibid.*, p. 159.

39 See Aronowitz and Giroux, *Education under Siege*, for a discussion of the importance of reappropriating the progressive education tradition.

40 Michael Calvin McGee, 'Secular Humanism: A Radical Reading of "Culture Industry" Productions,' *Critical Studies in Mass Communications* 1 (March 1984), 29.

41 I have discussed this in more detail in Michael W. Apple, 'Symposium on Philosophy and Education,' *Harvard Educational Review* 51 (August 1981), 419–23.

42 R. W. Connell, 'Theorizing Gender,' *Sociology*, in press, p. 20 in mimeo.

43 Pierre Bourdieu, *Distinction: A Social Critique of the Judgement of Taste* (Cambridge, Mass.: Harvard University Press, 1984), p. xiii.

44 See, for example, Apple, *Education and Power*, and Henry Giroux, *Theory and Resistance in Education* (South Hadley, Mass.: Bergin & Garvey, 1983).

45 Raphael Samuel, 'History and Theory,' in Raphael Samuel (ed.), *People's History and Socialist Theory* (Boston and London: Routledge & Kegan Paul, 1981), p. xliii.

46 Williams, *The Year 2000*, pp. 268–9.

BIBLIOGRAPHY

Acker, Sandra, 'Women and Teaching: A Semi-Detached Sociology of a Semi-Detached Profession,' in Stephen Walker and Len Barton (eds.), *Gender, Class and Education*, Barcombe, Sussex: Falmer Press, 1983, pp. 123–39.

Adler, Mortimer, *The Paideia Proposal*, New York: Macmillan, 1982.

Apple, Michael W., 'Against Reductionism,' *History of Education Quarterly* 24 (Summer 1984), 247–56.

Apple, Michael W., 'Common Curriculum and State Control,' *Discourse* 2 (No. 2, 1982), 1–10.

Apple, Michael W. (ed.), *Cultural and Economic Reproduction in Education: Essays on Class, Ideology and the State*, Boston and London: Routledge & Kegan Paul, 1982.

Apple, Michael W., 'Curriculum Conflict in the United States,' in Anthony Hartnett and Michael Naish (eds.), *Education and Society Today*, Barcombe, Sussex: Falmer Press, in press.

Apple, Michael W., 'Curriculum in the Year 2000: Tensions and Possibilities,' *Phi Delta Kappan* 64 (January 1983), 321–6.

Apple, Michael W., *Education and Power*, Boston and London: Routledge & Kegan Paul, 1982.

Apple, Michael W., *Ideology and Curriculum*, Boston and London: Routledge & Kegan Paul, 1979.

Apple, Michael W., 'Power and Culture in the Report of the Committee of Ten,' *New York University Education Quarterly*, 14 (Winter 1983), 28–32.

Apple, Michael W., 'State, Bureaucracy and Curriculum Control,' *Curriculum Inquiry* 11 (Winter 1981), 379–88.

Apple, Michael W., and Kenneth Teitelbaum, 'Are Teachers Losing Control of Their Skills and Curriculum?' *Journal of Curriculum Studies* 18 (April–June 1986), 177–84.

Apple, Michael W. and Lois Weis (eds.), *Ideology and Practice in Schooling*, Philadelphia: Temple University Press, 1983.

Barker, Jane, and Hazel Downing, 'Word Processing and the Transformation of the Patriarchal Relations of Control in the Office,' in Roger Dale, Geoff Esland, Ross Fergusson, and Madeleine MacDonald (eds.), *Education and the State, Vol. 2: Politics, Patriarchy and Practice*, Barcombe, Sussex: Falmer Press, 1981, pp. 229–56.

Barnes, James J., *Authors, Publishers and Politicians: The Quest for an Anglo-American Copyright Agreement 1815–1854*, Boston and London: Routledge & Kegan Paul, 1974.

Barrera, Mario, *Race and Class in the Southwest: A Theory of Racial Inequality*, Notre Dame, Ind.: Notre Dame University Press, 1979.

Barrett, Michele, *Women's Oppression Today*, London: New Left Books, 1980.

Barrett, Nancy S., 'Women in the Job Market: Occupations, Earnings, and Career Opportunities,' in Ralph E. Smith (ed.), *The Subtle Revolution: Women at Work*, Washington, D.C.: The Urban Institute, 1979.

Beechey, Veronica, 'The Sexual Division of Labour and the Labour Process: A Critical Assessment of Braverman,' in Stephen Wood (ed.), *The Degradation of Work?* London: Hutchinson, 1982, pp. 54–73.

Benson, Susan Porter, 'The Clerking Sisterhood: Rationalization and the Work Culture of Saleswomen in American Department Stores,' *Radical America* 12 (March/April 1978), 41–55.

Bergen, Barry H., 'Only a Schoolmaster: Gender, Class, and the Effort to Professionalize Elementary Teaching in England, 1870–1910,' *History of Education Quarterly* 22 (Spring 1982), 1–21.

Bernstein, Basil, *Class, Codes and Control Vol. 3*, Boston and London: Routledge & Kegan Paul, 1977.

Beyer, Landon, 'Aesthetic Education and Cultural Reproduction,' in Michael W. Apple and Lois Weis (eds.), *Ideology and Practice in Schooling*, Philadelphia: Temple University Press, 1983, pp. 89–113.

Boston Women's Teachers' Group, 'The Other End of The Corridor: The Effects of Teaching on Teachers,' *Radical Teacher* 23 (Spring 1983), 2–23.

Bourdieu, Pierre, *Distinction: A Social Critique of the Judgement of Taste*, Cambridge, Mass.: Harvard University Press, 1984.

Bourdieu, Pierre, and Jean-Claude Passeron, *Reproduction in Education, Society and Culture*, Beverly Hills: Sage, 1977.

Brenner, Johanna, and Maria Ramas, 'Rethinking Women's Oppression,' *New Left Review* 144 (March/April 1984), 33–71.

Brumberg, Joan Jacobs, 'The Feminization of Teaching: "Romantic Sexism" and American Protestant Denominationalism,' *History of Education Quarterly* 23 (Fall 1983), 379–84.

Bruner, Jerome, *The Process of Education*, New York: Vintage Books, 1960.

Buhle, Mari Jo, *Women and American Socialism, 1870–1920*, Urbana: University of Illinois Press, 1981.

Burawoy, Michael, *Manufacturing Consent*, Chicago: University of Chicago Press, 1979.

Buswell, Carol, 'Pedagogic Change and Social Change,' *British Journal of Sociology of Education* 1 (No. 3, 1980), 293–306.

Campbell, Patricia B., 'The Computer Revolution: Guess Who's Left Out?' *Interracial Books for Children Bulletin* 15 (No. 3, 1984), 3–6.

Carnoy, Martin, 'Education, Democracy and Social Conflict,' *Harvard Educational Review* 53 (November 1983), 398–402.

Carnoy, Martin, 'Education, Economy and the State,' in Michael W. Apple (ed.), *Cultural and Economic Reproduction in Education*, Boston and London: Routledge & Kegan Paul, 1982, pp. 79–126.

Carnoy, Martin, 'Marxism and Education,' in Bertell Ollman and Edward Vernoff (eds.), *The Left Academy: Marxist Scholarship on American Campuses, Vol. 2*, New York: Praeger, 1984, pp. 79–97.

Carnoy, Martin, *The State and Political Theory*, Princeton: Princeton University Press, 1984.

Carnoy, Martin, Derek Shearer, and Russell Rumberger, *A New Social Contract: The Economy and Government After Reagan*, New York: Harper & Row, 1983.

Castells, Manuel, *The Economic Crisis and American Society*, Princeton: Princeton University Press, 1980.

Center for Law and Education, 'Key Provision in New Law Reforms Vocational Education: Focus is on Broader Knowledge and Experience for Students/Workers,' *Center for Law and Education, Inc. D.C. Report*, December 28, 1984, 1–6.

Christian, Linda, 'Becoming a Woman Through Romance,' unpublished doctoral dissertation, University of Wisconsin, Madison, 1984.

Clarke, John, Chas Critcher, and Richard Johnson (eds.), *Working Class Culture: Studies in History and Theory*, London: Hutchinson, 1979.

Clawson, Daniel, *Bureaucracy and the Labor Process*, New York: Monthly Review Press, 1980.

Clifford, Giraldine, 'The Female Teacher and the Feminist Movement,' unpublished paper, University of California, Berkeley, 1981.

Cohen, G. A., *Karl Marx's Theory of History: A Defense*, Princeton: Princeton University Press, 1978.

Cohen, Joshua, and Joel Rogers, *On Democracy: Toward a Transformation of American Society*, New York: Penguin Books, 1983.

Compaine, Benjamin M., *The Book Industry in Transition: An Economic Study of Book Distribution and Marketing*, White Plains, N.Y.: Knowledge Industry Publications, 1978.

Connell, R. W., *et al. Making The Difference*, Boston and London: George Allen & Unwin, 1982.

Connell, R. W., *Teachers' Work*, Boston and London: George Allen & Unwin, 1985.

Connell, R. W., 'Theorizing Gender,' *Sociology*, in press.

Cook, Alice, *The Working Mother: A Survey of Problems and Programs in Nine Countries*, Ithaca: New York State School of Industrial Relations, Cornell University, 1978.

Copelman, Dina, 'The Politics of Professionalism: Women Teachers, 1904–1914,' unpublished paper, Department of History, University of Missouri, Columbia, 1985.

Copelman, Dina, 'We Do Not Want to Turn Men and Women into Mere Toiling Machines: Teachers, Teaching, and the Taught,' unpublished paper, Department of History, University of Missouri, Columbia, 1985.

Coser, Lewis, Charles Kadushin, and Walter Powell, *Books: The Culture and Commerce of Publishing*, New York: Basic Books, 1982.

Crompton, Rosemary, and Stuart Reid, 'The Deskilling of Clerical Work,' in Stephen Wood (ed.), *The Degradation of Work?* London: Hutchinson, 1982, pp. 163–78.

Dale, Roger, 'Education and the Capitalist State: Contributions and Contradictions,' in Michael W. Apple (ed.), *Cultural and Economic Reproduction in Education*, Boston: Routledge & Kegan Paul, 1982, pp. 127–61.

Dale, Roger, 'The State and Education: Some Theoretical Approaches,' in *The State and the Politics of Education*, Milton Keynes: The Open University Press, 1981.

Dale, Roger, Geoff Esland, Ross Furgusson, and Madeleine MacDonald (eds.), *Education and the State, Vol. 1: Schooling and the National Interest*, Barcombe, Sussex: Falmer Press, 1981.

Dale, Roger, Geoff Esland, Ross Fergusson, and Madeleine MacDonald (eds.), *Education and the State, Vol. 2: Politics, Patriarchy and Practice*, Barcombe, Sussex: Falmer Press, 1981.

Danylewycz, Marta, and Alison Prentice, 'Teachers, Gender, and Bureaucratizing School Systems in Nineteenth Century Montreal and Toronto,' *History of Education Quarterly* 24 (Spring 1984), 75–100.

David, Miriam, *The State, the Family and Education*, Boston and London: Routledge & Kegan Paul, 1980.

Davies, Margery, *Woman's Place Is at the Typewriter: Office Work and Office Workers, 1870–1930*, Philadelphia: Temple University Press, 1982.

Davis, Tricia, 'Stand By Your Men? Feminism and Socialism in the Eighties,' in George Bridges and Rosalind Brunt (eds.), *Silver Linings: Some Strategies for the Eighties*, London: Lawrence & Wishart, 1981, pp. 9–27.

Degler, Carl, *At Odds: Women and the Family in America from the Revolution to the Present*, New York: Oxford University Press, 1980.

Dessauer, John P., *Book Industry Trends, 1982*, New York: Book Industry Study Group, 1982.

Dickson, David, *The New Politics of Science*, New York: Pantheon Books, 1984.

DiMaggio, Paul, and Michael Useem, 'The Arts in Class Reproduction,' in Michael W. Apple (ed.), *Cultural and Economic Reproduction in Education*, Boston and London: Routledge & Kegan Paul, 1982, pp. 181–201.

Donald, James, 'Green Paper: Noise of a Crisis,' *Screen Education* 30 (Spring 1979), 13–49.

Dwyer, Peter, Bruce Wilson, and Roger Woock, *Confronting School and Work*, Boston and London: George Allen & Unwin, 1984.

Eaton, William Edward, *The American Federation of Teachers, 1916–1961*, Carbondale: Southern Illinois University Press, 1975.

Education Group of the Centre for Contemporary Cultural Studies, *Unpopular Education*, London: Hutchinson, 1981.

Edwards, Richard, *Contested Terrain: The Transformation of the Workplace in the Twentieth Century*, New York: Basic Books, 1979.

Elsbree, Willard S., *The American Teacher*, New York: American Book Co., 1939.

Everhart, Robert, *Reading, Writing and Resistance*, Boston and London: Routledge & Kegan Paul, 1983.

Febvre, Lucien, and Henri-Jean Martin, *The Coming of the Book*, London: New Left Books, 1976.

Feistritzer, C. Emily (ed.), *The American Teacher*, Washington, D.C.: Feistritzer Publications, 1983.

Ferguson, Kathy E., *The Feminist Case Against Bureaucracy*, Philadelphia: Temple University Press, 1984.

Fomin, Feodora, 'The Best and the Brightest: The Selective Function of Mathematics in the School Curriculum,' in Lesley Johnson and Deborah Tyler (eds.), *Cultural Politics: Papers in Contemporary Australian Education, Culture and Politics*, Melbourne: University of Melbourne Sociology Research Group in Cultural and Educational Studies, 1984, pp. 219–61.

Foster, Emery M., 'Statistical Summary of Education, 1929–30,' *Biennial Survey of Education 1928–1930, Vol. 2*, Washington, D.C.: U.S. Government Printing Office, 1932, pp. 1–12.

Frankenstein, Marilyn, and Louis Kampf, 'Preface to "The Other End of the Corridor",' *Radical Teacher* 23 (Spring 1983), 1–2.

Freedman, Sara, 'Master Teacher/Merit Pay – Weeding Out Women from "Women's True Profession": A Critique of the Commissions on Education,' *Radical Teacher* 25 (November 1983), 24–8.

Gilligan, Carol, *In a Different Voice: Psychological Theory and Women's Development*, Cambridge, Mass.: Harvard University Press, 1982.

Gintis, Herbert, 'Communication and Politics,' *Socialist Review* 10 (March/June 1980), 189–232.

Giroux, Henry, 'Public Philosophy and the Crisis in Education,' *Harvard Educational Review* 54 (May 1984), 186–94.

Giroux, Henry, 'Theories of Reproduction and Resistance in the New Sociology of Education: A Critical Analysis,' *Harvard Educational Review* 53 (August 1983), 257–93.

Gitlin, Andrew, 'School Structure and Teachers' Work,' in Michael W. Apple and Lois Weis (eds.), *Ideology and Practice in Schooling*, Philadelphia: Temple University Press, 1983, pp. 193–212.

Gitlin, Andrew, 'Understanding the Work of Teachers,' unpublished Ph.D. dissertation, University of Wisconsin, Madison, 1980.

Gitlin, Todd, 'Television's Screens: Hegemony in Transition,' in Michael W. Apple (ed.), *Cultural and Economic Reproduction in Education*, Boston and London: Routledge & Kegan Paul, 1982, pp. 202–46.

Goldstein, Paul, *Changing the American Schoolbook*, Lexington, Mass.: D. C. Heath, 1978.

Goodlad, John I., *A Place Called School*, New York: McGraw-Hill, 1983.

Gordon, David, Richard Edwards, and Michael Reich, *Segmented Work, Divided Workers: The Historical Transformation of Labor in the United States*, New York: Cambridge University Press, 1982.

Grace, Gerald, 'Judging Teachers: The Social and Political Contexts of Teacher Evaluation,' *British Journal of Sociology of Education* 6 (No. 1, 1985), 3–16.

Griswold, Wendy, 'American Character and the American Novel: An Expansion of Reflection Theory in the Sociology of Literature,' *American Journal of Sociology* 86 (January 1981), 740–65.

Grubb, W. Norton, 'The Bandwagon Once More: Vocational Preparation for High-Tech Occupations,' *Harvard Educational Review* 54 (November 1984), 429–51.

Hall, Stuart, 'The Whites of Their Eyes: Racist Ideologies in the Media,' in George Bridges and Rosalind Brunt (eds.), *Silver Linings: Some Strategies for the Eighties*, London: Lawrence & Wishart, 1981, pp. 28–52.

Harris, Kevin, *Teachers and Classes*, Boston and London: Routledge & Kegan Paul, 1982.

Hartmann, Heidi, 'The Unhappy Marriage of Marxism and Feminism: Towards a More Progressive Union,' in Roger Dale, Geoff Esland, Ross Fergusson, and Madeleine MacDonald (eds.), *Education and the State, Vol. 2: Politics, Patriarchy and Practice*, Barcombe, Sussex: Falmer Press, 1981, pp. 191–210.

Hearn, Jeff, 'Notes on Patriarchy: Professionalization and the Semi-Professions,' *Sociology* 16 (May 1982), 184–202.

Hirst, Paul, *On Law and Ideology*, London: Macmillan, 1979.

Hoffman, Nancy, *Women's 'True' Profession: Voices from the History of Teaching*, Old Westbury: Feminist Press, 1981.

Hogan, David, 'Education and Class Formation: The Peculiarities of the Americans,' in Michael W. Apple (ed.), *Cultural and Economic Reproduction in Education*, Boston and London: Routledge & Kegan Paul, 1982, 32–78.

Holland, Janet, 'Women's Occupational Choice: The Impact of Sexual Divisions in Society,' Department of Educational Research, Stockholm Institute of Education, Reports on Educational Psychology, 1980.

Hollands, Robert G., 'Working for the Best Ethnography,' unpublished paper, Centre for Contemporary Cultural Studies, University of Birmingham, n.d.

Hunter, Allen, 'Virtue with a Vengeance: The Pro-Family Politics of the New Right,' unpublished doctoral dissertation, Brandeis University, 1984.

Jencks, Christopher, *et al.*, *Who Gets Ahead?*, New York: Basic Books, 1979.

Jensen, Joan M., 'Not Only Ours But Others: The Quaker Teaching Daughters of the Mid-Atlantic, 1790–1850,' *History of Education Quarterly* 24 (Spring 1984), 3–19.

John, Angela V., 'Foreword' to Frances Widdowson, *Going Up into the Next Class: Women and Elementary Teacher Training 1840–1914*, London: Hutchinson, 1983, pp. 7–10.

Johnson, Richard, 'What Is Cultural Studies Anyway?' Occasional Paper SP No. 74, Centre for Contemporary Cultural Studies, University of Birmingham, September 1983.

Jungck, Susan, 'Doing Computer Literacy,' unpublished doctoral dissertation, University of Wisconsin, Madison, 1985.

Kaufman, Polly Welts, *Women Teachers on the Frontier*, New Haven: Yale University Press, 1984.

Keith, Sherry, 'Politics of Textbook Selection,' Institute for Research on Educational Finance and Governance, Stanford University, April 1981.

Kellner, Douglas, 'Network Television and American Society,' *Theory and Society* 10 (January 1981), 31–62.

Kelly, Gail, and Ann Nihlen, 'Schooling and the Reproduction of Patriarchy,' in Michael W. Apple (ed.), *Cultural and Economic Reproduction in Education*, Boston and London: Routledge & Kegan Paul, 1982, pp. 162–80.

Kelly, Michael, *White Collar Proletariat*, Boston and London: Routledge & Kegan Paul, 1980.

Kessler-Harris, Alice, *Out to Work: A History of Wage-Earning Women in the United States*, New York: Oxford University Press, 1982.

Kirst, Michael W., 'Choosing Textbooks: Reflections of a State Board President,' *American Educator* 8 (Summer 1984), 18–23.

Kliebard, Herbert, 'Bureaucracy and Curriculum Theory,' in Vernon Haubrich (ed.), *Freedom, Bureaucracy, and Schooling*, Washington: Association for Supervision and Curriculum Development, 1971, pp. 74–93.

Kliebard, Herbert, 'Education at the Turn of the Century: A Crucible for Curriculum Change,' *Educational Researcher* 11 (January 1982), 16–24.

Kliebard, Herbert, *The Struggle for the American Curriculum*, Boston and London: Routledge & Kegan Paul, 1986.

Kolesnik, Walter, *Mental Discipline in Modern Education*, Madison: University of Wisconsin Press, 1958.

Komisar, B. Paul and James E. McClellan, 'The Logic of Slogans,' in B. Othanel Smith and Robert H. Ennis (eds.), *Language and Concepts in Education*, Chicago: Rand McNally, 1961, pp. 195–214.

Larson, Magali, 'Monopolies of Competence and Bourgeois Ideology,' in Roger Dale, Geoff Esland, Ross Fergusson, and Madeleine MacDonald (eds.), *Education and the State, Vol. 2: Politics, Patriarchy and Practice*, Barcombe, Sussex: Falmer Press, 1981, pp. 323–47.

Larson, Magali, 'Proletarianization and Educated Labor,' *Theory and Society* 9 (No. 2, 1980), 131–75.

Lawn, Martin, and Jenny Ozga, 'Teachers: Professionalism, Class and Proletarianization,' unpublished paper, The Open University, 1981.

Leach, William, Transformations in the Culture of Consumption: Women in Department Stores, 1865–1900,' *Journal of American History* 71 (September 1984), 319–42.

Levin, Henry M., 'About Time for Education Reform,' *Educational Evaluation and Policy Analysis* 6 (Summer 1984), 151–63.

Lewis, Jane, *The Politics of Motherhood* London: Croom Helm, 1980.

Liston, Daniel, 'Are Critical Analyses of Curriculum Correct? Functional Explanation and Ethical Justification in Recent Curriculum Studies,' unpublished doctoral dissertation, University of Wisconsin, Madison, 1985.

Liston, Daniel, 'Have We Explained the Relationship Between Curriculum and Capitalism?' *Educational Theory* 34 (Summer 1984), 234–53.

Littler, Craig, 'Deskilling and Changing Structures of Control,' in Stephen Wood (ed.), *The Degradation of Work?*, London: Hutchinson, 1982, pp. 122–45.

Luke, Carmen, Suzanne Castell, and Alan Luke, 'Beyond Criticism: The Authority of the School Text,' *Curriculum Inquiry* 13 (Summer 1983), 111–27.

McNeil, Linda, 'Defensive Teaching and Classroom Control,' in Michael

W. Apple and Lois Weis (eds.), *Ideology and Practice in Schooling*, Philadelphia: Temple University Press, 1983, pp. 114–42.

Mattingly, Paul, *The Classless Profession*, New York: New York University Press, 1975.

Meiksins, Peter, 'Scientific Management and Class Relations,' *Theory and Society* 13 (March 1984), 177–201.

Melder, Keith E., 'Mask of Oppression: The Female Seminary Movement in the United States,' *New York History* 55 (July 1974), 261–79.

Melder, Keith E., 'Women's High Calling: The Teaching Profession in America, 1830–1860,' *American Studies* 12 (Fall 1972), 19–32.

Melosh, Barbara, *The Physician's Hand: Work Culture and Conflict in American Nursing*, Philadelphia: Temple University Press, 1982.

Montgomery, David, *Workers' Control in America*, New York: Cambridge University Press, 1979.

Murgatroyd, Linda, 'Gender and Occupational Stratification,' *Sociological Review* 30 (November 1982), 574–602.

National Commission on Excellence in Education, 'A Nation at Risk: An Imperative for Educational Reform,' *Education Week*, April 27, 1983, 12–16.

Noble, David, *Forces of Production: A Social History of Industrial Automation*, New York: Alfred A. Knopf, 1984.

Noble, Douglas, 'Computer Literacy and Ideology,' *Teachers College Record* 85 (Summer 1984), 602–14.

Noble, Douglas, 'Jumping Off the Computer Bandwagon,' *Education Week*, October 3, 1984, 24–5.

Noble, Douglas, 'The Underside of Computer Literacy,' *Raritan* 3 (Spring 1984), 37–64.

Olson, Paul, 'Who Computes? The Politics of Literacy,' unpublished paper, Ontario Institute for Studies in Education, Toronto, 1985.

Omi, Michael, and Howard Winant, 'By the Rivers of Babylon: Race in the United States,' *Socialist Review* 13 (September–October 1983), 31–65.

Omi, Michael, and Howard Winant, *Racial Formation in the United States*, New York and London: Routledge & Kegan Paul, 1986.

Ozga, Jenny, 'The Politics of the Teaching Profession,' in *The Politics of Schools and Teaching*, Milton Keynes: The Open University Press, 1981, pp. 9–48.

Peterson, Richard A., 'The Production of Cultural Change: The Case of Contemporary Country Music,' *Social Research* 45 (Summer 1978), 292–314.

Piven, Frances Fox, and Richard A. Cloward, *The New Class War*, New York: Pantheon Books, 1982.

Popkewitz, Thomas, B. Robert Tabachnick, and Gary Wehlage, *The Myth of Educational Reform*, Madison: University of Wisconsin Press, 1982.

Purvis, June, 'Women and Teaching in the Nineteenth Century,' in Roger Dale, Geoff Esland, Ross Fergusson, and Madeleine MacDonald (eds.), *Education and the State, Vol. 2: Politics, Patriarchy and Practice*, Barcombe, Sussex: Falmer Press, 1981, pp. 359–75.

Raskin, Marcus, *The Common Good*, New York and London: Routledge & Kegan Paul, 1986.

Reich, Michael, *Racial Inequality*, Princeton: Princeton University Press, 1981.

Reinecke, Ian, *Electronic Illusions*, New York: Penguin Books, 1984.

Rescher, Nicholas, *Unpopular Essays on Technological Progress*, Pittsburgh: University of Pittsburgh Press, 1980.

Richardson, John, and Brenda Wooden Hatcher, 'The Feminization of Public School Teaching, 1870–1920,' *Work and Occupations* 10 (February 1983), 81–99.

Rothman, Sheila, *Women's Proper Place*, New York: Basic Books, 1978.

Rowbotham, Sheila, *Hidden from History*, New York: Random House, 1974.

Rude, George, *Ideology and Popular Protest*, New York: Pantheon, 1980.

Rumberger, Russell, and Henry M. Levin, 'Forecasting the Impact of New Technologies on the Future Job Market,' Project Report No. 84-A4, Institute for Research on Educational Finance and Government, School of Education, Stanford University, 1984.

Rury, John L., 'Vocationalism for Home and Work: Women's Education in the United States, 1880–1930,' *History of Education Quarterly* 24 (Spring 1984), 21–44.

Sarason, Seymour, *The Culture of the School and the Problem of Change*, Boston: Allyn & Bacon, 1971.

Shatzkin, Leonard, *In Cold Type*, Boston: Houghton Mifflin, 1982.

Shor, Ira, *Critical Teaching and Everyday Life*, Boston: South End Press, 1980.

Shor, Ira, *Culture Wars: School and Society in the Conservative Restoration 1969–1984*, Boston and London: Routledge & Kegan Paul, 1986.

Sirotnik, Kenneth A., 'What You See Is What You Get: Consistency, Persistency, and Mediocrity in Classrooms,' *Harvard Educational Review* 53 (February 1983), 18–31.

Soltis, Jonas, *An Introduction to the Analysis of Educational Concepts*, Reading, Mass.: Addison-Wesley, 1978.

Spring, Joel, *The Sorting Machine*, New York: David McKay, 1976.

Stedman, Lawrence C., and Marshall S. Smith, 'Recent Reform Proposals for American Education,' *Contemporary Education Review* 2 (Fall 1983), 85–104.

Strasser, Susan, *Never Done: A History of American Housework*, New York: Pantheon, 1982.

Streibel, Michael J., 'A Critical Analysis of the Use of Computers in Education,' unpublished paper, Department of Curriculum and Instruction, University of Wisconsin, Madison, 1984.

Strober, Myra, 'Segregation by Gender in Public School Teaching: Toward a General Theory of Occupational Segregation in the Labor Market,' unpublished manuscript, Stanford University, 1982.

Strober, Myra, and David Tyack, 'Why Do Women Teach and Men Manage?: A Report on Research on Schools,' *Signs* 5 (Spring 1980), 494–503.

Sumner, Colin, *Reading Ideologies*, New York: Macmillan, 1979.

Therborn, Goran, *The Ideology of Power and the Power of Ideology*, London: New Left Books, 1980.

Thomas, Robert, 'Citizenship and Gender in Work Organization: Some Considerations for Theories of the Labor Process,' in Michael Burawoy and Theda Skocpol (eds.), *Marxist Inquiries: Studies of Labor, Class, and States*, Chicago: University of Chicago Press, 1982, pp. 86–112.

Tyler, Ralph, *Basic Principles of Curriculum and Instruction*, Chicago: University of Chicago Press, 1949.

Urban, Wayne J., *Why Teachers Organized*, Detroit: Wayne State University Press, 1982.

Valli, Linda, 'Becoming Clerical Workers: Business Education and the Culture of Femininity,' in Michael W. Apple and Lois Weis (eds.), *Ideology and Practice in Schooling*, Philadelphia: Temple University Press, 1983, pp. 213–34.

Valli, Linda, *Becoming Clerical Workers*, Boston and London: Routledge & Kegan Paul, 1986.

Vocational Studies Center, 'Instructional Strategies for Integrating the

Microcomputer into the Classroom,' University of Wisconsin, Madison, 1985.

Vogel, Lise, *Marxism and the Oppression of Women*, New Brunswick: Rutgers University Press, 1983.

Walker, James C., 'Materialist Pragmatism and Sociology of Education,' *British Journal of Sociology of Education* 6 (No. 1, 1985), 55–74.

Walker, James C., 'Romanticising Resistance; Romanticising Culture: Problems in Willis's Theory of Cultural Production,' unpublished paper, Department of Education, University of Sydney, n.d.

Walsh, Mary Roth, *Doctors Wanted, No Women Need Apply: Sexual Barriers in the Medical Profession, 1835–1975*, New Haven: Yale University Press, 1977.

Watt, Ian, *The Rise of the Novel*, Berkeley: University of California Press, 1974.

Weizenbaum, Joseph, 'The Computer in Your Future,' *New York Review of Books* 30 (October 27, 1983), 58–62.

Wexler, Philip, 'Structure, Text and Subject: A Critical Sociology of School Knowledge,' in Michael W. Apple (ed.), *Cultural and Economic Reproduction in Education*, Boston and London: Routledge & Kegan Paul, 1982, pp. 275–303.

Wexler, Philip, and Gene Grabiner, 'The Education Question: America During the Crisis,' unpublished paper, School of Education and Human Development, University of Rochester, 1984.

Widdowson, Frances, *Going Up into the Next Class: Women and Elementary Teacher Training, 1840–1914*, London: Hutchinson, 1983.

Williams, Raymond, *The Long Revolution*, London: Chatto & Windus, 1961.

Williams, Raymond, *Marxism and Literature*, New York: Oxford University Press, 1977.

Williams, Raymond, *The Year 2000*, New York: Pantheon Books, 1983.

Willis, Paul, *Learning to Labour*, Westmead: Saxon House, 1977.

Wise, Arthur, *Legislated Learning: The Bureaucratization of the American Classroom*, Berkeley: University of California Press, 1979.

Wolff, Janet, *The Social Production of Art*, London: Macmillan, 1981.

Wolpe, Ann Marie, 'The Official Ideology of Education for Girls,' in Michael Flude and John Ahier (eds.), *Educability, Schools and Ideology*, London: Halstead Press, 1974, pp. 138–59.

Woodward, Kathleen (ed.), *The Myths of Information: Technology and Postindustrial Culture*, Madison: Coda Press, 1980.

Wright, Erik Olin, *et al.*, 'The American Class Structure,' *American Sociological Review* 47 (December 1982), 709–26.

Wright, Erik Olin, *Class, Crisis and the State*, London: New Left Books, 1978.

Wright, Erik Olin, 'Class and Occupation,' *Theory and Society* 9 (No. 2, 1980).

Wright, Erik Olin, *Class Structure and Income Determination*, New York: Academic Press, 1979.

Wright, Erik Olin, and Joachim Singelmann, 'The Proletarianization of Work in American Capitalism,' University of Wisconsin-Madison Institute for Research on Poverty, Discussion paper no. 647-81, 1981.

Wright, Will, *Sixguns and Society*, Berkeley: University of California Press, 1975.

INDEX

LC191.4 .A67 1986
Apple, Michael W.
Teachers and texts : a politic
010101 000
0 2002 0007425 6
YORK COLLEGE OF PENNSYLVANIA 17403

LC 191.4 .A67 1986
Apple, Michael W.
Teachers and texts
DISCARDED
LIBRARY